GIS and Spatial Analysis for the Social Sciences
Coding, Mapping and Modeling

Robert Nash Parker (PhD, Duke University) is Professor of Sociology at the University of California, Riverside, and Co-Director of the Robert Presley Center for Crime and Justice Studies.

Emily K. Asencio (PhD, University of California, Riverside) is a Post-Doctoral Fellow at the Robert Presley Center for Crime and Justice Studies at the University of California, Riverside.

D1609222

Contemporary Sociological Perspectives
Edited by **Valerie Jenness**, University of California, Irvine and
Jodi O'Brien, Seattle University

This innovative series is for all readers interested in books that provide frameworks for making sense of the complexities of contemporary social life. Each of the books in this series uses a sociological lens to provide current critical and analytical perspectives on significant social issues, patterns and trends. The series consists of books that integrate the best ideas in sociological thought with an aim toward public education and engagement. These books are designed for use in the classroom as well as for scholars and socially curious general readers.

Published:

Political Justice and Religious Values by Charles F. Andrain

GIS and Spatial Analysis for the Social Sciences by Robert Nash Parker and Emily K. Asencio

Hoop Dreams on Wheels: Disability and the Competitive Wheelchair Athlete by Ronald J. Berger

Forthcoming:

The Internet and Inequality by James C. Witte

Media and Middle Class Moms by Lara Descartes and Conrad Kottak

Sociology of Music by Michael B. MacDonald

Race, Justice and the New Genetics by Sandra Soo-Jin Lee

Watching T.V. Is Not Required by Bernard McGrane and John Gunderson

Intimate Impostors: The Social Psychology of Romantic Deception by Sally Caldwell

Regression Unplugged by Sally Caldwell and Robert Abbey

Violence Against Women by Douglas Brownridge

GIS and Spatial Analysis for the Social Sciences

Coding, Mapping, and Modeling

Robert Nash Parker
University of California, Riverside

Emily K. Asencio
University of California, Riverside

 Routledge
Taylor & Francis Group

NEW YORK AND LONDON

What is included on the DVD and Companion Website?
Please see the authors' Overview on p. xvii for a complete description of the resources
and software included *both* on the DVD *and* the Companion Website at
www.routledge.com/textbooks/9780415989626 associated with this text.

First published 2008
by Routledge
270 Madison Avenue, New York NY 10016

Simultaneously published in the UK
by Routledge
2 Park Square, Milton Park, Abingdon, Oxon, OX14 4RN

Routledge is an imprint of the Taylor and Francis Group, an informa business

© 2009 Taylor & Francis

Mathematica and the Mathematica logo are registered trademarks of Wolfram Research,
Inc. ("WRI" – www.wolfram.com) and are used herein with WRI's permission. WRI did
not participate in the creation of this work beyond the inclusion of the accompanying
software, and offers it no endorsement beyond the inclusion of the accompanying software.

Typeset in Times by
Swales & Willis Ltd, Exeter, Devon
Printed and bound in the United States of America
on acid-free paper by Edwards Brothers Inc

Library of Congress Cataloging in Publication Data
A catalog record has been requested for this book

ISBN10: 0–415–98961–2 (hbk)
ISBN10: 0–415–98962–0 (pbk)
ISBN10: 0–203–92934–9 (ebk)

ISBN13: 978–0–415–98961–9 (hbk)
ISBN13: 978–0–415–98962–6 (pbk)
ISBN13: 978–0–203–92934–6 (ebk)

Brief Contents

Section 1   **Introduction to Geocoding and Mapping / 1**

Section 2   **Mapping for Analysis, Policy, and Decision Making / 84**

Section 3   **Geospatial Modeling and GIS / 201**

Appendix   **GIS Data sources / 235**

References / 237

Glossary/Index / 241

Contents in Detail

Preface   *viii*
Overview   *xiii*

Section 1   **Introduction to Geocoding and Mapping / 1**
How to Make a Pin Map / 2
The Basics of Geocoding / 3
   Example: The Process of Geocoding / 5
Geocoding Addresses / 12
Data Mining and GIS / 24
   Example: The Science and Art of Interactive Geocoding / 29
   Example: Exporting a Geocoded Map / 48
Thematic Maps / 51
   Example: Creating a Thematic Map from Sample Data / 52
   Example: Racial Profiling Thematic Map / 62
   Example: Juvenile Crime Thematic Map / 75
Conclusion / 83

Section 2   **Mapping for Analysis, Policy, and Decision Making / 84**
Basic Multivariate Displays / 84
Mapping Rates / 85
   Example: Classification of World Armed Rivalries / 88
   Example: Subsets of Youth Violence / 95
   Example: Maps for School Planning / 105
What is the Proper Unit of Analysis in GIS?—Using Tessellations and Related Database Issues / 112
   Example: Tessellations and Youth Violence / 115
Dynamic Maps: Showing Change over Time / 124
   Example: Rates of Poverty over Time in New Orleans / 124
Multiple Variable Maps / 128
   Example: Patterns of Residency by Ethnicity / 135
   Example: Diffusion of Innovation in the United States (3D map) / 141
   Example: Socioeconomic Conditions in 3D / 157
Using Complex Maps to Simplify and Support Better Decision Making / 160
Policies and Planning / 160
   Example: Homicide Patterns / 160
   Example: Alcohol Availability and Youth Violence, Perris / 164
   Example: Hurricane Katrina's Impact on Children and Schools / 166
   Example: HIV and Armed National Rivalries / 174

Example: Immigration and Unemployment in the U.S. / 175
Example: California Education System / 188
Conclusion / 200

Section 3   **Geospatial Modeling and GIS / 201**
Geospatial Modeling and GIS / 202
The Meaning of Space in Causal Modeling / 206
Measuring the Impact of Space and Spatial Relationships / 207
Statistical Issues in Spatial Modeling / 208
The Impact of Spatial Autocorrelations and Error Structures in Spatial
    Modeling / 212
Statistical Modeling of Spatial Data / 213
Types of Data Used in Spatial Models / 216
Choosing Software to Estimate Spatial Models / 217
    Example: A Cross Sectional Spatial Model: Gang Crime and Alcohol
        Availability / 219
    Example: Multisite Studies in Spatial Modeling / 225
    Example: Pooled Cross Sectional and Time-Series Spatial Models / 227
    Example: Spatial Models: Limitations, Issues, and Emerging
        Developments / 231
Substantive Issues in Spatial Modeling / 231
New Developments in Spatial Modeling / 232
Conclusion / 233

Appendix   **GIS Data Sources / 235**

References   237
Glossary/Index   241

Preface

This book was written to provide sociologists, criminologists, political scientists, public health specialists, anthropologists, economists, historians, and other social scientists that deal with data linked to geographic units and space an introduction to Geographic Information Systems, or GIS, and spatial analysis and statistical modeling. Increasingly specialists in these disciplines and those working in non-academic fields such as urban planning, disaster relief, military deployment, retail store location, health care delivery, and so on are realizing the potential of GIS and spatial analysis for the understanding of behavior, the planning of development, and the placement of assets and resources, physical, social, and economic. Researchers in the social sciences have also theorized about the importance of context, both social and physical, for a greater understanding of behavior and its causes. The issue of context and how it impacts outcomes of interest to sociologists, criminologists, urban sociologists, and others has become more and more necessary for the advancement of knowledge and understanding. This has engendered increasing interest in GIS, mapping, and spatial analysis, and some observers have predicted that GIS, mapping, and spatial analysis will transform the social sciences the way that the introduction of sophisticated statistical modeling transformed these disciplines and subjects in the 1960s and 1970s (Harris and Weiner, 1996; Goodchild and Janelle, 2004).

This book is also geared to mastering the use of a particular software package for GIS, ArcGIS, and related programs produced by the Environmental Sciences Research Institute, or ESRI, in Redlands, California. ESRI claims to be the industry leader in providing software for mapping and GIS (http://www.esri.com). Making maps and managing spatial data is a very complex set of tasks in a desktop computing environment, and so the programs are necessarily complex and sometimes difficult to master.

This degree of complexity is also not conducive to the successful transfer of GIS and spatial analysis to social sciences more broadly conceived. Thus, another aspect of the way we have designed this book is so that social science researchers and students can sit down in front of a computer and get started with GIS, without having to have a great deal of prior knowledge and experience with GIS and spatial analysis. Every presentation of an example is really an exercise, with step-by-step instructions; every example is designed so that the reader will be able to sit at a computer and produce exactly the same screens and results that they are shown in the book. The accompanying DVD contains all the data used in all the examples shown in the book, so readers can experience the examples as they go along. Our examples present practical applications that are meaningful for those conducting social science research, and for those who are trying to teach others how to use these tools to conduct social science research. We have found that the example-driven approach we take in this book works effectively in one-on-one instruction as well as in the classroom equipped with computers and ArcGIS software. In some cases our step-by-step instructions reveal information necessary to produce the type of maps we illustrate here, information which can be found in none of the available help menus on the desktop or online.

One of the reasons GIS software is so complex is that as a program like this develops and grows in capability, the system becomes more complex, and multi pathways develop for doing the same task. The has become a self-evident truth in desktop software development; witness the fact that Microsoft operating systems and productivity suites take up gigabytes of space on your hard drive, in contrast to the original versions that took up megabytes. In this book we illustrate the tasks and steps needed to make useful social science oriented maps and build GIS databases that can be effectively utilized in spatial analysis; in ArcGIS there may be five or more other ways to perform the tasks we illustrate. However, the reader does not need to know all five ways and to understand the subtle differences among them and the background in logic and computer programming that distinguishes them from each other; the social science reader wants to know how to produce a map like the one in Figure X. Our approach is to construct explanations of how to use GIS in such a way that readers can pick up the text, select an example, and plug their own data into the steps to easily produce a map. If a reader is more dedicated, they can develop their understanding of the GIS process from beginning to end as they re-create each step in the examples, in order, from the beginning of Section 1 to the end of Section 3. In either case, our philosophy is one of learning by doing.

This approach is an important characteristic of this book that distinguishes it from most books about GIS for the social sciences that are currently on the market. The senior author of this book has been lecturing on college campuses for more than 25 years, and the junior author has already had several years' experience in teaching in the large class (300-plus students) format at the college level, including taking on the senior author's Research Design Lecture class for undergraduates while he was on sabbatical working on this book. The combined wisdom we have gained from our lecture class experience is that lecturing is a limited way of learning about a topic, especially one as complex and detail driven as research methods and statistics in general, or GIS and spatial analysis in particular. You simply cannot learn to use GIS in your research, or learn to teach others to use GIS, by being the passive recipient of lectures about the topic. Yet most books on the market treat the subject of GIS and spatial analysis as highly conceptual and theoretical, and although they provide examples of maps and databases to illustrate the general points being made, this will not produce social scientists who can actually use GIS as a research and learning tool. Some books take on the shape and form of a beautiful coffee table book, full of complex and interesting maps that only someone with 20 years of experience could possibly begin to know how to produce and use effectively in their own research and teaching. Instead, in this book we allow social scientists to understand the GIS process from beginning to end as they re-create each step in the examples. If the result of each step does not produce the result that matches what we show in the text, the reader will know which step to examine or go back to see if an error was made, and where to start again in the process to produce the desired result. As a result, this book should be used in so-called "smart" classrooms, in which typically each student or maybe every pair of students have a computer, the instructor has a computer, and there is a big display at the front of the room that shows the instructor's screen for all to see and match on their own screen. A second approach would be to have a lecture followed by a computer lab session in which each student can take themselves through all the examples step by step and match the results given in the text after seeing the instructor demonstrate the examples in the lecture.

Either way, social scientists can learn the tools of GIS and spatial analysis using this book in a straightforward, example-driven way. The learn-by-doing approach we take will allow social scientists and related professionals and students to adopt GIS and spatial modeling on their own terms and in ways useful to their research and learning goals.

Note on data

Please note that some of the data presented in this book is not "real" data but manipulated data based on real information gathered in this project and others. We doctored the data with the goal of protecting privacy and human subject protocols that govern these projects, so that none of those protocols have been breached by the data used here; much of the data we use throughout the book is public domain information and readily available to any user; see the Appendix on GIS data sources as well as discussions of data access and importation into GIS throughout the text.

Acknowledgments

There are many people who helped us to conceive of and write this book. One such mentor is Karl Schuessler, who always used to say to me that if I wanted to be a statistician, get a PhD in that discipline, but if I wanted to be a sociologist, make sure that the methods and techniques I was learning were in the service of sociological ideas and research, not an end in and of themselves. We hope you will agree that we followed his advice to make the focus on substance, and on what GIS and spatial analysis methods can do in the service of social science substance. I would also like to acknowledge the influence of Colin Loftin, my very first mentor in sociology and criminology, whose interest in geography, expressed in one of the first articles published in mainstream sociology on geospatial analysis, and his interest in regional differences in homicide, had a lagged effect on my interest in context, physical and social.

I would also like to acknowledge the tremendous impact that my former colleague Paul Gruenewald, Prevention Research Center (PRC), Pacific Institute for Research and Evaluation (PIRE), in Berkeley, CA, had on my interests and development of a spatially oriented research agenda. Gruenewald and I were colleagues in the early to mid-1990s at the Prevention Research Center and together we started a Spatial Analysis and Mapping Group that has grown into a major center of focus at PRC and PIRE (www.prev.org). Initially, this group consisted of the two senior research scientists (Paul and Rob) and all of the employees directly under our supervision—research assistants and research associates working on grant projects that Paul or I were involved in as investigators. This was a small and intrepid group, and we began by reading some of the classic works in spatial modeling and trying, collectively, to figure out what they were all about. This effort led to the development of S^3, the spatial analysis package featured in Section 3 of the book and available on the accompanying DVD. The collaboration with Paul Gruenewald and the efforts of the spatial analysis group are the direct originators of my interest in spatial modeling and GIS and thus, the genesis of this book.

The next person I want to acknowledge is Emily K. Asencio, my co-author of this book and a number of other projects and papers that we have worked on over the past eight years. It has been an unmitigated pleasure to work with Emily, to see her develop her talents and abilities, to learn from working with her more than I have from any other student I have taught or supervised over the length of my career. Emily started working with me as a full-fledged expert in GIS from her many years as a stalwart of the Help Desk at ESRI, the company that publishes the software we feature in this book. Any time during the past and the present, especially during the creation of the book, Emily is my instant resource for GIS— "How do you do X again, Emily?" was the typical form of the question, phone call, or e-mail—she always knows the answer, and she usually knows more than one way to get the task done. It is truly the case that without my collaboration with Emily K. Asencio, this book would not have been possible.

Many other students and former students have contributed to the completion of this book, including Louis Tuthill, Kate Luther, Lisa Fahres Murphy, Deborah Plechner, Valerie Callanan, Doreen Anderson Facile, Holly Meade, Kay Kei-ho Pih, Randi S. Cartmill (a member of the original spatial analysis group at PRC), Olivia Seheult, Helen Ross, and Bryan Wilson. I would also like to thank Celeste Wojtalewicz with whom I collaborated on the Project Bridge evaluation, one of the sites in Irving Spergel's project to test the Comprehensive Model (Spergel and Alexander, 1993), which provided significant data for some of the examples and illustrations used in the book.

I would also like to thank the *Press-Enterprise*, a daily newspaper for the Inland Empire of California, with headquarters in Riverside; it was due to their intervention that the data on traffic tickets used in several examples and illustrations in the text was obtained from the Riverside Police Department.

I want to acknowledge the significant impact that Lisa Cuevas Shaw, formerly of SAGE Publications, had on the genesis of this book. She insisted on visiting with me at the Presley Center at UC-Riverside, and when I pitched the outline for the book to her, she jumped at the chance to issue a contract and to persuade me that writing this kind of book was a good idea. I never thought that I would write a book like this in my career. Although the relationship with SAGE fell through the cracks after Lisa Cuevas Shaw left, she and SAGE did play a major role in getting this project started.

In 2005 I was granted a sabbatical leave by the University of California, whose support for this book I hereby gratefully acknowledge. I also proudly declare that this book is part of the Tyler Collection of the Center for Advanced Study in the Behavioral Sciences, or CASBS as the center is widely known. Cecilia L. Ridgeway (my significant other and life partner for the last 20 years) of Stanford University was awarded a fellowship at CASBS for the 2005–06 academic year, and as I was able to obtain full salary sabbatical support from the University of California (my appreciation to the University of California for its support knows no bounds), I was able to take the entire year away from UC-Riverside and my faculty and administrative duties at the Presley Center without financial concerns. We started writing the manuscript in late August 2005 and the first draft was completed before I had to leave CASBS in the summer of 2006. CASBS, under Director Claude Steele and Associate Director Anne Petersen, with dedicated staff like Cynthia Brandt, Susan Mattos, Iris Wilson, Linda Jack, and last but not least Chef Extraordinaire Susan Beach, gave me full support almost as if I were a fellow, including office space, computer network access, a chance to present my work to the most distinguished group of scholars I will ever present to, and the opportunity to try out some of the examples from the book on fellows interested in learning more about GIS. I would particularly like to thank Eric Sheppard for some sage advice from a real geographer, and Ken Schultz, who allowed me access to his data so that I could try out some ideas for GIS examples using data from the entire world's polities. Finally, Ruth Katz provided me with the encouragement of a true scholar, and a renewed sense that the effort to be true to the ideas and methods that are fundamental to the scholarly enterprise is indeed worth the effort, despite the difficulties that can and often are the result of such a commitment. My time at CASBS was an incredible gift, and the atmosphere and conditions at CASBS really made it possible to complete the book.

I would like to truly and deeply thank Cecilia L. Ridgeway. Not only did we get to spend a fantastic year together full time in the same house, and to have lunch together just about every day, but the encouragement and advice she has given me during the course of this project has been essential and crucial for the completion of this project. The love and support she has given me in my life and my work makes everything possible. Jaqueline Ridgeway, Cecilia's mother, has also contributed significantly to this project by providing me with a wonderful situation during the time since the sabbatical, with lovely dinners every night and fabulous conversation, as well as a comfortable place to live and work while I was finishing this project.

We would both like to acknowledge the support of the Southern California Academic Center for Excellence on Youth Violence Prevention Research, funded by the Centers for Disease Control and Prevention, with Nancy Guerra, P.I., Kirk R. Williams, Co-P.I., Lyndee Knox, Co-P.I., and Robert Nash Parker, Co-P.I. The ACE project has provided material, moral, scientific, and personal support to both authors since 2000, including that provided to us both by Roxie Alcaraz, Project Manager. The Presley Center for Crime and Justice Studies, Donita McCants Carter and Nelda Thomas, staff, the Psychology Department, and the Sociology Department, including Cathy Carlson, Robin Whittington, Anna Wire, and Terry DeAnda, at the University of California, Riverside, have also provided material and academic support for this project, and have provided the authors with opportunities to offer workshops and short courses which have allowed us to test the instructional approach and the specific examples used throughout this book on actual students at all levels within the university setting.

Emily K. Asencio would like to acknowledge the first author of this book, Robert Nash Parker, for his continuing mentoring and encouragement. She would also like to acknowledge Aaron and Diego for their support during the process of writing this book. I would also like to acknowledge my parents for their unconditional help with any and all imaginable tasks. Finally, I would like to thank my dogs and cat for sitting by my side during countless hours of working on this book.

Overview

The book is divided into three sections: Section 1 covers geocoding and basic map making; Section 2 covers mapping with multiple variables, understanding and displaying relative risk and rates, using symbols and data to construct maps to support analyses and policy decision making, and three-dimensional maps; and Section 3 provides an introduction to spatial analysis and theory testing for research and practice, as well as discussing software for spatial analysis and illustrating the use of one available program. In this overview we discuss terms from geography, cartography, GIS, and spatial analysis that will help the reader who wants to go further into standard sources, and the reference section at the end gives sources of data and specific research studies cited in the book. The Appendix lists sources of data that can be used in GIS and Spatial Analysis. The accompanying DVD contains all of the examples used in the book in full color to overcome the limits of black and white printing in the textbook market. The DVD also contains all of the databases used in the examples as well as additional examples and resources for GIS and spatial analysis in the social sciences. The DVD also has versions of the ArcGIS software used in the book, S^3, the spatial analysis software used in Section 3, as well as the software package Mathematica (Version 5) which is needed to run S^3.

Each section of the book is built entirely on examples illustrating every point and type of map or analysis we present. The steps to construct the map or database shown are given in the text, with intermediate results also displayed in the screen shots and illustrations. In addition, after many of the examples we have given additional puzzles, questions, or assignments to the reader using the same data and asking the reader to produce a new or different variant of the maps and outcomes shown in the text. Instructors can use these to challenge their students, and individual readers can use these examples to see how well they have learned from the previous example how to make a particular type of map or construct a particular type of GIS database. The results of these additional examples are given on the website designed to support the book. The website also contains updates, additional software tips and tricks, and new developments in GIS, mapping, and analysis. The location of the website for the book can be found at www.routledge.com.

Some Basic Concepts from Geography and Cartography

In this section of the overview, we discuss some basic concepts and terminology from geography and cartography. Instructors may wish to ground their students more thoroughly in these concepts before starting then on how to make maps and conduct spatial analysis. We also refer to the terms and concepts discussed here in the main sections of the book and define them in bold face in the index.

We start with the most basic definition of what GIS actually means. Next, we present a brief history of the development of GIS, followed by an introduction to some basic terminology relevant to GIS.

Although this book is geared specifically toward those interested in using GIS to conduct research in the social sciences, GIS has many purposes outside of the social science arena. Among these are military and defense planning, ecological planning, urban planning, market analyses, disaster relief planning, and infinite other tasks associated with utilizing and organizing geographic space.

What is GIS?

Take a moment to think about the acronym GIS. Think about whether you actually know what each letter of the acronym stands for. The meaning behind the acronym itself provides insight into what it means to be a GIS. The first letter, G, stands for Geographic. This represents the purpose of a GIS in the simplest form: to manage data about geographic locations, including spatial relationships and spatial processes. The type of data in this category includes electronic maps and other electronic representations of geographic spaces. The second letter, I, stands for Information. This represents the ability of GIS to store information that can be used for purposes of analyses that are organized spatially. Information of this nature can be from any data source, from the U.S. Census data to police data regarding incidents of crime, to unemployment data, and beyond; any data source that can be organized along some geographically oriented basis, such as state or county borders. The final letter, S, stands for System, which acknowledges the ability of a GIS to work as a system for the storage, analyses, and presentation of geographically based data. Essentially, this refers to the ability of a GIS to take geographic data such as an electronic map file, and combine it based upon user-specified criteria with some information set to tell a story about a particular geographic region. For example, if a GIS user combines an electronic map file of the United States with U.S. Census data, the user can instruct the GIS to tell a story about the ethnic composition of the whole United States, or about some subset geographic region within the United States.

A GIS has the capacity to present many different types of analyses as specified by the user. One of the strengths of this approach is that once the user is aware of the potential and possibility of GIS, many types of data that have not typically been thought of as "geographic" in nature can be incorporated within a GIS. In other words, if we combine an electronic map file of the United States with U.S. Census data as mentioned previously, this will not allow us to understand how crime rates differ across the states. This is because crime is not a part of the data gathered by the U.S. Census Bureau. However, we can obtain data from the Federal Bureau of Investigation (FBI) on crimes by state, and incorporate these data into our GIS and display the rates of crime in the states, thus providing now a simple spatial analysis and mapped display of crime rates, combining the data from the map, the Census, and the FBI. This is a simple example of the new power that GIS gives researchers and students of the social sciences.

History of Mapping and GIS

The concept of associating attributes with an image, which underlies GIS, originated tens of thousands of years ago. Cave dwellers used drawings of animals and their associated migration routes to plan their hunting season. The concepts underlying GIS can be likened to a police chief placing pins at the locations of criminal incidents on a paper map that is mounted on the wall in order to look for a pattern among the incidents. Though these examples depict a much more simplistic form of associating images and attributes than modern-day GIS applications use, the basic goal is the same. GIS software applications available today allow for more complex data as well as analyses of data and more sophisticated displays of images and associated attributes than ever were imaginable by cave-dwelling hunters.

The historical development of GIS technology goes hand in hand with the development of computer technology. Prior to the availability of the computer technology to create a GIS application, mapping analyses were performed using layers of maps on different transparency sheets overlaid on top of one another. Each transparency represented a different layer of information with respect to the geographic region under study. The availability of database technology in the 1960s led to the development of the first wave of GIS applications, which allowed for management and analyses of massive databases such as the early U.S. Census data files. Much of the technology available in the early days of GIS required a large, mainframe computer. This limited the use of GIS to large organizations and institutions, such as the government and university research settings. Much of the GIS technology available during this time was created in the context of these settings for specific uses related to the needs of governments and universities.

Subsequently, private organizations began to develop more broad GIS applications in the late 1970s. Though a mainframe computer was still required to run these applications, therefore limiting the number and types of potential users, they could be used for more general kinds of analyses rather than the applications developed previously for specific purposes within the government and university settings. In the late 1980s computer technology became less cumbersome as personal computers started to replace mainframes and the cost of such equipment reduced drastically. This development in computer technology led to expansion of GIS applications, and they became widely implemented for land-use planning at the state and municipal level.

In the 1990s, the increased availability of personal computers for individuals led to the development of various levels of GIS technology with relevance to all levels of users. This expansion of GIS technology led to increased uses. By the late 1990s users of GIS included individuals ranging from federal government and university researchers, to commercial market analyzers, to local community planners and organizers. In the past five years, the widespread use of GIS has led to increased development in the capabilities of GIS. GIS analyses developed by individual researchers can now be shared and opened up for interactive contribution over the Internet. Nowadays, most of the statistical analyses techniques that originally had to be hand calculated and entered manually into the GIS application are done automatically by the application itself. Further, users can write their own programs and scripting to create sub-applications within the larger GIS system that meet specific requirements for data management and analyses.

Components of a GIS

The basic primary components required for conducting GIS analyses of any type include a GIS software package, a basemap file, and data that can be organized along some spatial boundary.

There are several manufacturers of GIS software applications. A search on the Internet will turn up at least a dozen retail and open source applications. At the time of this handbook, the two most popular retail GIS applications are ArcGIS and MapInfo. This book uses ArcGIS for all examples, and shows how to complete the steps to create specific map examples in ArcGIS. However, the maps shown in the book can be generated using the equivalent steps in MapInfo and/or most other GIS applications.

Basemap files are the files used by the GIS application to determine where to place particular attributes based upon some specified geographic criteria. Many basemap files are available from third-party resources. Basic basemap files can be created using the sample data provided with some GIS applications, as is shown in this handbook. Basemap data can also be created by the user by digitizing a hardcopy map using a computer-aided drafting (CAD) application. The basemap file must correspond to the data you want to analyze in terms of the available spatial attributes.

Data files are those files that contain the attributes that the user is interested in analyzing along geographic boundaries. Referencing the previous discussion, this would include data such as census data and police data. The preparation of such data is usually the most time-consuming task of a GIS researcher. As with any analyses software, data must be complete and consistent in order for the software package to make sense of it and conduct meaningful analyses. Data files can consist of spreadsheet files, such as .dbf files, global positioning system (GPS) data, remotely sensed data, and even scanned data. This handbook uses primarily the .dbf format data, as this is the type of data most often used in the context of social science research. The major requirement for data files used in a GIS (as alluded to in the previous discussion of basemap data) is that they contain some geographic attribute that the GIS application can use to place the objects in the data set on the basemap data for display purposes. For this reason, the geographic attributes of the data files used must correspond to at least one geographic attribute field of the basemap data. This attribute can consist of state, county, zip code, XY coordinates, or any other spatial attribute as long as the basemap and data files have at least one of these fields in common.

Related Concepts

The book introduces many concepts relative to GIS analyses for the social sciences in the context of the examples in subsequent sections. However, the following concepts are considered of particular importance for any GIS user to be aware of, thus they are defined here.

Map projections: a map projection is used to represent a three-dimensional curved surface such as the earth as a flat computer file, or flat map. Map projections allow for the preservation of the area, shape, direction, bearing, distance, and scale of the earth's curved surface while displaying the map as a flat file. There are many different map projections available, each of which preserves a different set of these attributes. For example, a projection that allows for the preservation of distance may distort the distance between countries. A user should base the decision about which map projection to apply on the purpose of the map they are creating. Further discussion of

Note: **Boldface** terms in the text are defined in the Glossary/Index.

projections is beyond the scope of this book; for more information see the link below.

Map scale: the map scale is the representation of the proportional ratio between distances on the map display and actual distances. For example, if a map scale is set to 1:100,000 with map units set to centimeters, this means that 1 centimeter on the map display is equal to 100,000 centimeters in actual distance. When using GIS, the map scale can be set for the display, as well as for the data.

Vector format: data in the vector format is data stored as geometries. Vector data stores features as lines, points, or polygons that represent objects on a map. Vector data takes up less storage space than raster data, but does not store the value for all points in a given polygon.

Raster format: data in the raster format is data stored as a series of cells with a single value contained in each cell. Raster format is most often used for storing images in a GIS, as it is able to store a value for all points in a given polygon. The raster format takes up more storage space than the vector format. The decision to use raster or vector is dependent upon the needs of the GIS user; further consideration of this issue is also beyond the scope of this book.

Spatial heterogeneity: spatial heterogeneity is the concept that spatial locations are not independent of other spatial locations divided by boundaries such as county and state lines. In reality, spatial locations divided in this manner vary along a continuum of spatial heterogeneity to spatial homogeneity, subject to the distance between them. For example, two spatial locations that are 100 miles from one another may be less independent than two spatial locations that are 500 miles from one another regardless of the official boundaries between the locations. These effects must be considered when conducting spatial analyses, particularly in the social sciences.

Internet Map Services (IMS): Internet Map Services provide the ability to produce dynamic GIS applications and publish them on the Internet. IMS can be used with standard web development tools to create an interactive mapping environment that allows for easy sharing of data with others via the Internet.

In addition to the terminology presented here, the Environmental Systems Research Institute (ESRI), the manufacturers of ArcGIS, hosts an online GIS dictionary at http://support.esri.com/index.cfm?fa=knowledgebase.gisDictionary .gateway. This dictionary can be accessed over the Internet for further explanation of these and any other GIS-related concepts and terms.

Companion DVD and Website

Readers who purchase a new copy of this book will find that a DVD is bundled with the book. This DVD contains a number of files and features that shall enhance the reader's experience using this book and the teacher and student interaction in cases where the book is being used in a classroom or workshop setting. We first describe in some detail the contents of the DVD, after which we shall describe the website that will be available to any interested reader.

Software

First and foremost, the DVD contains two software programs that are used in this book and to which the user will be provided at least some access to. In

Section 3 of this book, we use a spatial modeling program called S^3, a program written by Paul J. Gruenewald and William R. Ponicki of the Prevention Research Center of the Pacific Institute for Research and Evaluation. The latest version of the program along with the user's guide appear on the DVD as in a directory called "S3" and can directly be downloaded to the users' hard drive. Please read and follow the instructions in the users' guide to set up the program and the accompanying data and files.

Second, the DVD contains a trial version of Wolfram Research, Inc.'s Mathematica version 5, which is needed to run S^3; the trial is good for 30 days from the time it is installed on a computer. S^3 works as a module running under Mathematica, and Version 5 is known to work with S^3 under certain circumstances. These circumstances are documented in the S^3 User's Guide, on page 4, under System Requirements. The S^3 module will also work on older versions of Mathematica, specifically versions 3 and 4. Many universities have site licenses for Mathematica so that it is available to students and faculty for a very small fee, so if you use the trial version from our DVD and you wish to continue your spatial modeling with S^3, inquiry on your campus for additional access to Mathematica. The current version of Mathematica available from Wolfram Research is Version 6; please look to the website to be established for this book, **www.routledge.com/ textbooks/9780415989626**, which will be up and running by July 1, 2008, for further information regarding Mathematica Version 6 and its compatibility with S^3. If you want to purchase your own copy of Mathematica Version 6, if and when we can report on this book's website that it does work with S^3, you can contact Wolfram Research at http://store.wolfram.com/catalog/. For students, you can buy a single user license for $139.95; a 12-month timed version for $69.95, and a 6-month "semester" version for only $44.95 (prices are current as of April 2008 and are not guaranteed; see Wolfram Research website for the latest information).

Third, the DVD includes a link that allows the reader to contact ESRI, the makers of ArcGIS and the related GIS family of programs that this book is designed to teach you how to use, to request a free, fully functional copy of the software. This version of ArcGIS, including all the extensions demonstrated in this book, is available for a 60-day trial period. The link to the web page to request this software trial version is: http://www.esri.com/software/arcgis/arcview/eval/ evalcd.html. This trial version is a complete functional version of the software, and includes the following extensions, some of which are demonstrated in this book: 3D Analyst, including ArcGlobe; Geostatistical Analyst; Network Analyst; Spatial Analyst; Survey Analyst; Tracking Analyst; as well as several extensions that ESRI calls Productivity extensions. For more information, please use the link given here. The only requirement for the 60-day free trial is that you have an email address, and the trial is 60 days from the installation on a computer. As is the case with Mathematica, many universities and colleges, as well as many libraries and public institutions, have a site license for ArcGIS software. Computer labs at universities and colleges and in libraries, on campus and off, often have ArcGIS software installed for their users. If you run through your 60-day trial and want to continue to use and learn about GIS with ArcGIS software, please inquire at these institutions about continued access. Many universities and colleges have site licenses for individual faculty and students so that they can acquire and install ArcGIS on their own computers, usually for an annual fee of less than or about $100. As with Mathematica, you can also purchase your own copy of the ArcGIS software. For example, you can purchase a single user version of ArcView 9.2, which does not include any of the above extensions, for $1,500. This version includes all the basic coding, mapping, and database capabilities demonstrated in this book. For $2,500 more, you can get access to one extension of your choice. Once again, check the ESRI links given here for the latest guaranteed information.

For Sections 1 and 2, the ArcGIS software, along with basic productivity programs like Microsoft Word and Microsoft Excel, are all you need to do everything we have shown you how to do in the book. Currently, the ArcGIS software family is only certified to work with Windows XP, Windows 2000, and Windows NT. Check this book's website for information on how to work with ArcGIS software in a Windows Vista environment, something that is possible but not supported or endorsed by ESRI.

Mathematica and S^3 are used in Section 3 of this book, and so you can wait to install Mathematica and invoke the 30-day trial until you are ready to learn about spatial modeling.

Data, Figures, and Exercises

We have designed this book to be a hands-on learning tool, as we describe elsewhere in the Overview. As we taught workshops and seminars during the time we were developing the materials and examples used here, under ideal situations, we would have each student or perhaps two students sharing a computer equipped with ArcGIS and all of the data we use in the hundreds of examples shown in this book. This allowed our students to actually construct the maps we show in the book, and to follow along at each step and to see each submenu and/or intermediate map that leads up to the final product in each example. To make it possible for the teacher of a GIS course to use our book in the same way we designed it to be used, based on our own teaching experiences, or to allow an individual or small group of students who are trying to learn GIS with our book on their own to have the same learning experience, we have included over 2 gigabytes of data in a directory called GISdata, on the DVD. These data comprise all of the data we used in every example, map, submenu, screen, and exercise in this book. Each data set has the original name used in the step-by-step instructions that help the reader learn how each map was constructed, each address geocoded, and how each model was spatially tested. Using the book with these data allows you to reproduce every illustration included in this book.

In order to keep the price of this book reasonable, at least by today's standards, we decided to print the book entirely in black and white. Unfortunately, despite our best efforts, this has rendered some of the maps and figures difficult to read. However, we have included a directory on the DVD called Figures which contains a color version of every chart, map, submenu, or table included in the book, labeled with the same name and number that appears in the text, so that the reader can look from their ArcMap screen to the color image of the corresponding figure in this directory and be certain that they have successfully followed the instructions and arrived at the correct map or other outcome. Every figure is included here so that if the final one does not match, the reader can go back through the intermediate steps and their figures to check what went wrong. These files are TIFF format and can be displayed directly on any computer by simply double clicking on the image file you would like to display. In this case, the file name is the same as the figure label in the text, i.e., Figure 1.2 Census Bureau

Subregions of the United States is the file name to click on for a color version of Figure 1.2 in Section 1.

We have put a number of additional exercises for which we do not show the step-by-step instructions and for which we do not show the final outcome map, in a variety of places in Sections 1 and 2. We have included on the DVD a directory called Exercises, in which the reader can find the final maps that should have resulted if the reader was able to apply the knowledge gained from the step-by-step example in the text to produce the maps indicated by the exercise. These files are TIFF files like those in the Figures directory on the DVD and are labeled according to the page number in the text that the exercise was given, for example, on page 61 in Section 1, the reader is guided to produce Figure 1.72. At the bottom of page 61, an exercise is given which will require the reader to produce an alternative to Figure 1.72 for comparison. In the Exercises directory, the "answer" to this exercise is in a file titled, Exercise 1 page 161; double click on that file and compare the answer we came up with to yours.

Finally, you can check the website for the book, which will contain everything I have described here as being on the DVD, in addition to any new and updated information we would like to offer you about the text or GIS and spatial modeling. The URL for the website is: **www.routledge.com/textbooks/9780415989626**. On the website you can also find contact information for the authors, if you have any questions about the book, the DVD, or the website. Please contact us if you have any problems with the software included on this DVD and/or check the website for this book for tips and troubleshooting advice on the software included on this DVD. You can email us at: robnp@aol.com (Robert Nash Parker) or jemily@eathlink.net (Emily K. Asencio). You can call us at 951–827–4604; this is the number of the Presley Center for Crime and Justice Studies at the University of California, Riverside, where Robert Nash Parker is Co-Director and Emily K. Asencio is currently a Post-Doctoral Fellow. We hope you find these materials helpful and that you will be successful at learning and use GIS and spatial modeling in your work and life.

Section 1   Introduction to Geocoding and Mapping

This is a reference book for how to do Geographic Information Systems or GIS. So right away you have learned something you might not have known before reading this book—what the letters G, I, and S stand for in the acronym GIS. Of course, as with a lot of literal definitions, knowing what words the letters stand for does not really convey much new knowledge. The next question is, What do GIS techniques give us that we do not already have?

GIS is a methodological and conceptual approach that allows for the linking together of spatial data, or data that is based on a physical space, with non-spatial data, which can be thought of as any data that contains no direct reference to physical locations. For example, a survey of a representative sample of the population of a city or a nation is an example of non-spatial data. We have selected a sample (usually based on geographic location) of individuals who give us answers on survey questions which we have recorded. We can analyze the percentage of our sample that voted for a Republican presidential candidate, the percentage that take public transit to work, or the proportion that are married, single, or divorced. However, we do not know anything about where these respondents are located in the physical world, other than as a sample representing the U.S. population.

Suppose we add a question to the survey that asks each respondent to name the cross street nearest to their place of residence, including the name of the city and the zip code if we can get it. Now we can locate these respondents in geographic space—this is an example of a piece of spatial data. By including such a question, we have transformed our survey from a non-spatial data into spatial data.

Why would we want to do this? First, once we have the ability to locate a subject in physical space, we can create maps of our survey data. Maps are often a powerful way of displaying data in an interesting and compelling way—much more so that a dry and boring table. Figure 1.1 is a display of some data for each state in the United States; among the data shown here is the membership in the U.S. Census Bureau's sub-region classification system for each state, given in Column D.

FIGURE 1.1   **A Microsoft Excel spreadsheet**

	A	B	C	D	E	F	G
1	AREA	STATE_NAME	ST	SUB_REGION	STATE_ABBR	POP1990	POP2000
2	6380.614	Hawaii	15	Pacific	HI	1108229	1184688
3	67290.061	Washington	53	Pacific	WA	4866692	5835089
4	147244.653	Montana	30	Mtn	MT	799065	885795
5	32161.925	Maine	23	N Eng	ME	1227928	1257219
6	70812.056	North Dakota	38	W N Cen	ND	638800	631032
7	77195.055	South Dakota	46	W N Cen	SD	696004	734993
8	97803.199	Wyoming	56	Mtn	WY	453588	479673
9	56088.178	Wisconsin	55	E N Cen	WI	4891769	5277833
10	83343.643	Idaho	16	Mtn	ID	1006749	1273309
11	9603.272	Vermont	50	N Eng	VT	562758	596714
12	84520.490	Minnesota	27	W N Cen	MN	4375099	4820250
13	97073.594	Oregon	41	Pacific	OR	2842321	3356108
14	9259.527	New Hampshire	33	N Eng	NH	1109252	1215100
15	56257.965	Iowa	19	W N Cen	IA	2776755	2877060
16	8172.561	Massachusetts	25	N Eng	MA	6016425	6206482
17	77330.258	Nebraska	31	W N Cen	NE	1578385	1672199
18	48561.751	New York	36	Mid Atl	NY	17990455	18223519
19	45360.118	Pennsylvania	42	Mid Atl	PA	11881643	11986139

These data are spatial data because we can link the data, in this case what sub-region a state belongs to, to the physical location of the state in the United States. Displaying the same information in a map is more pleasing to the eye and better conveys the meaning of this particular piece of information, as shown in Figure 1.2.

FIGURE 1.2   **Census Bureau sub-regions of the United States; a layout view from ArcMap 9.1**

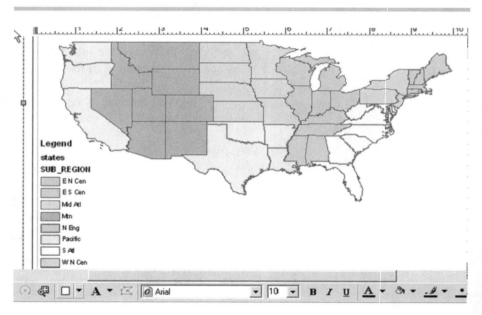

How to Make a Pin Map

A pin map is a geographic display of the location of a type of activity, organization, or event of interest to the map maker and the map viewers. The reference to the name comes from the fact that before computerized maps, you could make one of these displays by attaching a map to a wall and then pushing pins into the map at the location of each event, organization, or activity. For example, in Figure 1.3 we have a pin map of the United States, with a pin displayed on the map at the location of the capital city of each state.

FIGURE 1.3   **A pin map of the State capital cities in the continental United States**

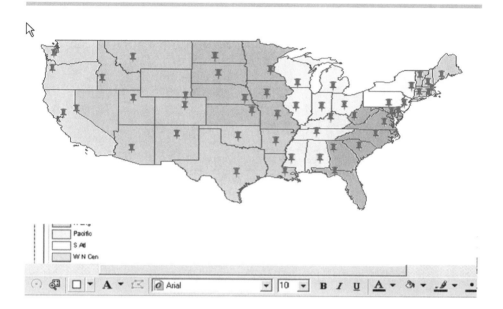

The Basics of Geocoding

How did we know where to put the pins in Figure 1.3? The process of identifying locations to be placed on a map is called **geocoding**, in other words, coding the location of an object, a place, an event, a building, or an address where something of interest took place. At its most basic, something can be geocoded by knowing its latitude and longitude; for example, the capital of California, Sacramento, is located at 38.581N latitude and −121.493W longitude. However, unless you really know your longitudes and latitudes, this is not very helpful if your task is to place Sacramento in the proper location. However, with ArcGIS software (and other GIS software packages) this can be useful information for geocoding the locations of the capitals. One of the useful options in ArcMap is the option to identify an object on the map. This option can be selected by clicking on the tool bar in the upper left-hand portion of the ArcMap screen as shown in Figure 1.4.

FIGURE 1.4   **The tool bars and the Identify tool**

The "i" inside the dark circle is the Identify tool. Once you activate the tool you can move it around the map to various objects; clicking on the object to reveal what the program knows about that object or location.

In Figure 1.5, you can see the result of clicking the object on the pin that is likely to be the capital of Utah, Salt Lake City.

FIGURE 1.5   **Identifying Salt Lake City**

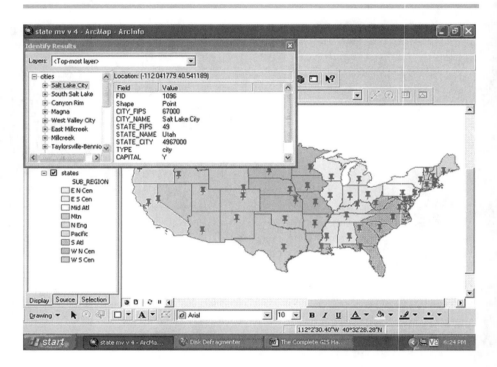

Among the information displayed in the drop down box labeled Identify Results is the longitude and latitude of Salt Lake City. Notice also at the bottom right of the screen another latitude and longitude is displayed; if you move the cursor around on a map, this line will display for you the longitude and latitude of wherever the cursor is pointing.

Most times, however, you will not have longitude and latitude as part of a database you want to link to a map. Another very common type of information you may have access to is a street address or an intersection of two streets. This kind of information can also be used to link objects, events, and structures to a map through the process of geocoding.

Before we get into the details of how to geocode addresses, why do we want to know the address of an event of sociological, criminological, or other disciplinary significance? How can this information be useful to us? Sociology and crimin-ology are disciplines that focus on the importance of context—as does public health and geography, and increasingly, public policy and other social sciences as well. But what does this really mean? In much of the history of these disciplines, the idea that context mattered for understanding social behavior, criminal behavior, health behavior, and so on was more platitude than a nexus for analytic understanding. Even when context really mattered, as in a theory such as Sutherland's (1947) differential association, in which the context created by your friends was seen to influence whether or not you developed attitudes unfavorable towards the legal code and whether or not you learned how to commit illegal acts, the physical context was not treated as part of "context" at all (see Matsueda, 1982). For example, you might find that, following Sutherland's approach, two individuals have the same number of and intensity of connections to delinquent peers, but in one case these peers all live within a block or two of the subject, while in the second case these peers are scattered all across the city. If the second subject showed fewer delinquent acts, this could be explained by the lack of concentrated access to these peers in the immediate environment. Being able to place the location of peer networks in physical proximity or not could make the difference in delinquency understandable; looking only at Sutherland's ideas as stated would not allow you to fully understand the differences in outcomes. Being able to "bring the context back in" with geocoding of the location of people, events, organizations, facilities, and so on is an important tool that GIS can bring to social and behavioral research for increased power and understanding.

In the following example we will examine youth violence in the city of Riverside, California. In terms of policy, it is very much in the city's interest and that of its police department to know where youth violence clusters. In such "hot spots" of crime (see Sherman and Berk, 1984) police can place extra patrols, and city officials can build neighborhood centers, increase after school programs, provide for public health nurse visits, and/or a host of other interventions that may reduce youth involvement in crime and violence. What GIS enables is the ability to "see" such patterns across a city's neighborhoods and thus guide city and police policies about where to deploy scarce resources and city expenditures.

Example: The Process of Geocoding

The basic procedure for geocoding address-based data into a map first involves obtaining a street database. A street database contains information that defines the lengths, shapes, directions, and address ranges for all the streets, roads, avenues, circles, culs-de-sac, and other such units that cities and towns use to label routes that have addresses located on them. The street database will also be linked to the other types of maps that can be created for a location—city, town, county, and so on. In Figure 1.6, the city of Riverside, California, circa 2000, is displayed with the U.S. Census Bureau block group units outlined.

FIGURE 1.6   **Riverside, California, circa 2000, U.S. Census block groups**

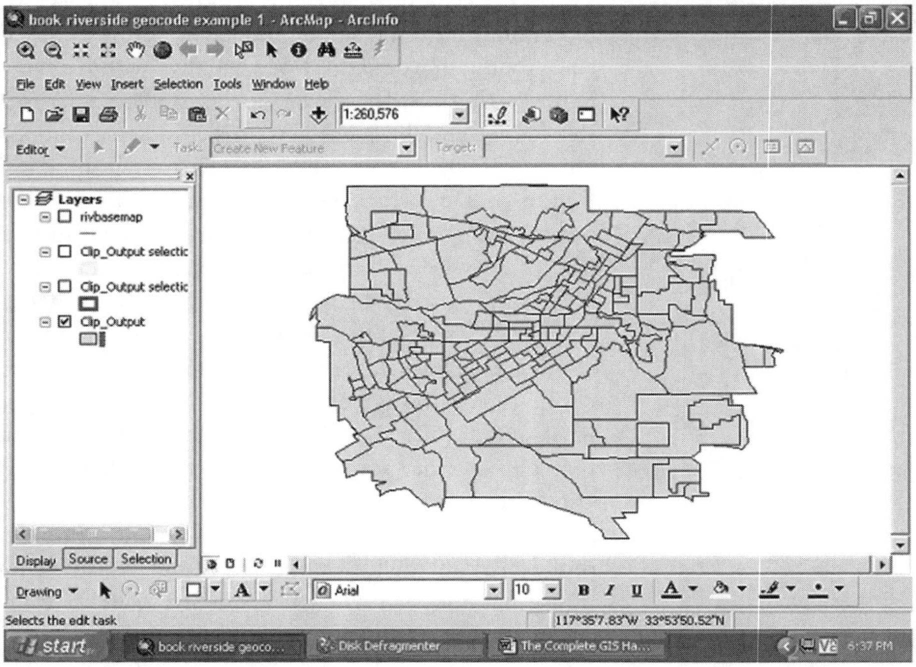

Block groups are units of measurement created by the Census Bureau for data collection and distribution for the decennial censuses—this map comes from the 2000 U.S. Census. Block groups in urban areas are made up of the familiar city block—about 4 to 8 blocks per block group, with a population in 2000 ranging from a few hundred people to about 2000 individuals. The block group is often the smallest unit of analysis for cities in the United States that you can be assured of getting the most data from; at the block level, the Census Bureau is concerned that someone could identify individuals by name from the Census data, so in many cases data like ethnicity, family composition and structure, income levels, and so on are missing in Census data sets released to the public and to researchers at the block level. The block group is usually large enough and has enough people in it to make it unnecessary to suppress any data of interest. Census tracts, perhaps a more familiar unit to some, are made up of block groups.

So a basic map for Riverside has been obtained from the Census Bureau (maps like this for the entire United States are included with the ArcGIS software); now what is needed is an address database. The U.S. Census Bureau once again is the data provider in this case. In order to try and count everyone where they live, the Census Bureau needs to have a pretty good idea of all the places people live in, and where such residences can be found on the map. The U.S. Constitution requires that certain information be gathered from a full count of individuals in the country, and in order to count people the Census Bureau needs to have an address where it can deliver a basic 100 percent Census form to each residence. If a Census form is mailed to a residence and the residents do not fill it out and send it back, the Census Bureau will send someone to that address to try and see who lives there and to get the basic information for the 100 percent count. However, the first step is to mail a Census form, and to do that the Bureau needs an address for every dwelling unit or residence in the country. So the Census Bureau also creates an address database every ten years for the decennial Census.

These address databases are also included with ArcGIS software and they can be obtained from the Census Bureau and other providers. Using the Streetmap database for 2000 from ArcGIS, we can add a **layer** to the map the represents all the known streets and addresses in Riverside, circa 2000.

To do this, we first add a new layer that contains the streets of Riverside to the map of Riverside block groups. We do this by selecting the Add layer command, the dark cross with a light background located on the tool bar third from the top, next to the map scale display (1 : 260,576).

FIGURE 1.7   **Adding a new layer in ArcMap**

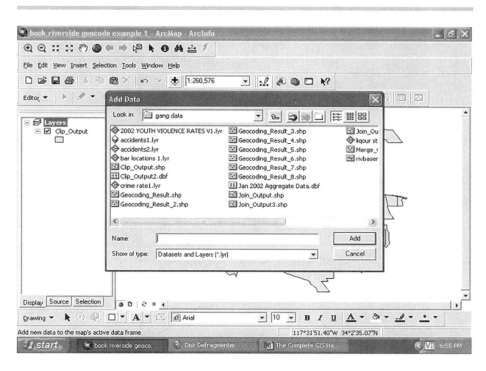

This opens up a menu of the available files and layers in the default directory (from where the first map was added to this session of ArcMap); we select one from the last column on the right called rivbasemap. Notice the symbol this file is displayed with—it looks like a tiny street map. The software has already identified this database as a street database. To add this street database to the map, click the database and click on Add.

FIGURE 1.8   **Adding a new database to a map**

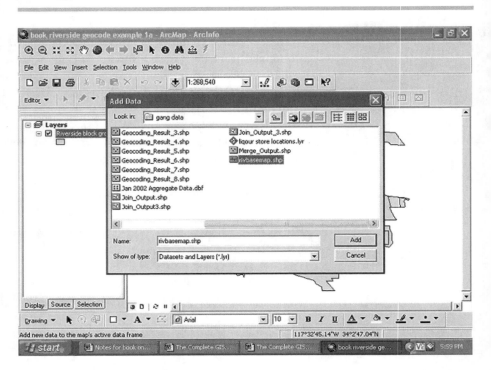

Note that the extension on this file is .shp; this is referred to as a **shape file**, and it is a file and accompanying data that contains information allowing these data, the streets in this case, to be displayed in a map of Riverside. We will discuss the locating and creating of shape files later in this section; having shape files makes the creation of maps much easier. Since this is a shape file, as soon as it is added to this session of ArcMap, the streets are displayed as a new layer overlaid on the block group map.

FIGURE 1.9   **New street map layer displayed as an overlay on the existing map**

The database for the streets contains the street names and all the recognized address ranges. Left-clicking on the street map in the table of contents window to the left of the map itself brings up a menu from which you can view the database associated with the map layer you left-clicked on.

FIGURE 1.10   **Popup menu for map layer**

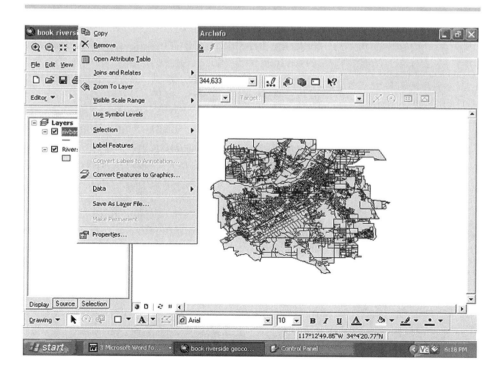

The menu in Figure 1.10 has a number of useful options, one of which is to display the attribute table. This is a spreadsheet version of the data associated with the map layer, in this case the street database. Click on Open Attribute Table to access these data.

FIGURE 1.11   **Attribute table for Riverside streets**

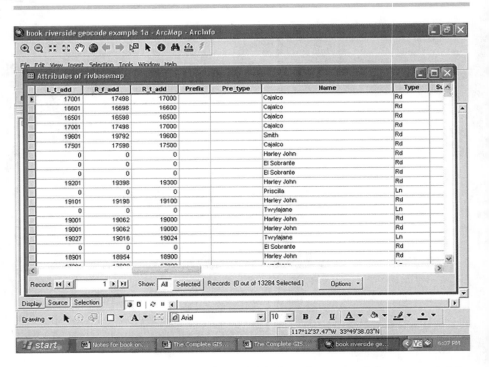

The sixth column from the left in Figure 1.11 gives the name of the street, and the next column to the left gives the type of street—Ln for Lane, Rd for Road, Dr for Drive, St for Street, Wy for Way, and so on. These types are really part of the name of the street, so in Figure 1.11 if you want to find the street on a map you look for Priscilla Lane. The types can become important for the process of geocoding because addresses recorded by people are often not as accurate as the address databases compiled by the Census Bureau (although some errors can exist in these databases as we will illustrate later). For example, someone may record an event as happening at 19792 Smith *St*, when the actual name of the street is Smith *Rd*, or Road, as shown in line 5 of the attribute table in Figure 1.11. This can cause difficulties in the geocoding process, and it is a detail that the geocoder can fix via address editing, as we will see below.

The attribute table also shows the address ranges on the right and left sides of the street (columns labeled "R_f_add" and "L_t_add" in Figure 1.11). Traditionally, left side addresses are odd and right side addresses are even, and the address range is listed, so for example for Smith Rd, the address range on the right or even side of the street is from 19600 to 19792. On the left or odd side, the range is from 19601 to 19793, parallel to the right or even side addresses. These are addresses that were known to exist on that street when the database was assembled.

The menu in Figure 1.10 also has a selection for labeling the data displayed on the map. In the case of the street map this is a very useful function as it toggles on and off the street names, so that you can locate a street by name. At the level of magnification in Figure 1.10, such labels would be hard to read. The magnification level can be changed in or out by selecting the magnifying glass icon from the tool bar at the top left of the ArcMap screen; + (plus) for making the image more detailed (Figure 1.12), and − (minus) for decreasing the detail.

FIGURE 1.12   **A detailed view of the streets of Riverside**

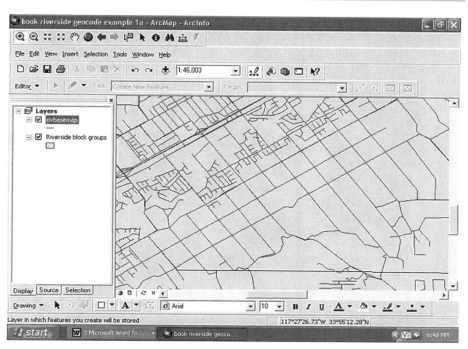

Now if we display the menu in Figure 1.10, and click on Label Features, we can activate the street name labels.

FIGURE 1.13   **Streets of Riverside labeled**

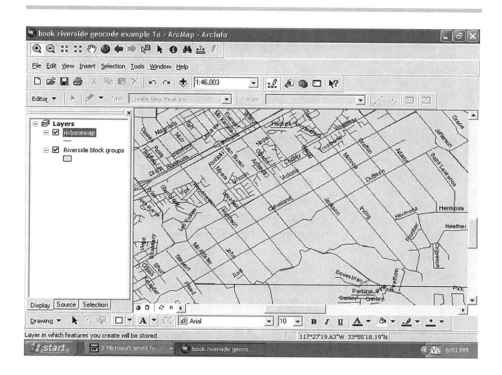

In Figure 1.13 you can see Cleveland Street right in the middle running at about a 45 degree angle across the map, and as you go from the lower left to the upper right, Cleveland crosses Monroe; a number of streets in this section of the city seem to be named after U.S. presidents. The streets are displayed in gray, while the black lines that sometimes overlap with the streets are the block group boundaries. In the table of contents window on the left side of the screen, you can turn off and on the display of each layer of the map by clicking on the check mark to the left of the name of the layer. We can turn off the block group map and just display the streets.

FIGURE 1.14   **Streets of Riverside**

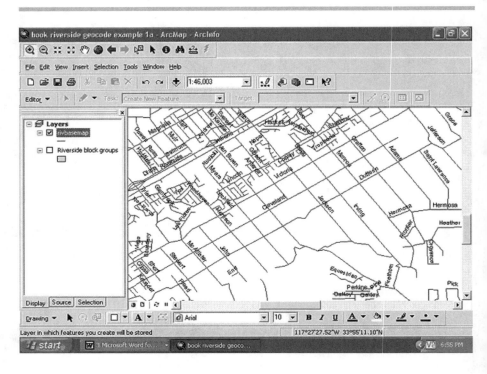

In Figure 1.14 you can see that not only are the darker boundary lines gone from the display, but the background color of the block group layer is also gone.

Geocoding Addresses

What kind of addresses can be geocoded? Software like ArcGIS can deal with addresses in a number of formats. A standard address would be something like 1922 Jones St, and an address in this format is potentially geocodable. An address in the form of 22nd St and Bowman Ave, indicating an intersection, can also be codable. Sometimes the conjunction between the two streets in an intersection can cause the address not to be recognized, but in ArcGIS there is some flexibility in the recognition of conjunctions: ampersands can be used (&), slashes can be used (/), as well as the word "and." The user has control of this process and can specify alternative forms. What if an address is misspelled? The geocoding engine of ArcGIS can be set to varying levels of sensitivity, that is to how much of an exact match the address has to be to what is in the database in order for the program to geocode the address successfully. Once you are familiar with the forms of address expected by the software, you can edit the set of addresses you want to geocode to more closely conform to the expectations of the software.

There are two kinds of geocoding, automatic and interactive. In the automatic method, issue such as sensitivity and the form of intersections are very important, because the software will try to geocode every address without any input from the investigator. However, depending on the sensitivity settings and the accuracy of the source of the addresses to be geocoded, the success rate for automatic geocoding could vary from 20 percent to 80 percent of the addresses you would like to locate on a map.

Interactive geocoding is the way you make up for the failures of automatic geocoding. In interactive mode, ArcMap presents you with a list of addresses it was not able to decide where to code. The program may also list some possible locations for the uncoded address, and you can investigate these locations by zooming to the map. However, before we can illustrate the process of geocoding, we must create what ArcGIS calls an address locator. An address locator is a set of commands and descriptions that together inform ArcGIS about the format of the address database you are using and how to use that database to compare with the address you wish to geocode and make automatic geocoding decisions. In order to begin this process, click on the icon for the Toolbox on the tool bar to the left of the help button (arrow with a question mark), as in Figure 1.15.

FIGURE 1.15   **ArcGIS Toolbox menu**

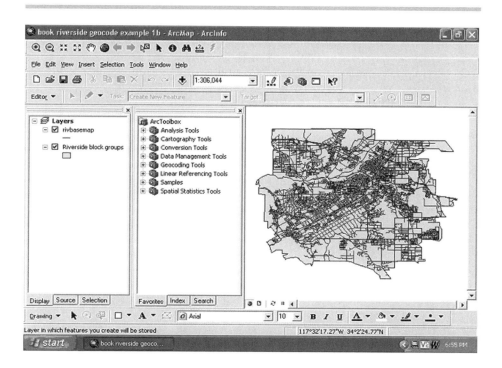

Locate the geocoding sub-toolbox on the menu, and click on it.

FIGURE 1.16   **Selecting the command to create an address locator**

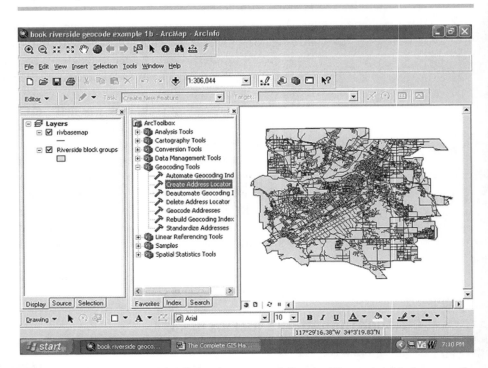

Double-clicking on the highlighted command line in Figure 1.16 brings up the Address Locator submenu. A number of selections and identifications are made on this submenu to create the address locator for geocoding.

FIGURE 1.17   **Creating an address locator**

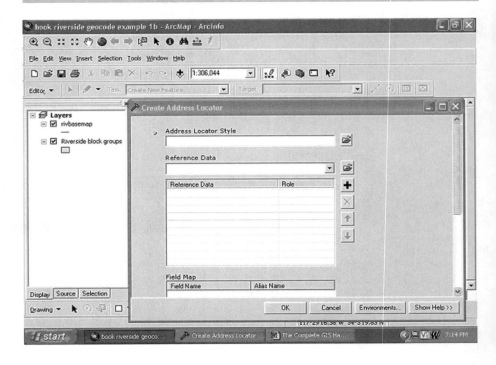

First, click on the folder icon to the right of the line below "Address Locator Style," to designate the style of address locator database to be used here. There are a number of options that make for a flexible system: the address database we are using here and shown in Figure 1.14 above are U.S. streets in a file; you can also designate a location for the address locator file, either on your own hard drive (local) or on a server (ArcSDE Server).

FIGURE 1.18   **Address Locator Style selection**

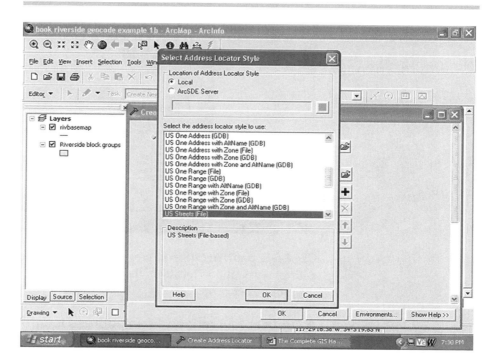

Next, click on the file icon to the right of the box labeled "**Reference Data**" and identify the location of the street map database; clicking on the downward arrow next to the box reveals the possible databases that ArcGIS has already located as possible reference files. The next selection is to identify the role that this database will play in the process of geocoding. As you can see from the number of lines in this box, it is possible to specify a number of address reference files. In some cases, the files may each provide reference to one address element that you wish to consider in the coding process—for example, street may be in one file, city council district in another, and U.S. congressional district in another database. If your addresses to be coded contain fields for all of these, you could include this information from multiple sources in the process. Notice that once the database and its role are established, the field map at the bottom of this menu is filled out—in the left-hand column are the specifications from the type of locater we selected, U.S. Streets—such as "house from left," "house to right," and "street name"—and in the right-hand column are the fields in the database we are using, as shown in Figure 1.11 above, that correspond to those specifications; e.g. "house to left" is equated with L_T_ADD in the table shown in Figure 1.19 for our address database.

FIGURE 1.19   **Specifying the details of the address locator**

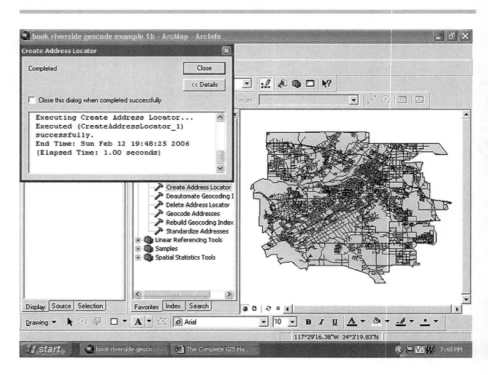

Click OK and ArcGIS will create an address locator to use in geocoding the addresses we want to locate on the map of Riverside. Figure 1.20 shows the end of the process being successful.

FIGURE 1.20   **A successful creation of an address locator**

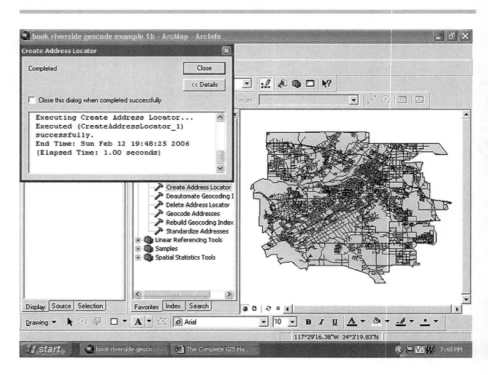

Now that an address locator has been established, the next step is to bring the data with addresses to geocode into the ArcMap workspace. We can do this by adding these data to the table of contents using the Add Data command (black cross on a light background) as illustrated in Figure 1.7. In many cases such data will be in the form of an Excel spreadsheet, as in Figure 1.21. In order to bring these data into ArcGIS, the file needs to be saved in database format, with an extension of ".dbf." Figure 1.21 illustrates how you can do this in Excel.

FIGURE 1.21   **Saving a spreadsheet in database format (DBF) with Excel**

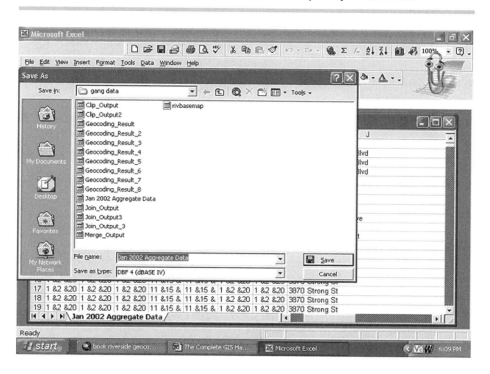

Once these data, which contain the locations of youth involved violent incidents from the Riverside Police Department, are saved in database format, these data can be added to the map as a new layer; once they are added to the map, they can be geocoded using the address locator we established previously. Using the Add Data command, these data are added to the map in Figure 1.22.

FIGURE 1.22   **Adding the database format file to the map; the file has the same name as in Figure 1.21 but with the .dbf extension**

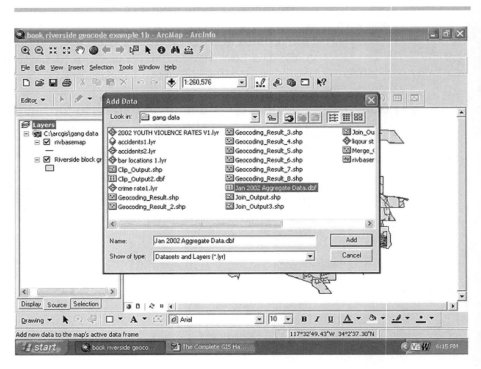

The next step is to authorize the automatic geocoding of the location column in this file, which as you can see in Figure 1.21 gives the street address where each incident occurred. There are sometimes multiple listings at the same address adjacent to each other in the file—this is because there is a line in the file for each violation of the law recorded in connection with the incident. If one youth assaulted another with a weapon and stole money and a bicycle, there would be multiple entries—one for the assault, for the bicycle theft, and another if the attacker used a weapon.

We can begin the process as in Figure 1.23, by clicking on Tools, Geocoding, and Geocode Addresses.

FIGURE 1.23   **A step in the geocoding process**

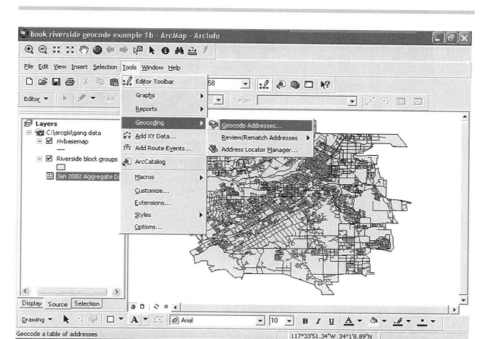

Notice that the table of contents window to the left is now on the "Source" tab at the bottom of the window; this occurred automatically when we added the "Jan 2002 . . ." file with the addresses to be coded. The reason this happens is that the spreadsheet table with the addresses is not displayed on the map, so if you click on the display tab, this file is not listed in the table of contents window.

Once you click on Tools, Geocoding, and Geocode Addresses, a menu comes up asking you to add an address locator; Figure 1.24 shows that you must point to the ArcGIS catalog, select address locators and double-click to bring up the list of available address locators.

FIGURE 1.24   **Address locator submenu**

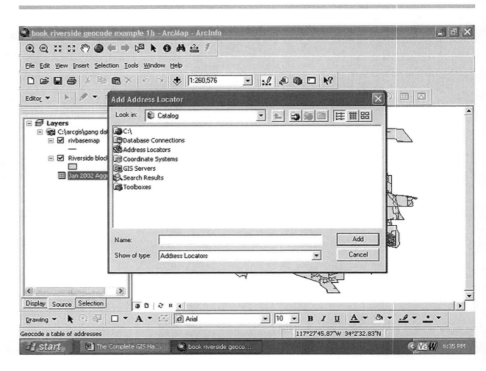

You can see there are two listed in Figure 1.25; both are the same, so you can select either one. A different address locator would have a different name after the user name (Rob in this case).

FIGURE 1.25   **Selecting the address locator**

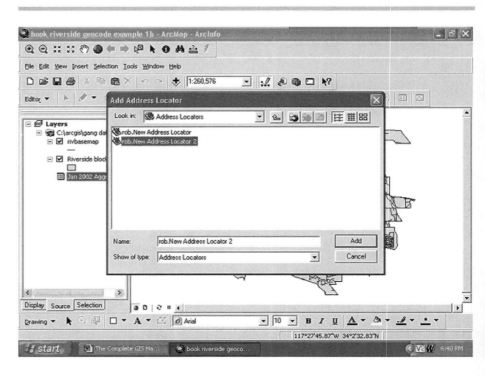

Click on Add and you are one step closer to starting the process of geocoding. Figure 1.26 shows what happens next; you can now tell ArcGIS about your address file—in what column is the street name and number given?

FIGURE 1.26   **Specifying the details of the automatic geocoding process**

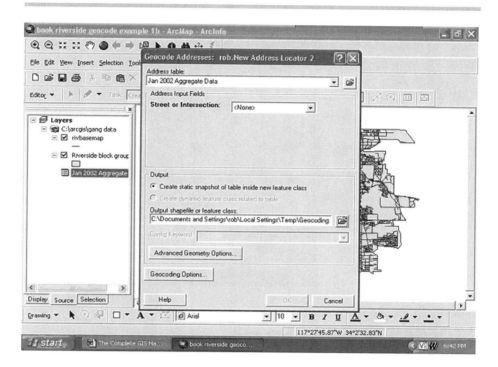

First, you click on the drop down menu to identify the column in the database that gives the addresses—in this case, location (as seen in Figure 1.28). If you want to change the default location and file name for the geocoded layer, click on the file symbol next to the listing under "Output shapefile or feature class." You can also modify the options that control how the automatic geocoding gets accomplished by clicking on the button labeled Geocoding Options. Let's examine these further in Figure 1.27.

FIGURE 1.27   **Geocoding Options submenu**

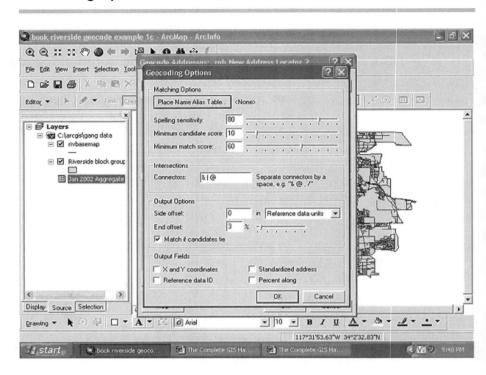

As we discussed above, the automatic process for geocoding addresses will use the information in the address locator to attempt to match the location of each address in the column "location" in the table of youth violent incidents we have asked ArcGIS to code. The addresses being examined were compiled from police department records based on the reports of each police officer in the field—one of the pieces of information officers always record is the address of the incident. However, police officers are human, and they have a lot to do when confronting the scene of an incident, and so the address may be incomplete or abbreviated in a way that the officers understand, but which may not match the address locator database information, which has usually been based on U.S. Census Bureau address collections and verified by Census workers and local officials. The automatic geocoding process creates a score for each address to be matched, from 0 to 100, where 100 would be an exact match to the information in the address locator database. Various modifications or abbreviations in the address to be geocoded can result in a lower score. For example, if in the address locator database a street has a direction North, East, West, or South, such as West 3rd Street, the address locator may expect that the direction is spelled fully; the address recorded by the officer may be in the form of W. 3rd st. This abbreviated version is understood by all officers and observers alike to be the same as West 3rd Street, but the address locator is now less certain of the correspondence, and so it will lower the score a certain amount. Suppose the address was known as 234 Robinson Ave in the address locator, and the officer records 234 Robnson ave instead—the misspelling of the street name would lower the score further. The officer might record 2267 Jones Ave., when the street in question is actually Jones Drive—again, if there were no other roadways named Jones in the locator database, the program would lower the score; if there were two such streets, Jones Ave. and Jones Drive, the program might match the wrong one, but more likely, as the address range on

Jones Drive includes 2267 and that for Jones Ave. ends at 1945, the score would lower again. You can see on the menu in Figure 1.27 that you can set the sensitivity of the automatic process higher or lower depending on your confidence about the nature of the errors or abbreviations made and any mistakes that may be in the addresses to be coded. The program has a default of 80 for spelling, a minimum match score of 60, and a score of 10 to be considered a candidate. This latter score is for the interactive process that comes after the automatic process has run; more about this below.

You can also specify a table of aliases for your street names if you have such information. You could specify in a spreadsheet that has a column in it in which you list aliases or alternative names for streets in the location column we are trying to geocode—such information could increase the score in the face of an initial comparison that shows an abbreviation or a misspelling.

Intersections are also a major issue in geocoding of address-based data. The program has three default symbols that it will interpret as indicating an intersection: an ampersand (&), a vertical line, and the at sign used in Internet addresses (@). However, you can add additional ones on the line in this submenu as shown in Figure 1.27. Sometimes addresses simply use the form "Jones and Taylor" to indicate an intersection. If you add the word "and" as indicated in this command, the program will now successfully code all of your intersections with "and" providing they are actually intersections that the address locator recognizes. Some officers may record an intersection that does not exist according to the address locator, in which case that address will come up for interactive geocoding.

Another consideration is the address number itself. Many times an address will not successfully code because the address range in the address locator database does not include the number given on the address to be coded. This could happen for a number of reasons, but two main reasons tend to explain these cases: (1) new construction, so that the end of the street was extended, new lots defined, and new housing built after the map was constructed. The further you get from the decennial census year, in this case 2000, the more this can be a problem if you are working with a geographic location that is growing in population and expanding its housing stock, such as Southern California; (2) the address number recorded is in error. If either of these things is true, the automatic process will usually reject the address and bring it up in the interactive process.

In many cases there will be multiple candidates identified depending on the magnitude of the error or the misspellings. Another option is to match if there is a tie in the score; this is indicated in a check-off box towards the lower left of the Geocoding Options submenu. For example, the address range on the right may include 2236, and on the left 2239, but address in the data to be coded is 2237. The program may decide that both of the existing addresses in the address locator are candidates, and it may decide they have an equal likelihood of being correct, so there will be a tie. If you check this box, and the score is above the threshold you select for matching, the program will geocode the address at the first location in the address locator of the pair that tied. Maybe someone who owned a big lot at 2239 decided to subdivide their lot and sold half to a developer, who built a new house at 2237. If the tie listed 2239 first, this would be a very accurate coding; if it listed 2236 first, it might still be very close but on the wrong side of the street. The impact of such an error depends on your goals in geocoding and in the larger project for which you are using the geocoded data.

In the case of the project we are illustrating here, the purpose of geocoding these youth violent incidents is to place each one inside a block group, the unit of analysis shown in Figure 1.6. Once we have succeeded in geocoding each one into a block group, we can then use the population of youths in each block group as measured by the U.S. Census to construct a youth violence rate per 1000 youth. This can in turn be used as a dependent variable in research. We can try and explain the reason for the variation in this rate of violence across all the block groups that we are likely to observe once we construct the rates. This then allows us to test theories about the causes of youth violence and, if we have made any attempts to intervene to prevent or reduce youth violence in certain areas defined by block groups, we can test over time whether or not these interventions have been successful at reducing youth violence in the block groups where the intervention occurred.

So, in this case, if the coding placed the new house on the wrong side of the street, chances are very high that it would still be in the same block group, and thus for the purposes of this study the error is of no consequence. If you were studying whether violence was more likely on the right or the left side of the streets, however, such an error would be of major consequence.

This example shows how careful we should be in adjusting the sensitivity of the automatic procedure. If we lower the sensitivity and the minimum match score too far, the automatic geocoding procedure will make too many errors, and some of those errors, in our case, may place violent incidents in the wrong block group, distorting the rates we observe. In Section 3 of this handbook, when we discuss **spatial modeling** of data such as these, this topic will come up again and we will discuss different statistical corrections we can apply for this problem. In the case of geocoding, the more accurate we can be the better for every type of mapping or analysis that comes afterwards. So while we hope the automatic geocoding succeeds in finding matches, we should not lower the sensitivity too much so that errors are increased. Any candidate that the automatic process will not match becomes the subject of an interactive geocoding process, where we can in essence check up on the automatic process. It is better to err on the side of having too strict match criteria than too lenient, because if you make the criteria too lenient you are likely to increase the errors made and, because the process is automated, you will never be able to check every geocoded point, especially if you have hundreds or thousands of them. When you make the criteria on the strict side, you may get too many addresses rejected, but you can match these to your satisfaction, with a minimal amount of error, through the interactive process.

Data Mining and GIS

One of the challenges of GIS is finding the data you need to make the kinds of maps you would like to make for your project. In this case, data were obtained from the city police department as part of a project designed to evaluate a gang prevention effort (Spergel, 1996). Once the data were obtained, they were converted to the .dbf format as shown above, and in the course of the geocoding we edited some of the entries in the location column so that ArcMap would more easily recognize intersections and we corrected some data entry errors along the way, such as misspelled street names, incorrect street types (blvd vs. bld), and, in one case, we corrected an error in the street map database; a street was misnamed in the database compared to the actual name in use in the city. These are examples of the process of data mining: finding and preparing data for use in GIS. For more information about data sources, please check out the Appendix on this subject.

To get a sense of how geocoding is done, please follow the examples set out here on the computer yourself. We have designed each example in this book actually to be conducted as you go along in the text. Some of you may be taking a course, we hope in a fully computerized "smart" classroom, in which each student or perhaps each team of two or three students is in front of a computer, and perhaps the instructor is also at a computer, doing each example for the class as the students follow along on their own computer screen, looking up to the instructor's projected screen for reference. Perhaps you saw the instructor demonstrate this example, and now you are in a lab class with a computer equipped with ArcMap and the data from the DVD that comes with this book. Perhaps you are learning GIS on your own for your school work, your research, your thesis, or some other reason. In any case, please find an opportunity to follow the examples in this book as step-by-step exercises. These examples were designed to be used in this way, for you to follow along by doing the same thing on your own computer, with the same data we used, and to check your screen's appearance to that shown in the examples. Occasionally, we will also give you an additional example that we do not illustrate directly with these same data, at the end of an example, to further illustrate a technique or approach. But please do not forget that each example we present is designed to be an exercise for the student of GIS, so that you can learn by doing and be able to check what you have achieved step by step and screen by screen. Our experience is that if you go through this text in this way, you will really learn to be a master of GIS. You will also then be able to adapt your own data and research questions to the techniques you learn by doing in this book. You can begin the process by loading the DVD that came with the book, or by accessing it where your instructor has indicated on your local computer network, and using Microsoft Excel open the spreadsheet shown in Figure 1.28, "Jan 2002 Aggregate Data.dbf."

Now let's see how these decisions and selections work in an example. Looking at Figure 1.28, we see the street names given in the location column of the data we wish to geocode.

FIGURE 1.28   **Data to be geocoded**

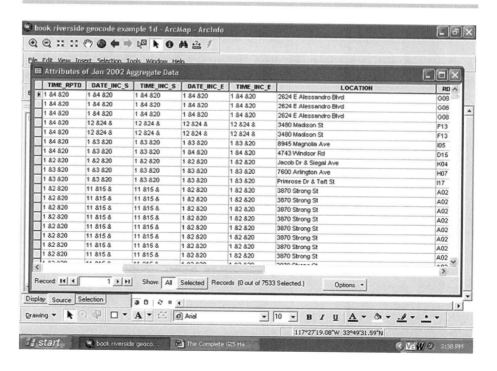

Notice some of the features of these addresses. For example, the first one is "E Alessandro Blvd"; the "E" is an abbreviation for East, and "Blvd" is an abbreviation for Boulevard. If our address locator is set up to accept "East" and not "E", we have a problem already, and we may not know in advance how boulevard should be abbreviated. Notice also that the intersections are indicated by an ampersand, "&", as in "Jacob Dr & Siegal Ave." We could search the address file to see if any "and" indicators remain, and edit those out of the file. At this point, however, it makes sense to run the automatic geocoding process and see what happens.

FIGURE 1.29   **Automatic geocoding in process**

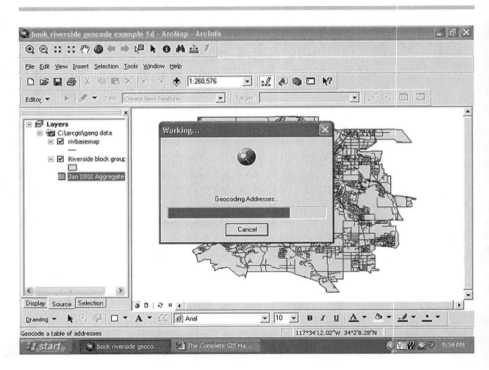

In Figure 1.29 you can see the display showing geocoding in process; the little magnifying glass searches over the little glob again and again as the process proceeds.

FIGURE 1.30   **Report of results from automatic geocoding process**

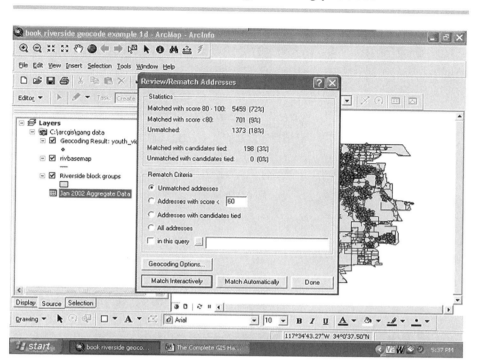

The popup shown in Figure 1.30 appears after the automatic geocoding process is completed, and gives a report as to the success and failure of the procedure. For example, we see that 72 percent or 5459 of the addresses coded successfully with a score of more that 80 out of a possible 100. In addition, another 9 percent or 701 addresses were matched with a score between 80 and 60, the point where the low point was set in the Geocoding Options menu shown in Figure 1.27. So a total of 81 percent of the addresses were matched and placed on the map. This is a very good result; experienced geocoders report success rates on the first automated pass anywhere from 20 percent to 80 percent using the stricter criteria and sensitivity we have used in this example. This means, however, that 19 percent of the addresses, or 1373, remain unmatched, and are candidates for interactive geocoding. Figure 1.31 shows the results of the automatic geocoding on the map of Riverside.

FIGURE 1.31   **Results of automatic geocoding process**

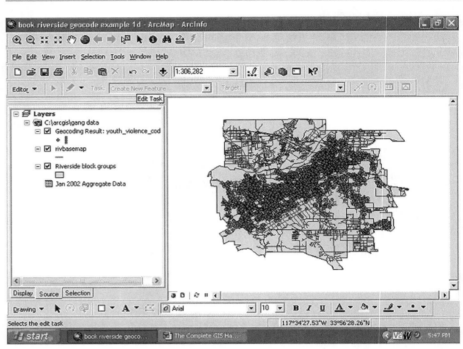

Each dot represents at least one violent incident reported in these data; as there is often overlap, or more than one incident at an address, dots can represent more than one coded incident. A pattern is already obvious from the distribution of dots on the map—there is a central core of the city running from the lower left of the map to the upper right in the middle of the city that seems to have a large concentration of violent incidents. There is also a secondary concentration along a line running from the central core down and to the right, with a side shoot that takes off to the right from that concentration to the right up to the border of the city. A few scattered incidents occur elsewhere outside these areas of concentration, and some areas at the extremes of the city have no dots at all. This may change after the interactive geocoding, as all the reported incidents have yet to be represented. However, we have already learned something about the distribution of these incidents by geocoding them to the extent we have thus far. What is it about those central areas that cause them to have more violent incidents? What is it about the outlying areas that explain the lack of incidents? There are many theories and hypotheses that can be discussed, and many of these can be explored once we have geocoded these data completely and accurately. Mapping these data will allow us to geographically link information about the nature of the populations that live in each block group, and the kinds of economic and social activities that go on there, and we will be able to develop and empirically examine such possibilities. None of this is possible without successful geocoding, which in this case, as in most cases, requires interactive geocoding to finish the job appropriately.

Example: The Science and Art of Interactive Geocoding

There are many reasons why an address does not geocode automatically. We have already mentioned some of these issues, such as address ranges, misspellings on the street names and types of streets, and of course, just plain old human error. The process of interactive geocoding is one of applying logic, knowledge, and good judgment to each address to place it appropriately on the map. In order to proceed, one needs access to a good independent source for geographic information, such as an atlas or an online service like Mapquest. These are necessary additional sources of information that may be more up to date than the address locator database, and they also provide the geocoder with another perspective on the map, streets, and address ranges they are working with. One also needs to keep in mind the goal of the geocoding project. In this case, we are trying to place all the violent crime incidents in the U.S. Census block groups in order to compute the rate of violence in each block group. Thus any decision made in interactive geocoding that places an incident across a boundary line of one block group to the other may be a source of error being introduced by human action. In most types of human activity, accuracy is valuable, and we should not undermine it deliberately or carelessly. Let's see how these ideas work in an actual application of interactive geocoding. However, before we get started, double-click on the street map database in the table of contents window, and then click on Label Features, if you have not already done so. The street labels will be useful in interactive geocoding.

First, click on Tools, next on Geocoding, and then select Review/Rematch Addresses. The results from your automatic geocoder will appear to the right; move the cursor to highlight that file, and click.

FIGURE 1.32   **Beginning an interactive geocoding session**

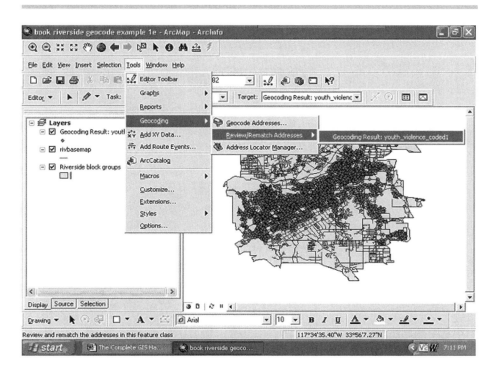

When you click on the file with your automatic geocoding results, the interactive geocoding menu will appear.

FIGURE 1.33   **Review/Rematch submenu**

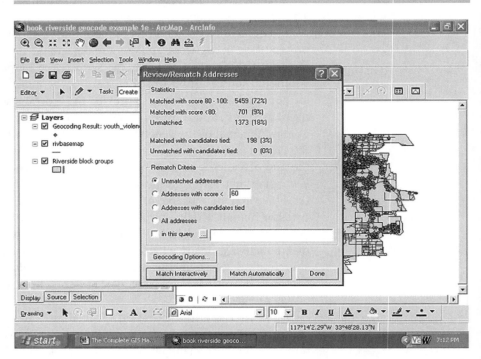

You may be asked if you want to edit the database, click on OK and the menu will appear. Make sure that the circle to the left of "Unmatched addresses" is selected, and click on Match Interactively.

FIGURE 1.34   **Interactive geocoding, Alessandro Blvd**

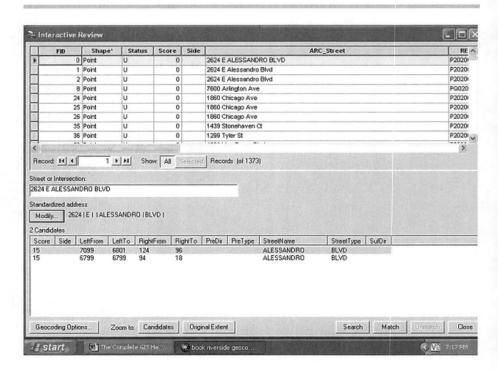

The screen in Figure 1.34 illustrates the many issues involved in interactive geocoding. At the top of the screen are the first nine unmatched addresses from the automatic procedure. The first candidate is selected and given in the box labeled "Street or Intersection." As you can see, it is 2624 E Alessandro Blvd; the address is broken down into the components recognized by the address locator to the right of the box labeled "Modify," that is the number, the directional prefix (E), the name, and the street type suffix (Boulevard abbreviated as BLVD). The next box indicates that in the address locator there are two candidates that the program identified, but neither had a very high score—in fact they were both scored 15 out of 100 on the sensitivity match score. The address number may be the problem, as the address locator has ranges of numbers on either left or right that do not include the number given in this address record. There is a set of low numbers— 124 and down on the right of the street, and some high address ranges on the left—6799 to 7099 in this case. This is a case where you need a good paper atlas of the area that can give you an indication of address ranges, or access to an online atlas for the place you are geocoding addresses from. Web-based mapping programs like Mapquest or Yahoo can be useful, as well as a GPS system.

The first thing to do is to see where these candidates are on your map in ArcMap. This can give you an idea of what the problem might be in geocoding this address. To do this, click on the first address in the "candidate" window, and click below on Zoom to: Candidates. Minimize the geocoding window and you will see the map, zoomed in to the exact location that the street database wants to put this address; remember that this may not be the right place for this address, however.

FIGURE 1.35   **Candidates for geocoding on the map**

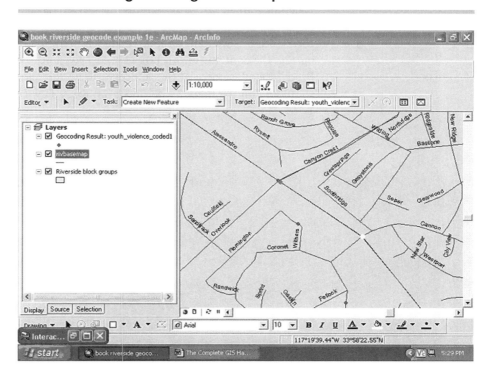

The light dot symbol is the candidate address, or where the street database thinks it should go; notice a larger dark symbol by the intersection of Canyon Crest and Alessandro; this is the other candidate for geocoding. If we were to go back to the geocoding menu and zoom to the second candidate, it would appear light on the map and the current light symbol would become dark.

In Figure 1.35, some of the streets appear darker than others; this is because these streets are also block group boundaries—an example is Alessandro or Canyon Crest. It could be the case that selecting one of these candidates might put the crime incident in one block group, and selecting the other candidate might shift the location to another block group. This is a case where accuracy is very important in interactive geocoding.

What does our atlas source tell us? Putting in this address as recorded, or looking up this block on the paper atlas, we can easily see that the street database is considerably off from where the atlas places this address, by about three miles. Instead of intersecting with Canyon Crest or Cannon, the atlas view shows that this address is nearer to the intersection of Alessandro and Sycamore Canyon Blvd. Why would this be the case? As mentioned above, one of the reasons why an address will fail to code is the fact that new construction adds to the possible address ranges along a street. The program knows what address ranges it has, and if it is asked to geocode one that is outside the known ranges, the program attempts to fit the unknown address with the known—but with little confidence that it is correct, hence the low score. In Riverside this area has been undeveloped until a few years ago, and therefore this is a prime candidate for an area with new address ranges that are not in the 2000 Census database.

Now that we have updated information about where this address is located, what can we do with that information? We can use our options for interactive geocoding to modify this address to better reflect the information we have at hand. If we go to the window on the left middle of the screen labeled "Street or Intersection," we can see that it displays the address being considered. If we modify the contents of this box to read, "Sycamore Canyon Blvd & E Alessandro Blud," the placement of this address will be very close to where the atlas shows it should be on the map. Doing this produces a new candidate, as shown in Figure 1.36.

FIGURE 1.36   **A modified street address and a new candidate for geocoding**

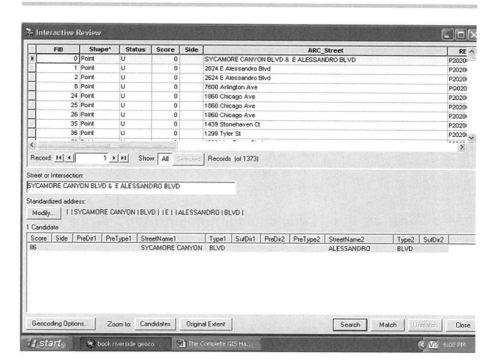

Selecting the new candidate, which has a score of 86, high enough to be matched automatically, and zooming to this location, shows the result of the process of interactive geocoding in Figure 1.37.

FIGURE 1.37   **Zooming to the new candidate on the map**

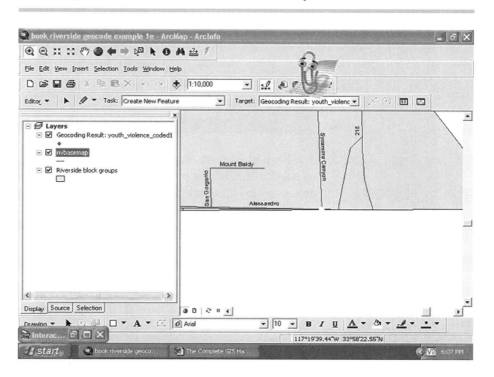

This location is literally within a few feet of the location shown in the atlas, and as long as the youth violent incident is within the city limits, it can only be in one block group being located where it is. The only step remaining is to go back to the interactive window and click on the Match key. The other two incidents at the exact same address can be handled in the same way, so that now three additional addresses have been successfully geocoded.

Looking back to Figure 1.36, the next address that is uncoded is on Arlington. Here, the address range given is only one single number away from the address we wish to code—7599 in the range vs. 7600 in the address. Zooming to the candidate shows that while a block group boundary is nearby, there is only one logical place for this address to be on the map. A check of the atlas confirms that this location is near Harold Way, as shown in Figure 1.38, so we can declare another match for this address.

FIGURE 1.38   **Candidate for Arlington Ave**

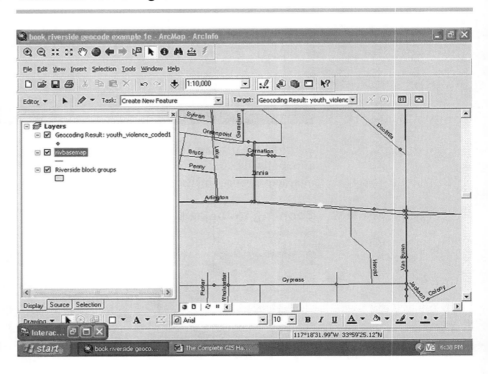

The next set of three unmatched addresses are from Chicago Ave; examining the location of candidates places these incidents well within the boundaries of a block group, so deciding to accept this location will have few consequences for the overall study; another three addresses coded. The next address, on Stonehaven Ct, presents a different kind of geocoding situation.

FIGURE 1.39   **An address with no likely candidates: 1439 Stonehaven Ct**

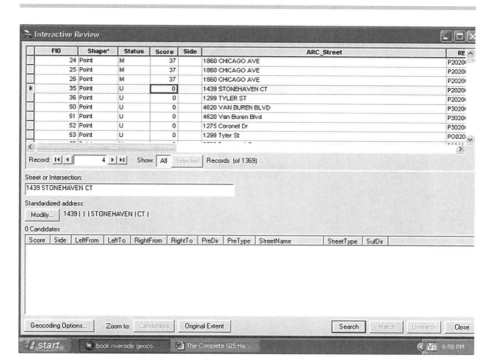

In this situation, there are no candidates to examine. This is a situation in which having another atlas that is more up to date is very important. Checking the atlas rules out all kinds of possibilities—that the street does not exist, that the number is way off from the range, that the street is not a "Court" but something else, and so on. So why does this address generate no candidates? A more important question is what can we do about this? It is unclear why the program may not produce any candidates, but we can examine the location in more detail and come up with an approach that is logical and appropriate given the goals of our project. In focusing in on this location in ArcMap (using the magnifying glass with the plus sign icon) we note that Stonehaven intersects with Allendale, and that there are no nearby block group boundaries. What if we modified the address to the intersection of Stonehaven and Allendale? Stonehaven is a very short street, so we could not be too far off, and placing the address at the intersection makes no errors in terms of which block group the incident happened in. Figure 1.40 shows what happens when we modify the address and a candidate is zoomed to.

FIGURE 1.40   **A nearby intersection generates a candidate for geocoding**

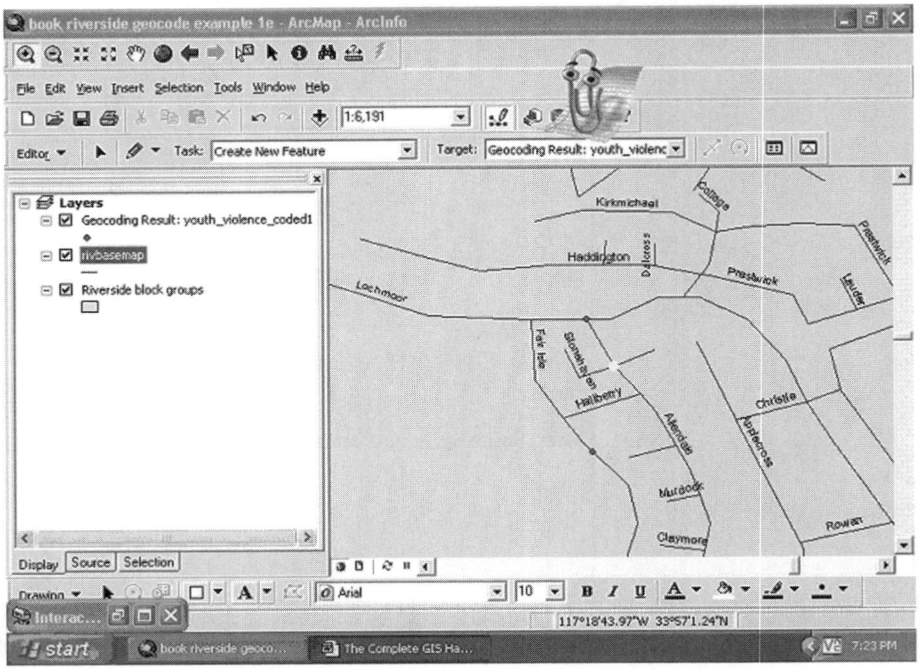

Even in the case of an address that should be coded automatically, and where there are no obvious reasons why it has not been coded automatically, we can use interactive geocoding to rectify the situation. Now we have coded an additional address.

Although you should expect to geocode every address successfully with interactive geocoding, there will be some addresses that are impossible to code. Although it is possible to force an address onto the map, this is not always justified given the logic of geocoding, the information you have in hand, and the impact such a decision might have on the ultimate goal of your project. If you end up with 5 percent or fewer addresses uncoded, you have probably done a very thorough job of geocoding, and any biases you introduce by not coding certain addresses is probably minimized. This is particularly the case if those uncoded addresses are roughly randomly distributed across the space you are examining; the likelihood of repeat crime incidents at the same address would tend to undermine this idea of randomness. This is one of the tensions that interactive geocoding creates, and it is a tradeoff that the geocoder is often faced with. The choice is between maximizing the information available to geocode more addresses, minimizing the errors of assuming too much about an address, and the loss of information in giving up being able to place an address on the map. The next address in these data illustrates some of these issues.

As seen in Figure 1.41, the next address also produces no candidates for consideration—1299 Tyler St.

FIGURE 1.41 **No candidates for geocoding**

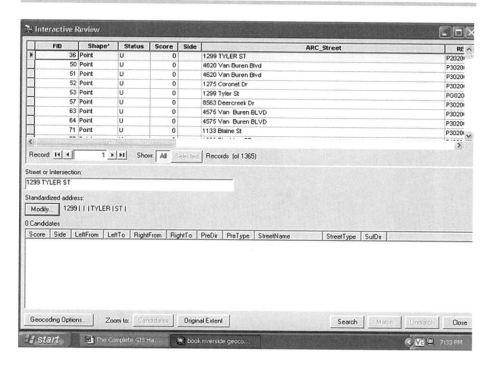

By editing the contents of the "Street or Intersection" box to remove the address number, the total range of addresses in the database for Tyler St becomes visible, and a likely reason for the lack of automatic geocoding is revealed: the address given is outside the range of addresses on this street in the database.

FIGURE 1.42 **Full address range available for Tyler St**

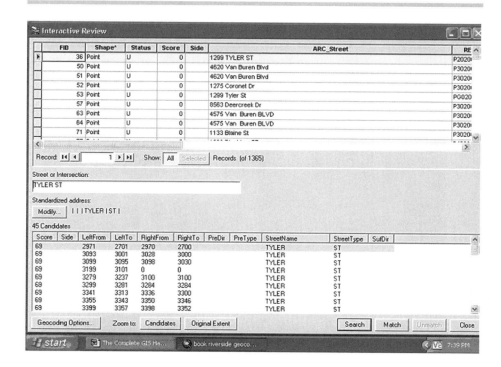

Notice that the lowest address range is for numbers in the 2700s, and the original address was 1299—not very similar; if the address to be coded was 2650, and you had 2701 as the lowest in an address range, it might be reasonable to declare a match. The difference here is too great for such an assumption. We can examine on the map the location of this lowest range by clicking on this range and zooming to the candidate.

FIGURE 1.43   **Addresses on Tyler Street, Riverside**

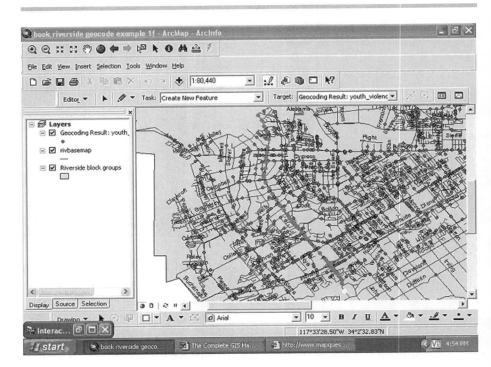

The light dot shows the block of Tyler Street with the smallest address number in the range recognized by the database—from Figure 1.42, you can see that this is 2700 Tyler Street. The address to be coded, 1299 Tyler, is quite some distance from this, and it would make no sense to assume that 1299 and 2700 are in the same block group, the ultimate unit of analysis here, so that we could code them as being similar. Figure 1.44 shows a close-up view of this section of the map; this was obtained by saving and exiting the interactive geocoding menu, using the magnifying glass tool to zoom in to the intersection of Tyler Street and Victoria. Next select the drawing tool from the tool bar at the bottom of the screen, as shown in Figure 1.44, and select the dot option from this collection of drawing

FIGURE 1.44   **The drawing tool selection popup menu**

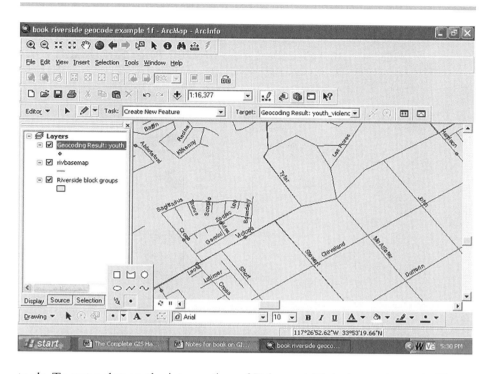

tools. To put a dot on the intersection of Tyler and Victoria, as shown in Figure 1.46, place the cursor on the intersection and left-click once; double-click to bring up the properties menu to change the size and color of the dot you just placed on the map, as in Figure 1.45.

FIGURE 1.45   **The symbol properties popup**

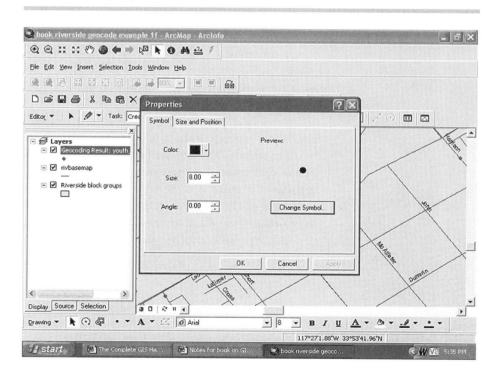

You can see in Figure 1.46 that Tyler Street does not start again to the southeast (see below to learn how to put a compass sign on your map) after dead-ending at Victoria.

FIGURE 1.46   **Detailed map of 2700 Tyler Street and surrounding area**

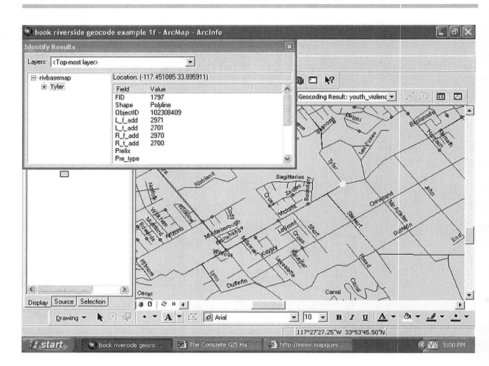

Sometimes you cannot make any assumption or adjustment that can make sense of an address, and you have to drop this address from the geocoding process and from the map. Perhaps it was recorded in error, or perhaps this is an address not in the city of Riverside; in either case, this address cannot be coded given the information at hand. Perhaps after an initial geocoding, you could get together with a representative from the organization that provided these data, and show them a list of uncoded addresses. These files could be reexamined to see if any additional information is available which could help resolve this record and allow it to be coded.

In this case, the record can be skipped and the next address be subjected to interactive geocoding. In this way, following the steps described here, the entire list of uncoded addresses can be processed and, in most cases, successfully coded. The next address of interest shows some of the ways you can use the information you have to make a reasonable decision to modify an address and achieve a successful geocode. The interactive geocoding menu for these data in Figure 1.47 shows that there are three possible candidates for 1275 Coronet Dr, an address that did not automatically geocode.

FIGURE 1.47   **Interactive geocoding for 1275 Coronet Dr**

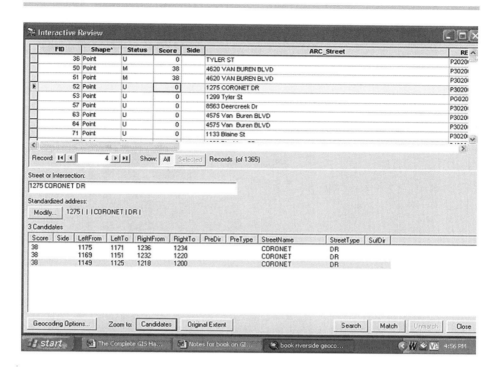

Highlighting the middle candidate in the bottom of Figure 1.47, clicking on the Zoom to: Candidates button, and minimizing the interactive geocoding menu reveals the three locations of these candidates, shown in Figure 1.48 in the larger symbols. This map also shows that a youth violent incident has already been coded near these three candidates. You can use this information to help make a better decision about how to geocode 1275 Coronet.

FIGURE 1.48   **Three candidates for 1275 Coronet and a previously geocoded incident nearby (smaller symbol)**

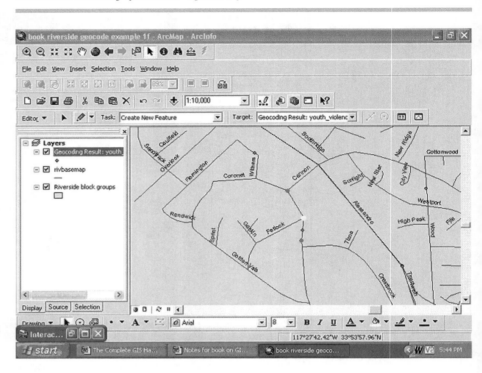

First, maximize the interactive geocoding menu, and click Close on the lower right of the screen (see Figure 1.47). Next, exit the geocoding process by clicking Done on the lower right hand of the Review/Rematch window you now see in front of the map. Now you see the main map, and you should click the selection drop down on the main tool bar; in Figure 1.49, you can see the drop down, and you should click on Select by Attributes.

FIGURE 1.49   **Selection tool drop down menu**

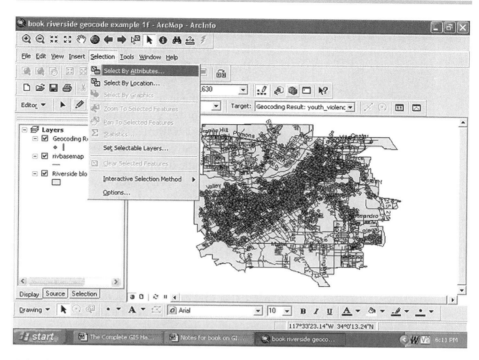

Selecting by attributes brings up the menu shown in Figure 1.50.

FIGURE 1.50   **Selection by attributes**

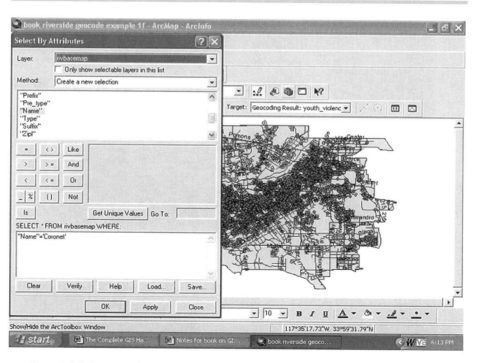

Step 1 Make sure the layer name containing the street database is shown in the Layer box at the top of the menu; if not, click on the drop down and select the proper layer.

Step 2   The large box below the Method drop down (which should be set on "Create a new selection" as shown in Figure 1.50) will give the columns in the attribute table for this layer; you should recognize them from the interactive geocoding menu as shown in Figure 1.47. Double-click on the column labeled "Name" and the column "Name" will appear in the box at the bottom of the menu where you will specify the selection formula.

Step 3   Click on the icon for the equal sign, and place your cursor in the box to the right of the equal sign, and type a single quote, type the name of the street you want to select (in this case, Coronet) with no type of suffix like Street, Dr, Blvd—just the street name itself, and then close with a single quote.

Step 4   Click on the verify button, and the program will tell you if you have specified the formula properly, and it will give you a message if no records would be selected by this formula—in which case, something is wrong; perhaps you misspelled the name or perhaps you left out an equal sign or a quote. In any event, once you have it correctly specified, the message will say, "Expression was successfully verified."

Step 5   Click OK on this window, and click Apply on the lowest set of buttons, and your selection will be made.

Step 6   Click Close, and the main map reappears on the screen. Click on the Selection drop down, and if you have made a selection successfully, you should be able to select the command, "Zoom to selected features"; this should reveal a detailed map of Coronet Dr with one previously geocoded incident shown, as in Figure 1.51.

FIGURE 1.51   **Coronet Drive highlighted, along with one previously geocoded incident**

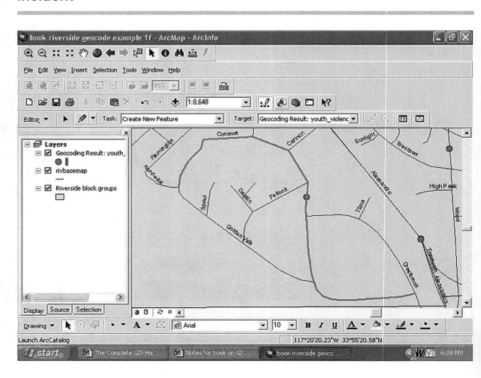

Step 7 Select the Identify tool from the tool bar at the top of the window; this is a dark circle with a light "i" inside it. Move the cursor to the previously geocoded incident and right-click; a box in the upper left of the screen will show the address of this incident, as in Figure 1.52.

FIGURE 1.52   **Identifying a geocoded incident on Coronet Dr**

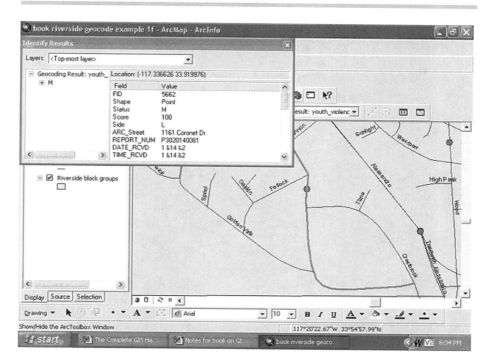

The address of this previously geocoded youth violent incident, 1161 Coronet Dr, can now help us to decide where to put the address we are trying to interactively geocode, 1275 Coronet Dr.

Step 1 Navigate back into the interactive geocoding menu, by clicking on Tools, moving the cursor to Geocoding, Review/Rematch Addresses, and finally to Geocoding Result: youth_violence_coded1, as in Figure 1.53; this opens the interactive geocoding window once again.

FIGURE 1.53   **Navigating the menus back to the interactive geocoding window**

Step 2 Click on Match Interactively, to bring up the uncoded address list.

Step 3 Click on 1275 Coronet Dr to bring up the address ranges; click on the first range, and click on Zoom to: Candidates.

You can see that this candidate is near the previously coded address of 1161 Coronet Dr, and is closest to the listed range of addresses on the right side of Coronet Dr. This address is on the left side of the street (even addresses on the right side, odd addresses on the left), but the other two candidates (indicated on the map in Figure 1.54) have ranges that are further away than the first one from 1161 and presumably from 1275 Coronet Dr. A reasonable conclusion is that this location is a good one for 1275 Coronet.

FIGURE 1.54   **Candidates for 1275 Coronet Dr**

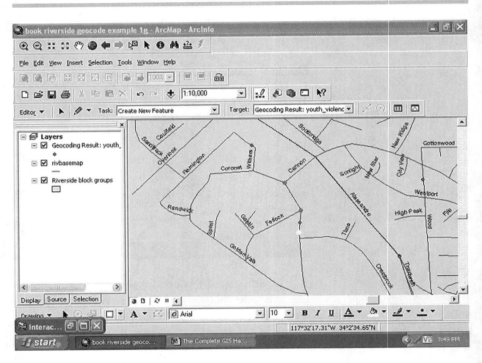

Step 4 Maximize the uncoded address list window, make sure the first candidate is highlighted, and click Match to accept this location for 1275 Coronet Dr.

The process of geocoding is a challenging one, but following the principles and examples we have shown here, any set of addresses can be successfully geocoded. As you have seen, some addresses just cannot be coded by any reasonable set of assumptions and procedures, but with some diligence you can expect to successfully and reasonably code 90 percent of the addresses in your database, and most analysts would agree that to adequately represent your data and to avoid the introduction of biases, you should achieve at least 90 percent coded at a minimum. Any less than that could introduce bias into your data and your maps, as the addresses you are unable to code may share some unknown but systematic characteristic or set of characteristics that make the events and data associated with the uncoded addresses significantly different than the ones you successfully code. Coding almost all of the addresses you have will insure that bias does not enter into your research project as a result of the geocoding procedures you have implemented.

Once the geocoding process has been completed, you will want to save your edits and save the files associated with this map and data, and you may want to export the map for inclusion in a report produced by a word-processing program like Microsoft Word, or perhaps a presentation program like Microsoft Power-Point. The next example shows how to do this for any maps constructed in ArcMap.

To save your geocoding, you first save the edits you have made to the addresses as you proceeded with the interactive geocoding phase. To do this, follow these steps:

Step 1 Click on the Editor drop down menu, and click on Save Edits, as shown in Figure 1.55. This will save your edits to the street addresses you made during the process of geocoding interactively.

FIGURE 1.55   **The Editor drop down menu**

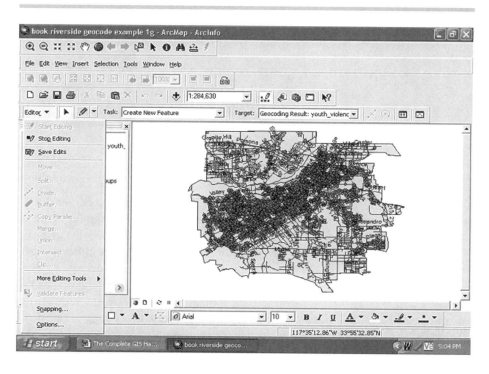

Step 2 Click on File > Save As, and select an appropriate name and folder to save your map document in. The file, with extension .mxd, has links to all the component files your map was built from, so that every time you load the .mxd file, all the components that are needed to construct the map as you saved it are accessible.

Step 3 Click on Save to complete the operation, as in Figure 1.56.

FIGURE 1.56   **Saving an ArcMap file**

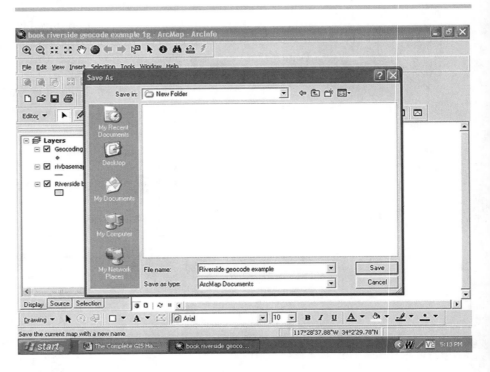

Example: Exporting a Geocoded Map

Now you are ready to export the map to be used in other software applications.

Step 1 Click on File, and move the cursor down to Export Map.

Step 2 The current name of the map file is given in the File name window, as well as the location on your hard disk that the computer is currently pointed to. You can change either or both of these to save the exported map in a convenient location.

Step 3 The default format is EMF—enhanced meta file—but there is a drop down menu which gives you a number of options, including JPEG, TIFF, PDF, BMP, PNG, and so on. If you have a preference, or know your software likes a particular form, you can select it. Then click on Save to export the map file, as in Figure 1.57.

FIGURE 1.57   **Exporting the map**

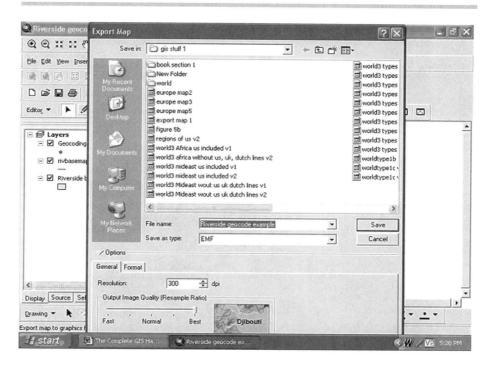

Now you are ready to import your exported map into another application, such as Microsoft PowerPoint.

Step 1 Minimize ArcMap, and open PowerPoint.

Step 2 Select a presentation style with a title on the top and the rest of the slide blank.

Step 3 Click on Insert, Picture, and from file; locate the file we just exported from ArcMap, and click on Insert to complete this action, as in Figure 1.58.

FIGURE 1.58   **Exporting a map to PowerPoint**

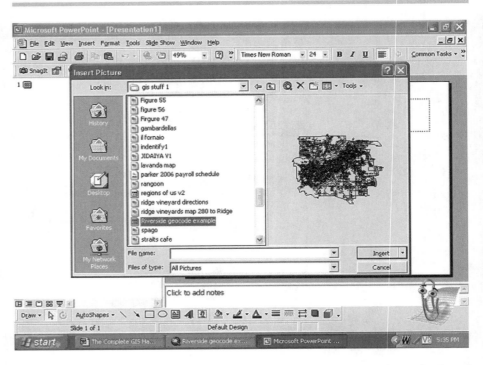

The map will now appear on a PowerPoint slide, and can be resized and repositioned in the usual fashion in that software application. The final version might look something like the slide in Figure 1.59.

FIGURE 1.59   **PowerPoint image of the map created in ArcMap**

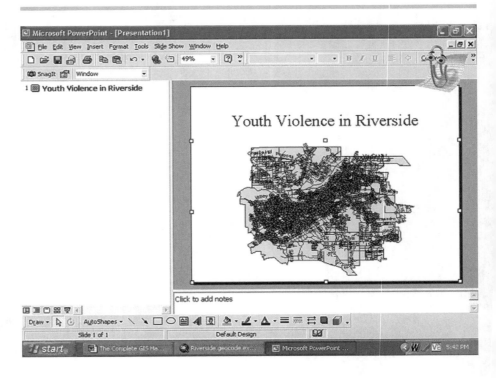

Now that you know how to build the basic maps, save, and export them into report or presentation applications, you are ready to take your maps further in terms of the visual display of meaningful information. This leads to the topic of **thematic maps**, how to make them and how to interpret them, which we examine in the next section of this book.

Thematic Maps

A thematic map is a visual representation of characteristics of a given geographic location. The characteristics illustrated within the map may consist of a wide variety of properties of interest to the researcher. These include, but are not limited to, quantitative properties of the geographic region, such as population and demographic information, as well as qualitative properties, such as descriptive information about specific types of crime occurring in the region. Data for use in a thematic map may be from an existing source, such as census or police data, it may be original data collected by the researcher him or herself, or some combination of both.

Thematic maps may be used to provide such information as the difference in the number of homicides between one county and another through a single glance at a map. They can show the audience about the differences in income, age, and ethnicity of the population in a particular city. Information provided on thematic maps can be at the level of global region, state, county, city, or even as small as a census block group.

Researchers can use their own existing data sets within the GIS software to create thematic maps. The software allows you to present visual representations of statistical analyses of data in the form of a thematic map. For example, a researcher may instruct the GIS application to calculate the number of robberies per hundred residents for each census block group in a particular city. Once the calculation is performed, the GIS application provides different options for presentation of the results in a thematic map. The differing rates may be presented using different colors to allow the audience to easily distinguish between the rates of robberies in different block groups with a single glance.

The accuracy of the map is dependent upon the accuracy of the data, as with geocoding. Thus, the major work on the part of the researcher lies in data preparation as with any type of analysis. The researcher who creates a thematic map depicting the differences in the number of robberies per one hundred residents between census block groups must be sure that the data set used to provide information about robberies is accurate to begin with. If the data incorrectly reports the number of robberies, the resulting thematic map will subsequently report the incorrect number of robberies as well.

An additional consideration with GIS is the accuracy of the underlying reference map data. This is the data used by the application (as specified by the researcher) to represent the applicable geographic location. Typically, the reference data consists of maps of countries, states, cities, or any other geographic region. ArcGIS comes with some geographic map data that can be used as reference data. However, there are many third-party sources for data of this kind (including ESRI, the manufacturer of ArcGIS) that extends far beyond that of the data provided in the sample data sets with ArcGIS. Data of this nature may be divided along a variety of borders, including but not limited to: country borders, census boundaries, state lines, county lines, political boundaries, and so on. It is essential for the researcher to be aware of the nature of the boundaries of the reference data as this will have an effect on the analyses and subsequent results as presented in the thematic map.

Example: Creating a Thematic Map from Sample Data

Figure 1.60 shows a simple thematic map created from the sample data provided with ArcGIS. The map illustrates the difference in population between all 50 states in the United States according to the data for Census 2000. This map was created using a single field from a single layer of data provided with the sample data installed with ArcGIS. This is the most basic example of a thematic map. We will now go through the steps used to create this map, which you can follow along with if you have ArcGIS installed. Once we go through the steps to create the most basic type of thematic map, we will use the skills learned to build more complex thematic maps.

FIGURE 1.60   **Sample thematic map of the United States**

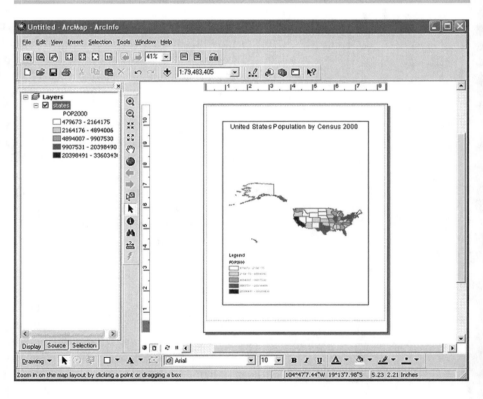

Step 1 Use the Start menu on your computer to launch ArcMap.

Step 2 On the Welcome screen check the radio button for "A new empty map" and click OK.

Step 3 Use the Add Data button (dark cross on a light background) to browse to the location on your computer where the sample data is stored. By default this data will be stored at: \ArcGIS\Bin\TemplateData.

Step 4 Select the file called "states.shp" from the USA folder and click Add to add the file to ArcMap as shown in Figure 1.61.

FIGURE 1.61   **Selecting a shape file**

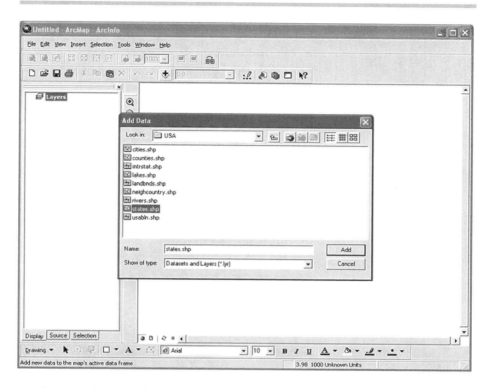

A map of the United States should appear in your ArcMap dataframe as shown in Figure 1.62.

FIGURE 1.62   **A basic map**

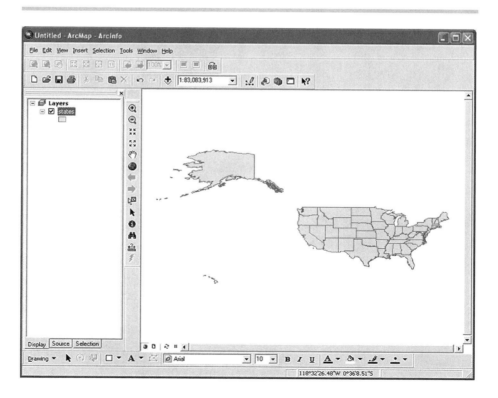

The sample data set "states.shp" is associated with data from the United States Census Bureau. To view the attributes associated with this file right-click the mouse on the layer name in the table of contents and select Open Attribute Table. Go ahead and use the scroll bar to scroll across the table and view the available information. For the purposes of this basic example we are going to use the field named "POP2000" to create a thematic map displaying the differences in population between the states according to the U.S. Census data 2000. Now, we will create the thematic map. Use the X in the corner of the attribute table to close the table.

Step 5 Double-click on the states layer name to open up the Layer Properties dialog box.

Step 6 Select the Symbology tab in the Layer Properties dialog. Within the Symbology tab, select Quantities from the show panel as in Figure 1.63.

FIGURE 1.63   **Symbology tab options**

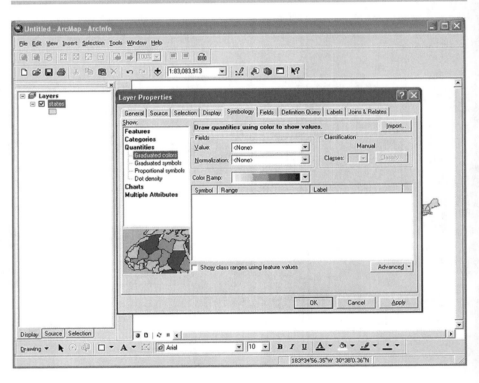

You will see that by default the Graduated colors option is selected. However, there are the additional options of Graduated symbols, Proportional symbols, and Dot density that can be selected instead if these are more appropriate for your data. We will see examples of the graduated symbols and proportional symbols options later in this section. We will also explore some of the other available options for the Symbology tab in subsequent examples. Since we are currently interested in creating a simple thematic map showing the population differences between states according to the U.S. Census 2000, we need to specify which field from the attribute table ArcGIS should use to base the symbology upon.

Step 7 Use the pulldown menu next to Value in the Fields box to select the field "POP2000."

FIGURE 1.64   **Selecting the variable to display**

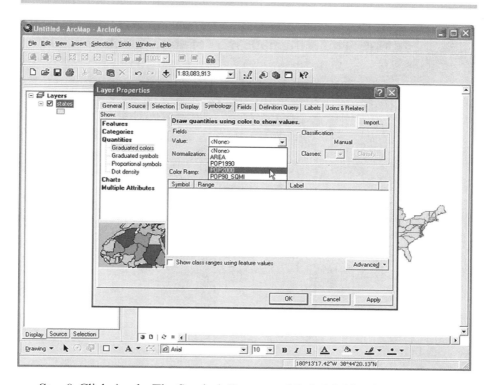

Step 8 Click Apply. The Symbol, Range, and Label fields will automatically populate according to the default settings for ArcGIS, as shown in Figure 1.65.

FIGURE 1.65   **Details of the Symbology tab**

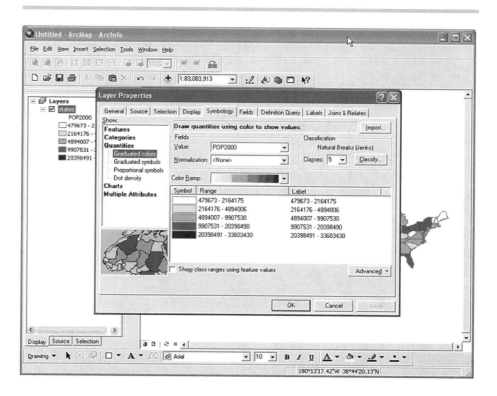

Step 9 Click OK.

The map will appear in the ArcMap dataframe, as shown in Figure 1.66.

FIGURE 1.66   **A thematic map of state population, 2000**

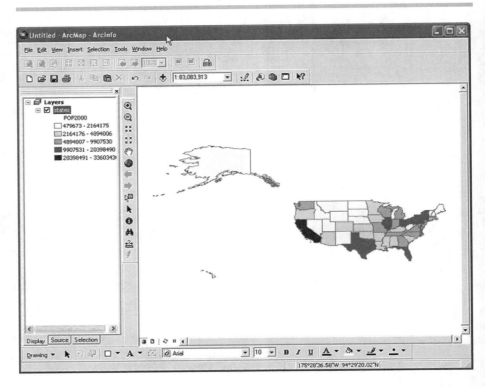

If you compare these results to the initial map presented at the beginning of this section (Figure 1.60) you will notice that the two are different. The map you just created does not contain the title and the **legend** that appear on the initial map. These are features that are added to the map before presentation in order to make them more clear to the audience. These features cannot be added in the data view of ArcGIS. Instead, we must use the layout view in order to specify how we want ArcGIS to layout our map presentation.

Use the Layout View button on the bottom of the ArcMap dataframe to switch over to the layout view of your map (Figure 1.67).

FIGURE 1.67   **The layout view**

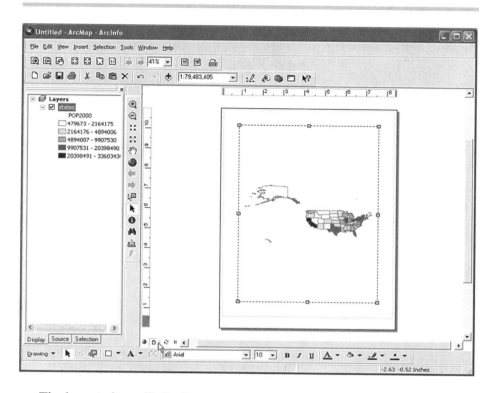

The layout view will display on your screen. The layout view will show ruler guides along the left and top margins to provide a frame of reference for printing purposes. You can use the left mouse button to reset margins as needed. Now, we can add our title and legend to provide a more clear presentation of the data contained in our map.

Step 10 Use the Insert menu in the layout view and select Legend as shown in Figure 1.68.

FIGURE 1.68   **Adding a legend to the map**

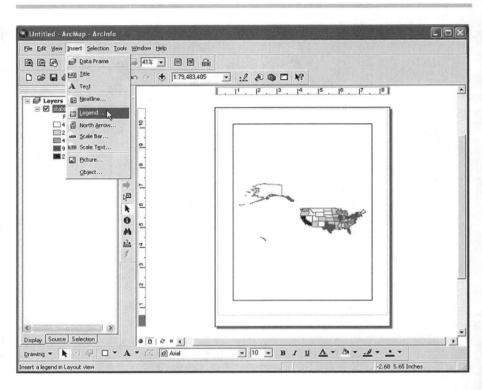

Note that the Insert menu provides the option of inserting various components that may be useful in creating maps for presentation. These include north arrows, text, scale bars, and even pictures. Explore these options on your own to gain insight into the creative options available for map presentation.

The Legend Wizard will appear on your screen. Since we are only working with a single layer of data for this example it is not necessary to select which layers to include in the legend. In this case only the states layer appears in the Map Layers dialog and it is included in the Legend Items by default. If there were multiple data layers contained in our map we would need to use the Legend Wizard to specify which layers to include in the legend. Go ahead and use the Preview button to see a preview of the default legend ArcGIS creates for this map. It may be necessary to adjust the position of the Legend editor window in order to view the preview on the map layout underneath as shown in Figure 1.69.

FIGURE 1.69   **The Legend Wizard**

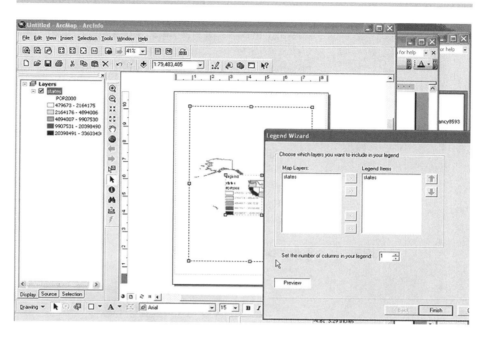

Select Finish to add the legend to your map. Once the legend appears in the map you can use the left mouse button to move it around on the map until you find the desired position. You can also use the mouse to resize the legend. By double-clicking on the legend you will have access to the Legend Properties dialog (Figure 1.70). The Legend Properties dialog can be used to set specific properties of your legend. Take a moment to explore each of the four tabs to get a sense of the available options for the properties of the legend.

FIGURE 1.70   **Legend Properties**

These properties may be used to customize your legend as well as make the items in the legend more clear to the specific audience to whom you are presenting your map. As with any method of data presentation, there may be different relevant aspects of the data you wish to highlight depending on the audience. Using GIS to present your data often means that a simple change in the legend presentation is all you need to tailor your data according to your audience.

The default legend style used to create the legend for our map includes the layer name. In this case, the layer name "states" seems unnecessary to include as part of the legend. We can specify that we are viewing the United States in our title instead. To remove the layer name from this legend, choose the Items tab in the Legend Properties dialog. Then, choose the Style button to see the available options for the legend style. Choose several different styles to see how they differ in appearance and information presented. After you have explored the various options, choose the style called "Horizontal with Heading and Labels" as shown in Figure 1.71.

FIGURE 1.71   **Legend Item Selector**

This option eliminates the layer name while still presenting the name of the field used to be clear about what the categories in the legend represent. Click OK in the Legend Item Selector to apply the selected style to the legend in the map layout. Click OK in the Legend Properties to dismiss the dialog and view your map with the updated legend. The Legend Properties dialog provides a simple, straightforward method of adjusting the legend as needed.

Now, we are ready to add a title to our map to add to the clarity of the data presentation for the audience.

Step 11   Use the Insert menu in the Layout view and select Title instead of Legend.

Step 12   Type the following text in the title box on the map: "United States Populations by Census 2000."

Step 13   Use the Enter key on the keyboard once the title is typed in. The properties of the title can be edited in a similar manner to those of the legend. Double-clicking on the title text will launch the Properties box for the title. Here, properties such as text style, size, and position can be altered as needed. Take a minute to explore the available options in the Properties dialog for the title. Click Cancel when you are finished reviewing these options.

Step 14 Use the mouse to drag the title into a center position on the map layout until it appears as shown in Figure 1.72.

FIGURE 1.72   **A thematic map with legend added**

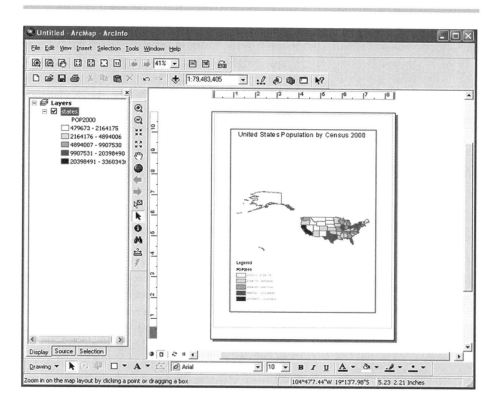

Congratulations! You have successfully created a thematic map clearly depicting the United States population according to the U.S. Census for 2000. If you want to export this map with the title and legend to a program such as Microsoft PowerPoint, you can use the procedure we followed in Figure 1.59. To start this process, click on File, and then on export map from the layout window.

Now that you have completed the map you should save it to a safe location.

Step 15 Use the File > Save As option to save this map document (.mxd) to a location on disk for retrieval at a later time. For reference, name the map "U.S. Population by Census 2000."

The basic steps used to create this simple map of the U.S. population are the building blocks needed to create GIS illustrations of more complex data and analyses.

One of the strengths of GIS is that it allows for the comparison of geographic units over time on a variable or set of observations with relative ease and clarity. As an exercise, follow the same steps described in the previous example and construct the same map of the U.S. population, only this time use the "POP1990" column in the attribute table shown in Figure 1.64. This will allow you to compare the map you just made in this example with the map for 1990; patterns of change during the decade between 1990 and 2000 will be readily apparent, much more so than if you looked at two columns in the spreadsheet or attribute table.

Example: Racial Profiling Thematic Map

Let's discuss an example of the use of GIS with more complex data and analyses. The topic of racial profiling is one that is widely studied by sociologists and criminologists in the United States. The concept of racial profiling represents the notion that law enforcement officers use visual signs of ethnicity to target certain ethnic groups for traffic stops and other kinds of arrests. Theorists argue that it is the disproportionate number of stops and arrests for certain ethnic groups that accounts for the disproportionate representation of different ethnic groups in jail or prison in the United States, rather than a disproportionate amount of criminal behavior by members of certain ethnic groups. Studies on racial profiling show statistically significant differences between the number of police detainments for African Americans and Whites in several major U.S. cities (Harris, 1997; Ramirez et al., 2000; Warren et al., 2006). In these studies, African Americans were consistently more likely to be detained by police than Whites in the same geographic areas.

One study in particular presented a GIS analysis of the racial profiling phenomenon to make a clear presentation of the differences in the rates of tickets issued to different ethnic groups within the same geographic location (Parker et al., 2004b). Parker and colleagues used data collected on the differences in the number of traffic tickets issued to different ethnic groups as an indicator of racial profiling on the part of the police department in Riverside, CA, in 1998. The results revealed significant differences in the likelihood of different racial groups receiving a disproportionate number of traffic citations relative to their representation in the local population. The study showed that African Americans were the most likely of all ethnic groups to receive traffic citations in the city of Riverside regardless of the socioeconomic characteristics of the neighborhood in which they were stopped. Results of this nature are of great interest to the scientific community, law enforcement agencies, and the general public.

Thematic mapping offers a useful way for researchers to present such findings about racial profiling in a straightforward manner such that individuals of all levels of knowledge and interest can gain a clear understanding of the data presented. The examples below are thematic maps that illustrate the rate of traffic citations issued to African Americans per 1000 residents, Latinos per 1000 residents, and Whites per 1000 residents in the city of Riverside, CA, in 1998. Take a minute to look over the maps and compare the results of each.

FIGURE 1.73   **Tickets given to African-American drivers**

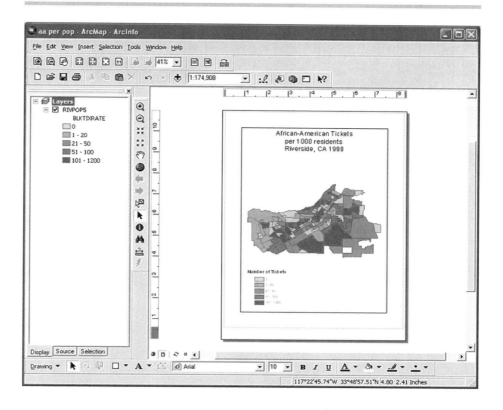

FIGURE 1.74   **Tickets given to Latino drivers**

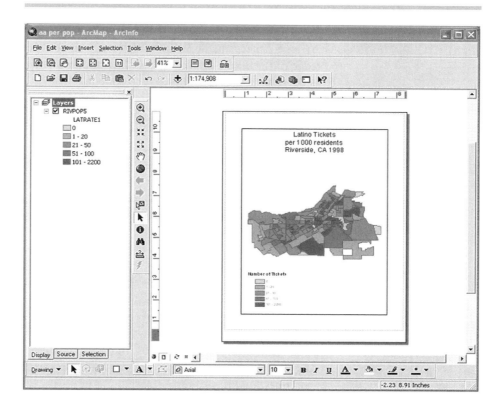

FIGURE 1.75   **Tickets given to White drivers**

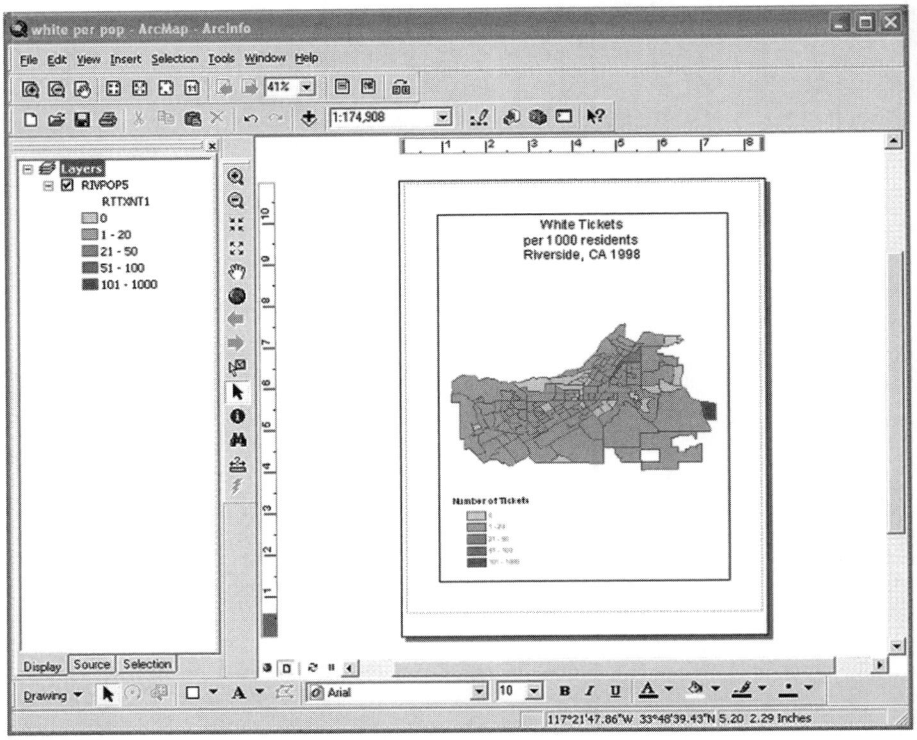

The graduated color scheme used to symbolize the ticket rates for Riverside, CA, in 1998 clearly illustrates that African Americans were more likely to receive tickets than both Latinos and Whites. Further, Latinos were far more likely than Whites to receive tickets. This is despite the fact that according to the census data for Riverside at the time of the study only 6.9 percent of the population was African American, 24.1 percent Latino, and 66.7 percent White. With the knowledge of the ethnic breakdown of the population (also contained in the map data) at the time of the study it is easy to conclude from the ticket distributions reported in the maps that African Americans and Latinos received a disproportionate number of traffic citations during this period.

Before exploring these data in detail, a discussion of the data mining necessary to obtain and prepare these data for GIS is appropriate. How did Parker and colleagues obtain these data and prepare them for the production of the thematic maps shown here? The story of how these data were obtained is an interesting one, full of twists and turns—and it shows that in order to get data for GIS analysis that is really important for the social sciences, one sometimes has to be persistent and opportunistic.

The interest for the examination of traffic stops by race and ethnicity in Riverside came out of the reaction of the community and the city to a terrible tragedy and a great offense against people of color in Riverside. The incident was the traffic death of a young African-American woman named Tyisha Mille; she was 19 years old at the time of her death. She was killed by four police officers who fired 27 times into her car; she was struck 12 times from four different angles. The police officers, all employed by the Riverside Police Department, were either Anglo or Latino, and none of them had very much experience on the job (see Pitchford and Hill, 2002).

The reaction of the community and the city of Riverside was, after the initial shock, to empower a commission to investigate the circumstances of this incident and what might be the causes, with an eye towards coming up with policy changes that might prevent such violence in the future. One of the recommendations of the commission was to conduct a study of racial profiling in police practice to see if profiling was occurring and, if so, to gain some insight into how to reduce or prevent racial profiling. The City Manager's office approached the Presley Center for Crime and Justice Studies at the University of California, Riverside, directed by Parker, to see if it would help design and carry out such a study. The negotiations proceeded to such a point where the city offered a draft contract to Parker. The draft was suddenly withdrawn with no explanation, although some speculation was that the victim's family had sued the city for damages and the city's legal council had objected to the study because it might be used against the city in such a legal case.

Several months later, Parker received a call from an editor at the *Press-Enterprise*, a daily newspaper headquartered in Riverside, inviting him to lunch to discuss the issue of racial profiling by the Riverside Police Department. The editor proposed something unusual—if the newspaper could get the data for the study the city and Parker had originally agreed to, would Parker do the same study for the newspaper? The editor talked about data-based journalism, and it transpired that there was a long history of the newspaper asking for data from the city government, the city refusing to provide the information, the newspaper suing the city, and the city losing in court and having to pay legal costs as well as hand over the data. So the city was prepared to hand over the traffic ticket data, and avoid the legal contest this time. A deal was made; this was just the beginning of the data mining.

The city had agreed to cooperate, but did not have the support of the police department in this, so the cooperation was tepid at best. Months and months of delays, then came a delivery of boxes of badly Xeroxed hardly legible copies of the traffic tickets in random order. There were about 20,000 tickets for the year (1998) given to Parker and associates. As they were in random order, they had to be sorted three times in order to establish a sampling frame for selecting a random sample; not all numbers in the sequences were included, so the sampling had to be repeated random sampling with replacement. We finally selected a 1 in 5 sample for about 4000 tickets. These had to be read, and decisions made about interpreting faded copy, then coded and entered into the computer, and organized into a GIS-compatible spreadsheet; tasks that took more than two years. This was a most challenging data mining experience.

Now we will trace the steps used by Parker and associates to produce the thematic maps presented in Figures 1.73, 1.74, and 1.75. First, data from the city's police department were collected regarding all traffic citations issued in the City of Riverside for 1998. Data from the citations included the ethnicity of the driver as perceived by the officer issuing the ticket. Additionally, the type and severity of offense were recorded. The data were entered into a spreadsheet format such that they could be converted to many other file formats for analysis. ArcGIS is compatible with many file types including but not limited to .xls, .dbf, and .csv.

Next, researchers obtained reference data to serve as the base map for the geographic location. For this particular analysis, sample data provided with Arc-GIS were used to create the base map. Researchers selected the sub-area of the city of Riverside, CA, from the larger street map of the United States and saved it as a separate file. This file was subsequently used as the reference data for this project. The citation data file was joined to the basemap data file to create a single data file "RIVPOP5" containing both the attributes of the map of Riverside, including census block group boundaries, and the attributes of the traffic citation data set. Using this single data file researchers were easily able to create thematic maps representing the differences in the number of traffic citations issued to the different ethnic groups in Riverside as shown in Figures 1.73, 1.74, and 1.75.

Now we will use the basic steps learned to re-create the U.S. population by Census 2000 map (Figure 1.72) in the previous example to re-create the analytical map of the difference in the rates of traffic citations issued to the different ethnic groups in Riverside for 1998. As you work through this example, you will notice that some of the steps are left open for you to use the knowledge gained from the previous example to fill in on your own. In cases where you are not able to recall these steps, please turn to these pages for the details on how to complete the steps.

Step 1 Start ArcMap with a new, empty map.
Step 2 Use the Add Data button and browse to the location where the book data is stored. Add the file called "RIVPOP5."

The following map, showing the city of Riverside, CA, and its census block group boundaries should appear in your ArcMap dataframe, as shown in Figure 1.76.

FIGURE 1.76 **U.S. Census block groups, Riverside**

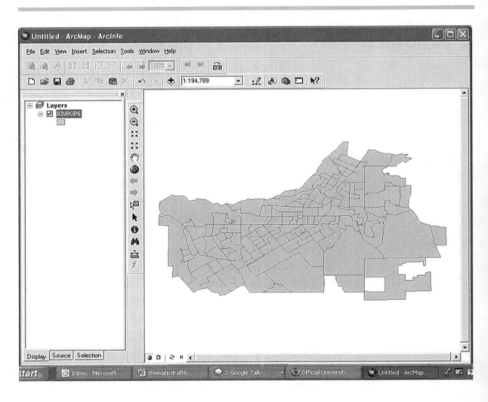

Right-click on the layer name "RIVPOP" and open the attribute table for these data. Scroll through the table to see what type of information is available. The data contain fields from the 1990 U.S. Census (the most current census data available at the time of the study), as well as the data input from the traffic citations issued by the Riverside Police Department. Any of the fields contained in the table can be used on its own or in combination with other fields to represent different characteristics about this region. As with any type of data analyses, knowing what information is available within the data set is helpful in deciding what type of thematic map to create.

Before we can create the maps shown in the three examples (Figures 1.73, 1.74, and 1.75), we must calculate the rates of tickets issued per ethnic group by population. We can use ArcGIS to calculate this rate directly within the RIVPOP5 data layer. Use the following steps:

Step 1 Use the options button on the bottom right of the attribute table and choose Add Field, as shown in Figure 1.77.

FIGURE 1.77   **Attribute table for "RIVPOP5"**

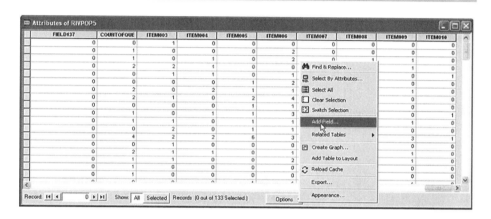

Step 2 In the Add Field dialog type "AA_Rate" for the Name, and select Long Integer for the Type and click OK (Figure 1.78).

FIGURE 1.78   **Adding a field (column) to an attribute table**

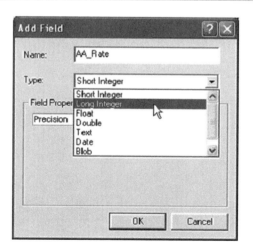

View the attribute table to find that your newly added field "AA_Rate" now appears at the end of the table. Now we can populate the AA_Rate field with the rate of traffic citations issued to African Americans in Riverside, CA, in 1998.

Step 3 Right-click on the AA_Rate field and select Calculate Values.

Step 4 In the message box from the Field Calculator warning that edits performed outside of an edit session can be undone, click Yes (Figure 1.79).

FIGURE 1.79   **Warning message about calculation methods in ArcMap**

Although edits cannot be "undone" when editing with this method, you can delete a field and re-create it if necessary. You also have the option of adding more new fields as needed.

You should now see the Field Calculator window on your screen. We will use the calculator to compute the values for the AA_Rate field. Since we are interested in the rate of tickets issued to African Americans per 1000 African-American residents in Riverside, CA, in 1998, we will need to combine fields from the U.S. Census data with fields from the traffic citation data.

Step 5 Use the mouse to select the appropriate fields (reference codebook) and calculations in the Field Calculator so that ArcGIS can calculate and populate the values accordingly. In order to get the rate of tickets issued to African Americans per 1000 residents in Riverside, CA, we will need to divide the number of tickets issued to African Americans by the number of residents, and multiply this result by 1000. The Field Calculator will appear as in Figure 1.80 if you have entered the calculation correctly.

FIGURE 1.80   **Field Calculator screen**

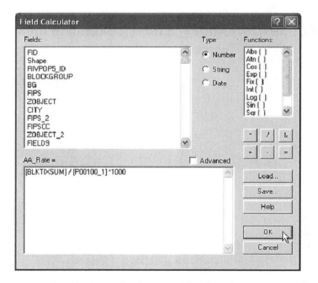

Once you have populated the calculator with the above expression, click OK. Note that the Field Calculator provides options for loading previously saved syntax files, and also has the ability to process VBA code for more advanced calculations. The AA_Rate field should now be populated. The attributes contained in the field represent the rate of tickets issued to African Americans per 1000 residents in the city of Riverside in 1998.

Now you will use the steps to create and populate the rate of African-American tickets from above to create and populate the rates of Latino tickets and White tickets per 1000 residents. Use the previous model and replace the "BLKTIXSUM" field with the corresponding "TOTLAT1" to create the Latino rate, and "CNTWHT1" to create the rate for Whites. When you have finished creating the additional fields scroll down the table to view the differences in the rates of traffic citations issued between these three ethnic categories, then close the table.

The data are now ready for you to re-create the three maps presented at the beginning of this section. First, you will create the map showing the rate of African-American tickets issued per 1000 residents.

Step 6 Open the Layer Properties dialog and select Quantities > Graduated colors. If you have trouble remembering how to accomplish this, refer to steps 5 and 6 from the U.S. Census 2000 example.

Step 7 Use the pulldown menu to select the desired color ramp. Selecting an appropriate color ramp often depends on your data structure. In this case, since the characteristic of primary interest are the "hot spots," or areas where many tickets are being issued, the authors suggest using a "hot" color such as red (darker shade here) to represent the areas where the most tickets are issued. You may choose to represent the data with any colors you wish, but using the color scheme to represent the theoretical logic adds to the clarity of the presentation.

Step 8 Use the pulldown to populate the Field Value box with the AA_Rate field.

You should see the results as in Figure 1.81.

FIGURE 1.81 **Symbology tab**

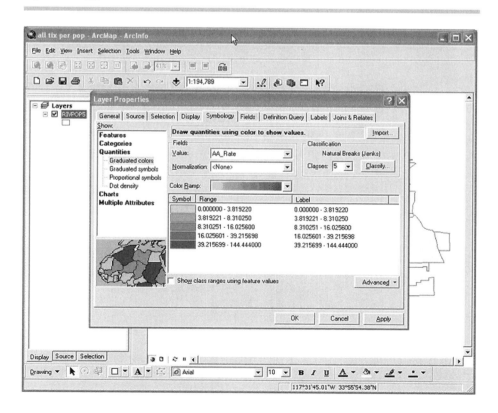

In order to maintain consistency between the different maps you are going to create, you will need to customize the symbol ranges and labels. For this example, we are going to use the same symbology scheme for each map. However, there may be cases where a different symbology strategy provides more meaning to your audience. This will have to be a judgment call on the part of the researcher. You can change symbology values manually by clicking the mouse in the appropriate area of the range column and typing in the desired values.

Step 9 Use the manual entry method described above to populate the Symbology tab as shown in Figure 1.82.

FIGURE 1.82   **Creating the thematic map**

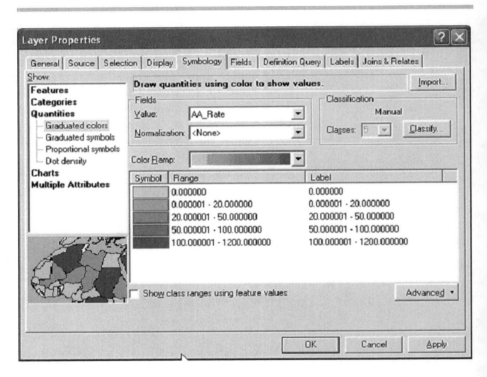

To change the number format for the labels you can left-click the mouse on the Label button and specify the number of significant digits as well as other properties about how the label should appear, as shown in Figure 1.83.

FIGURE 1.83   **Selecting details for labeling a thematic map**

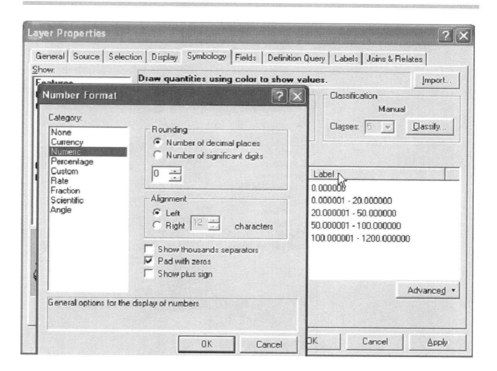

Step 10 Click Apply. Click OK.

Congratulations! You have successfully created a map showing the rate of tickets issued to African Americans in Riverside, CA, in 1998.

Now, you need to add a legend and a title for clarity.

Step 11 Go to the layout view in ArcMap. (Hint: use the button on the bottom left corner.)

Step 12 Use the Insert menu in the layout view to insert a legend with an acceptable style.

Step 13 Use the Insert menu in the layout view to insert the title "African-American tickets per 1000 residents in Riverside, CA 1998."

If you cannot remember how to accomplish these tasks, please refer to steps 10–14 of the previous example for detailed instructions.

Step 14 Once the legend and title are created use the File > Save As option to save your newly created map as "African-American tickets 1998" to a location on disk for retrieval and use at a later time.

The exact same steps you used to create the map representing the rate of traffic citations issued to African-American drivers in Riverside, CA, in 1998 can be used to create the additional maps showing the rate of traffic citations issued to Latino and White drivers in Riverside during 1998. The only change will be the variable used to symbolize the data in the map.

Step 1 Use the button on the bottom left corner of the dataframe to switch back to the data view in ArcMap.

Step 2 Double-click on the layer name to open the Layer Properties dialog and select the Symbology tab.

Step 3 Use the value pulldown menu to specify that values should be
symbolized using the field Lat_Rate instead of AA_Rate, as shown in
Figure 1.84.

FIGURE 1.84 **Selecting a variable for a thematic map**

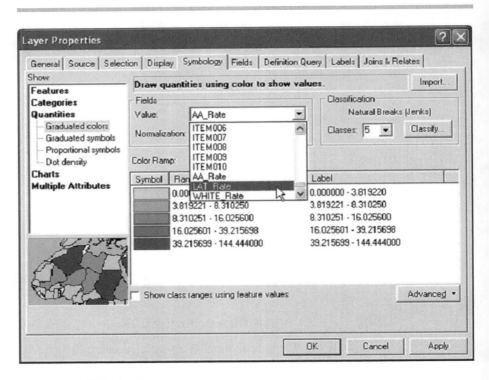

Step 4 Click Apply.

You will notice the map behind the layer properties changing slightly to reflect
the newly specified symbology. Next, you need to specify a symbol range that is
the same as the range used for the map showing the rate of tickets issued to
African-American drivers for a more meaningful comparison across maps.

Step 5 Use the procedure discussed in the above example (steps 8–9) to
manually populate the symbol range column and display zero
significant digits as shown in Figure 1.85.

FIGURE 1.85   **Constructing another thematic map**

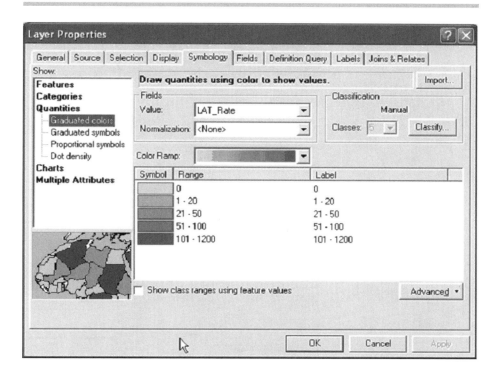

Step 6 Click Apply, then OK.

The map display will update to reflect your changes and show the rate of tickets issued to Latino drivers in Riverside during 1998. You have just created another thematic map. Next are the finishing touches of the legend and title.

Step 7   Switch to the layout view of ArcMap. You will notice that since you did not close the previous .mxd file showing the rate of tickets issued to African-American drivers, the legend and the title remain in the layout view. This makes your job easier. Notice that the legend has updated itself to reflect the new symbol range (max is now 1200 instead of 200 as in the previous example). This is due to the live link between the ArcMap data view and layout view. Since the legend is already in place, we only need to change the title to reflect the current map and save the file.

Step 8   Double-click on the title in the ArcMap layout to bring up the properties in an editable window. Replace the existing title with "Latino tickets per 1000 residents in Riverside, CA 1998."

Step 9   Click Apply and notice the title update on the screen.

Step 10 Use the File > Save As option to save the file with an appropriate name to a location on disk for use later.

Now you will create the last map in the series for this example on your own using the steps presented in the previous two map examples. Use the steps for creating the maps of the rate of citations issued to African-American and Latino drivers in Riverside during 1998 to create the map showing the rate of citations issued to White drivers in Riverside during 1998. When you complete this map, be sure to save it as you did with the previous maps. Your final product should look like the map shown in Figure 1.86.

FIGURE 1.86   **Layout view of thematic map with legend**

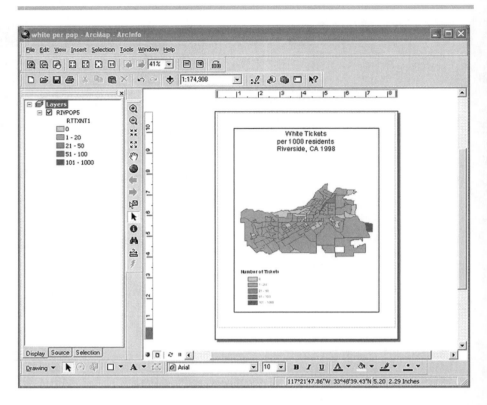

Now, as an exercise, you will create one more example using the same data from the racial profiling example on your own. Suppose researchers want to report to the general public the total number of traffic citations per 1000 residents issued to drivers of all ethnic groups who were stopped for traffic violations in Riverside in 1998 by census block group. Recall our previous examples and the options available for creating thematic maps in ArcGIS. With these options in mind, which variable/s from the RIVPOP5 data set could we use to create a thematic map that represents the number of citations issued in total per 1000 residents in Riverside in 1998? Write your answer down and then read below to see if you are correct. Try using the knowledge you gained from the previous section to create the resulting thematic map in ArcGIS; your results should look similar to Figure 1.87.

FIGURE 1.87   **Using the rate of getting a ticket to display relationships in a map**

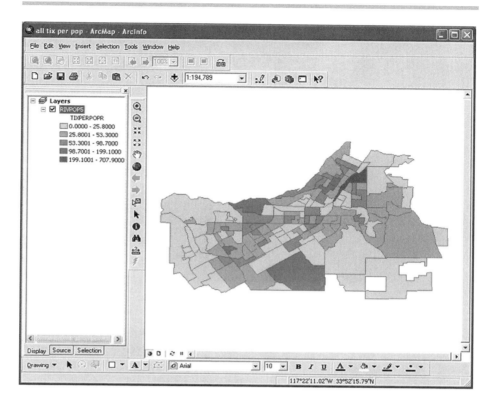

Now, add a legend and a title to this map in the layout view and save the results as "All Tickets per 1000 Residents." Refer to the steps in the previous examples if you need to refresh your memory about how to add the legend and the title to your map. Once you complete this map, save the results with an appropriate name to a location on disk. (Answer: to create the thematic map above you needed to use the variable called "TIXPERPOP" from the RIVPOP5 data set.)

In the previous section of this book, you learned the steps involved in the process of geocoding addresses to create what is known as a "pin map." Thematic mapping can take a geocoded map one step further in creating a detailed visual representation of the characteristics of interest in a given geographic region. Recall the example from the previous section in which addresses indicating instances of juvenile crime in Riverside, CA, were geocoded to create a pin map. Using this same geocoded map you will now create a thematic map indicating differences in crime rates between census block groups in Riverside, CA.

Example: Juvenile Crime Thematic Map

First, browse to the location on your computer where you have stored the geocoded map of juvenile crime that you created in the previous section and double-click on the filename to open this map in ArcGIS. Your .mxd file should look similar to Figure 1.88.

FIGURE 1.88   **Pin map of youth violent incidents, Riverside**

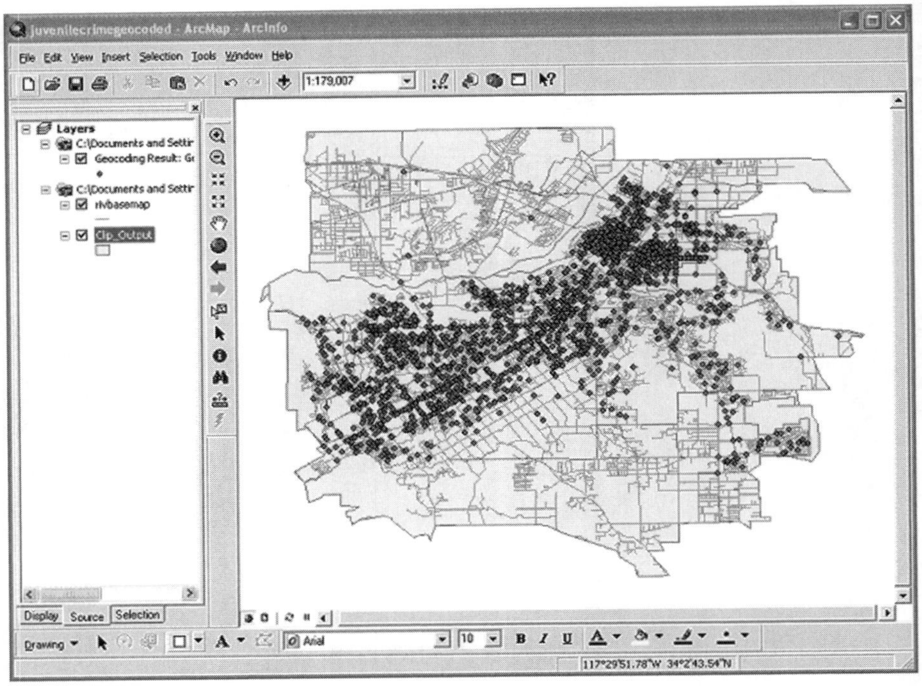

Now you will learn how to create a thematic map demonstrating differences in rates of juvenile crime in Riverside, CA, in 2002, by building from the existing geocoded map you created in the previous section.

First, we will need to join the polygon layer containing the block group divisions for Riverside to the point layer containing the geocoded incidents of juvenile crime in Riverside for 2002.

Step 1   Right-click the mouse on the name of the layer containing the polygon data (in this case it is clip_output) in the open .mxd file. Select Joins and Relates > Join as shown in Figure 1.89.

FIGURE 1.89   **The Join submenu**

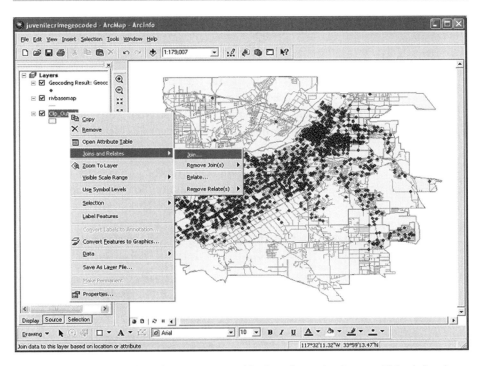

Step 2 Use the Join submenu to specify that the point layer will be joined to the polygon layer based on spatial location. Turn on the radio button specifying that each polygon will contain all attributes of the point data set and specify the location and filename to save the result of the join as in the example in Figure 1.90.

FIGURE 1.90   **Placing geocoded data into spatial units on the map**

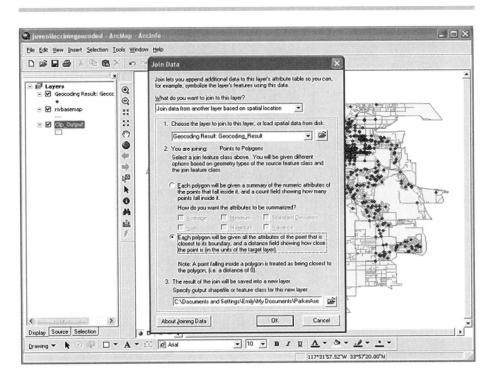

Note that ArcGIS also provides the option to associate a summary format of the attributes of the join layer, which may be useful under some conditions. For the purposes of this example it is necessary to carry all attributes over from the point layer.

ArcGIS will automatically add the resulting joined layer to the map for you. Open up the attribute table of the joined layer to see that the fields from both the polygon layer and the point layer are now contained in one joined layer. Join can be used to combine attributes from multiple sources to create a single layer that can be used for analyses. Now you can create the thematic map showing the differential juvenile crime rates between census block groups for Riverside in 2002.

> *Step 3* Right-click on the joined layer name and select properties. The Layer Properties dialog box should appear. Select the Symbology tab as shown in Figure 1.91.

FIGURE 1.91   **A thematic map from the geocoded data**

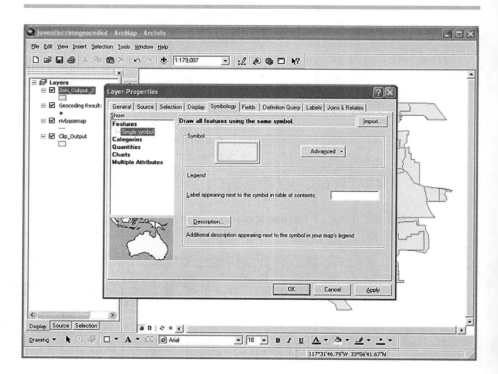

In the show panel, select Quantities. Then, select Graduated colors.

Use the Color Ramp pulldown to browse through the available color options as in Figure 1.92. Select the color ramp of your choice.

FIGURE 1.92   **Graduate colors for a thematic map**

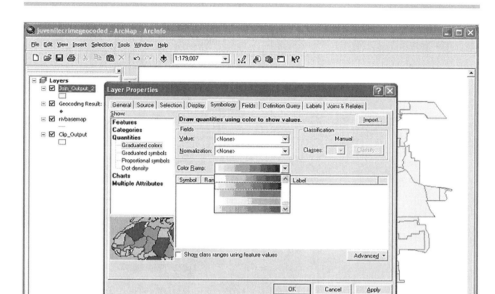

Step 4 In the Value drop down, select the Score field. The dialog will automatically populate with the number of values in each class according to the number of classes specified in the classes box, as shown in Figure 1.93.

FIGURE 1.93   **Finalizing the nature of a thematic map**

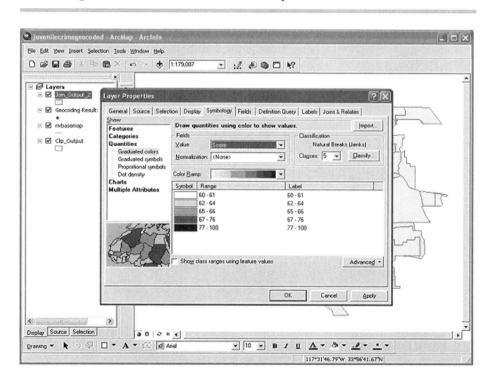

Use the classes pulldown to experiment with the different number of classes that can be used with the automatic classes option. ArcGIS is set to the "Natural Breaks" option for classes by default. Click on the Classify and use the Method pulldown to see additional options for classification. The most appropriate method of classification will depend upon the data you are presenting, and the audience to whom you are presenting. The syntax used for the various methods can be found in the ArcGIS online help (Figure 1.94).

FIGURE 1.94   **Selecting category boundaries for a thematic map**

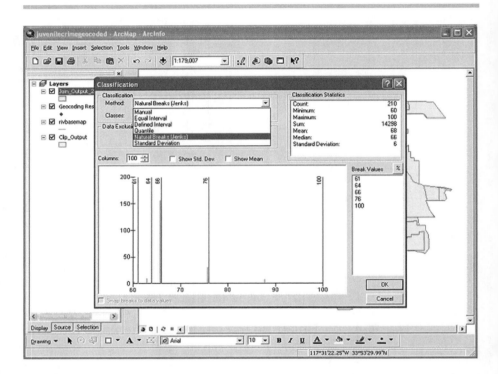

The Break Values in the box on the right can also be edited manually by clicking with the mouse and then using the keyboard to enter the desired values. After taking a minute to explore the Classification dialog box, click cancel to return to the Symbology tab of the Layer Properties dialog box. In the Layer Properties box, click Apply. You will see some changes occurring in the map behind the dialog box. Click OK to dismiss the dialog box and display your thematic map as shown in Figure 1.95.

FIGURE 1.95   **A new thematic map**

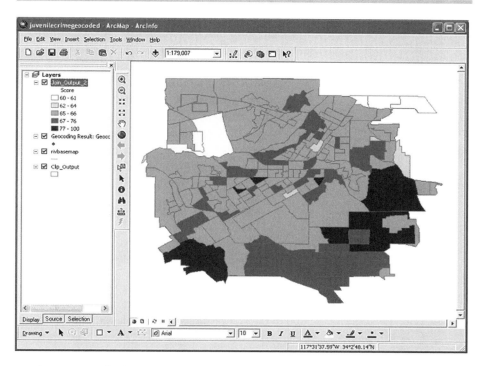

Step 5 Use the layout view to add a legend and title. Once finished, save your work. Your finished product should look similar to the map in Figure 1.96.

FIGURE 1.96   **Hot spots of juvenile violence**

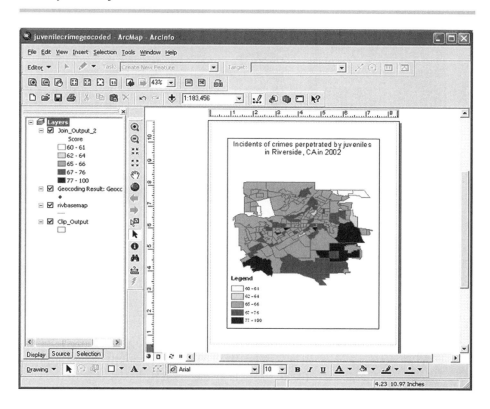

A simple look at our map of instances of juvenile crime reveals several "hot spots" where these incidents are more prevalent. Specifically, the lower west end and the mid to lower east end of town have significantly larger amounts of juvenile crime than other areas of the city. Additionally, there are two areas that seem particularly low in comparison to the hot spots. It might be of interest to the researcher to pursue further investigation into these areas in terms of specific characteristics that might lead to these differential rates. For example, by taking a look at the census block group data, a researcher could examine the number of divorced parents in these areas to see if there is a difference in this rate that correlates with the difference in juvenile perpetrated crime.

Since we have census data associated with the files we are currently using, we can use the current map to take a quick look at the divorce rates by block group to see an illustration of how this type of comparison would work.

Step 1 Double-click on the layer name Join_Output_2 to open up the Layer Properties. Select the Symbology tab.

Step 2 Replace Score for the value field with Divorced using the pulldown menu. Click Apply. Click OK.

Notice the changes in the map. The symbology now reflects the number of divorced individuals by block group in Riverside as according to the U.S. Census 2000 data. The results should look something like the map in Figure 1.97.

FIGURE 1.97   **Thematic map of divorce, Riverside, 2000**

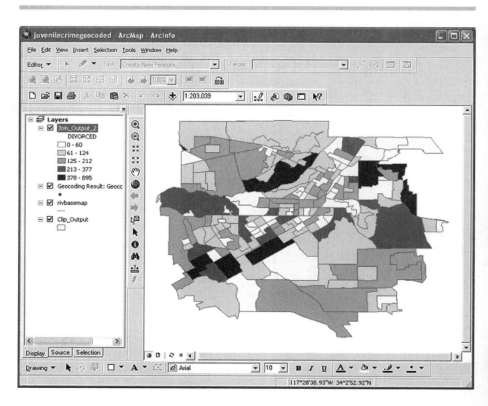

Compare the results of the map of divorces with the map of the instances of juvenile crime to look for correlations. The comparison shows that while the areas of high juvenile crime are not the areas with the highest number of divorces, they are in areas with relatively high divorce when compared to the areas lower in juvenile crime. Using the additional census variables contained in the data, experiment with different symbology schemes to find out if any of the other census variables have a significant relationship with the instances of juvenile crime. When you are finished, you may exit out of ArcMap without saving the maps of the census variables. You have completed the thematic mapping section.

Conclusion

In this section you have learned a great deal about coding, and the basics of how to get your data into a map. You have also learned how to display these data in useful ways with the thematic map, and along the way you have done some basic analysis of the relationships the data show when examined in a geographic context. You can see already the powerful way relationships and the differences across space and geographic, political, or administrative boundaries can be shown on these maps. But this is only the basics; you can now use the techniques you have learned to produce some very powerful and interesting maps that address public policy, history, social relations, and economic and political change—at the neighborhood level, the city level, the state level, the national level, and across the world.

Section 2 explores the power of maps for combining data from different sources and many variables and relationships simultaneously. Once you learn how to make maps that convey complex information in accessible and powerful forms, you will begin to see the benefits of GIS as a tool for research, policy, and making the places we live in better, safer, and healthier. However, all of the techniques in the next section are based on the knowledge you have gained by the end of Section 1. Proceed to Section 2 and see how what you have learned can be put to powerful uses.

Section 2 Mapping for Analysis, Policy, and Decision Making

The maps we have discussed in this book so far have been basic, displaying one set of data, one variable, at one time period, in a straightforward way. However, the conceptual framework of GIS is a very powerful one, in which data can be manipulated, classified, and displayed in innovative and interesting ways. There are many instances where social science researchers will want to combine data from several different sources to create a visual presentation of multiple phenomena in the same map. Multiple variables can be displayed, relationships can be mapped, transitions over time can be displayed, and GIS can support some very powerful research questions and important public policies and decision making in a wide variety of fields such as criminology, urban planning, and disaster relief. In this section you will see a number of examples of the types of data that can be constructed and displayed, the types of maps that can be developed, and the range of decisions and questions that can be answered. Along the way you will learn a powerful set of mapping and database tools that can be applied to any area of knowledge or life, with exciting and important consequences. Having the right data and displaying it in the right form can make the difference between a puzzle and a solution, a successful policy and a failed intervention, tragedies prevented and life lost—all this with GIS and the skills you will learn in this section.

Now that you have the basic skills required to create pin maps and thematic maps, you can apply these techniques to producing more complex maps. This section will present several examples of maps that are more analytical in nature than those we looked at in the first section. To begin with, you will see the finished map product and the analytical reasoning behind it, then the steps to create the map will be presented for you to duplicate the map on your own.

Basic Multivariate Displays

The last map in Section 1, Figure 1.97, showed the number of divorced residents of each block group in the year 2000 in the city of Riverside, California. As interesting as this information is, it begs the question of the relative numbers of divorced people in these units of analysis. It may be very important to know that there are less than 10 divorced individuals in one location, for example, if you are a divorce lawyer and you want to market your services, but it would also be important in that decision to target your marketing efforts in a few places across the city rather than everywhere in the city if you knew how many adults lived in that particular area. If there were 10 divorced people, and only 11 adults living there, it would be a waste of time to market your services there as more than 90 percent of those who could be divorced are already divorced! So knowing the percentage of divorced individuals, which is just the proportion of divorced people divided by the total number of people who could possibly be divorced, namely adults, is useful in such a situation. This is a special case of a more general idea involving the concept of relative risk. The risk of something happening is the number of actual occurrences of the thing that have happened, divided by the possible number of cases in which that thing could happen; another expression for this is the rate of something happening. So we talk about the divorce rate as the number of divorces relative to the number of people who are married, since in fact only married people can become divorced. Usually these rates are expressed for a particular time period, such as in the year 2000, and for a particular place, such as the city of Riverside. Rates are very common in discussions of events in public and private, in research, newspapers, policy discussions, economics, and just about any field of activity. The birth rate (number of children born to women in the childbearing years in a country in a year), the death rate (number of deaths divided by the number of living people in a place in a time period), the crime rate (number of crimes committed divided by the number of people living in a city in a year), and so on—these are the basic building blocks of everyday knowledge and scientific research.

The rate of something, or the relative risk of something happening, may be very different from the number of events of this type that have happened, especially in their geographic distribution. For example, if you tell me that 10,000 Toyota Camry automobiles were stolen last year, I would ask, "well, what is the relative risk of a Camry being stolen?" Just knowing the number does not help me decide whether to buy a Camry based on whether or not it will be stolen. If there are 50,000 Camrys on the road, then the relative risk of a Camry being stolen is 10,000/50,000 or 0.20 (a percentage can be made by multiplying this result by 100; rates are often standardized by multiplying them by a constant, as in the crime rate per 100,000 population, or the divorce rate per 1000 married couples, and so on). On the other hand, if you also tell me that there are 100 Porche Boxters stolen in the same year, I will ask the same question—if there are only 250 Boxters on the road (at 60K per Boxter this could well be the case), you would say, "Oh, the Camry is much more likely to be stolen than the Boxter," but you would be wrong because the relative risk for Boxters is 100/250 = 0.4. So, in fact, the relative risk of a Boxter being stolen is twice that of a Camry being stolen. The use of rates is a simple but powerful tool to gain understanding about the world around us.

Mapping Rates

If you have data that allow you to know the number of some event that happened and the population at risk for having such an event, then you can map the rate of that event happening across geographic space in a very straightforward manner. This method of calculation is useful for many different purposes. For example, an urban planner who is designing the layout of a new community may want to know the rate of elementary school age children residing in a given area in order to decide whether or not to place an elementary school in that area. Another useful function for mapping rates is disaster relief planning. In the process of planning an effort to evacuate potential victims of a hurricane it would be useful to know the rate at which hurricanes tend to affect the geographic region in which the evacuation is to occur. Rate mapping is also useful for market analyses. If you are deciding whether or not to open a restaurant franchise at a particular location, it would be helpful to have a map showing the rate at which diners eat out at other restaurants in the vicinity of your potential location.

We will now go through the steps to create a map of rates of divorce.

Step 1　Open the Layer Properties menu by double-clicking on the map you are displaying, and select the Symbology tab as in Figure 2.1:

FIGURE 2.1　**Layer Properties and Symbology tab**

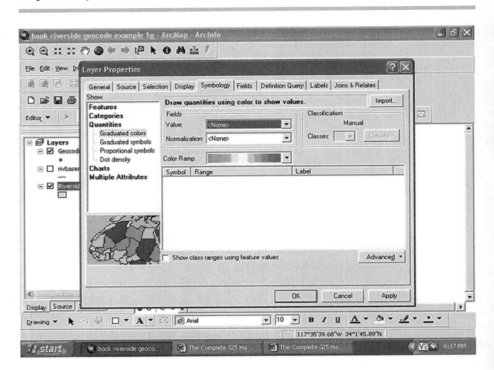

Click on quantities, and notice that the option is given to use a field as the value, and another field as the "**normalization**"; this is another word for the denominator in a calculation of the rate or relative risk ratio. Click on Value, and put Divorce in the box; click on Normalization and put Married in the box. Click on Apply, and OK at the bottom of the symbology tab, and the map displayed should look like Figure 2.2.

FIGURE 2.2   **Divorced residents relative to married residents**

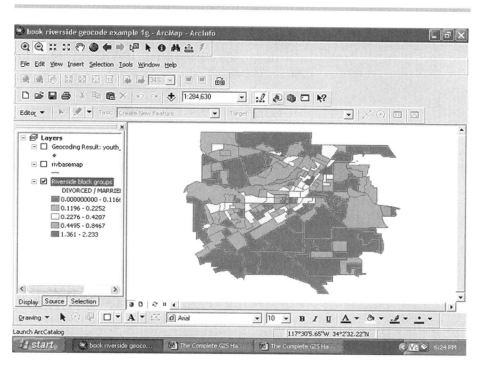

Comparing this figure to Figure 1.97 shows a rather different picture—here we can see that in most cases the rate of divorce is very low in Riverside—most places are below 25 percent divorced relative to married individuals. In only a very few places is the number of divorced people greater than the number of married people (the darkest area), with a range above 1.0 for the rate. Demographers will question this calculation, as just using divorced people over married people may not accurately capture the true risk—we need to know when people were married, as we know from experience and the data confirm that people who have been married for many years are less likely to get divorced than relative newly wed couples are. There are a number of alternative ways to better measure the relative risk of divorce than the simple rate we have displayed here.

However, even this simple rate shows that understanding the rate at which something happens relative to the population at risk for this event is a powerful tool for understanding reality and making good decisions about interventions and policies.

Basic Multivariable Maps: Classification and Subsetting

One of the ways in which social and behavioral research has made significant progress in understanding behavioral patterns in social life has been by classifying general and relative common phenomena into smaller, more homogeneous sub-classes of patterns and behaviors. These efforts to classify from the more general to the more specific often result in a great deal of new understanding and knowledge, as the goal of classification is to group examples together in subclasses that share the largest number of common traits, traits that serve to distinguish this group of behaviors or actions or opinions from other groups. One researcher recently began to consider the type of rivalries and conflicts in which nations around the world get involved, and the focus here was on one subtype out of all such disagreements and disputes: those that lead to armed conflict or the explicit threat thereof (Schulz, 2006). However, even this classification still leaves a very general category—ranging from a skirmish on the border or increasing military maneuvers on the border to a full-scale invasion of another nation. Can we learn something from classifying these types according to the factors that help to bring about the rivalry in the first place?

Example: Classification of World Armed Rivalries

Figure 2.3 shows a classification of rivalries into three types: those based on spatial conflicts, that is those in which the disagreement is about territory, the demarcation of the border, or a disputed island off the coast (the red lines appear as black lines on the map below); those based on the desire on the part of one nation to change or overthrow the regime in power in another nation (green or light-colored lines); and those based on the desire of one rival to change or influence the policies of another nation (blue or mid-colored lines). In addition, the map in Figure 2.3 also shows in the background which nations have been involved in rivalries of these types since 1950 and those who have not.

FIGURE 2.3   **World Armed Rivalries, 1950–2003, Classified into Three Types**

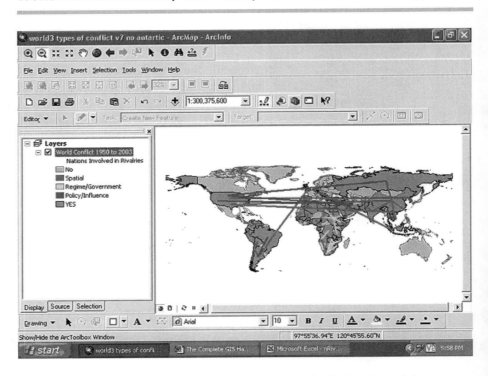

One of the first interesting things about this map is the location of the patterns in the background colors: gray for those who have been involved in armed rivalries, and light gray (blue) for those who have not. There is a clear regional pattern revealed in this simple two-way classification: Europe, Australia, and North America (with the exception of the United States), have been almost exclusively uninvolved in these types of armed rivalries. Given the long-term history of many of the nations represented in these places, this would not be an obvious conclusion, yet it is striking how consistent this pattern is over the last 50 years.

The three classifications of the causes of these rivalries also reveal significant patterns. For example, it is apparent that conflicts in Asia are almost exclusively about territory—almost every line that ends or starts in Asia is black (red). In addition, with the exception of two conflicts involving the United States and a couple in the Middle East, almost all the rivalries about regime change have occurred in Africa, with two "hot spots" standing out: the Sudan, the site of several major internal and external disputes today, and South Africa, which used to have a very repressive regime under a White minority government, until Nelson Mandela came to power in 1994.

Another pattern that is revealed in Figure 2.3 is that most rivalries are short distance in nature—this makes sense, as if you want to have your army fight with another countries' army, you need to be close by in order to get the armies to a place where they can fight each other. The one obvious exception to this is the United States. The United States has not had very many wars or armed rivalries with its neighbors (with the exceptions of Cuba and Nicaragua); most of the rivalries the United States has become involved in are with countries a great distance from North America. As the world's richest nation, perhaps only the United States can afford to send its Armed Services to fight with or threaten other potential superpower and proxy countries thousands of miles from home.

This map is really made up of one basic map of the world displaying whether countries get involved in these rivalries or not, with an overlay of lines coded to show the two nations involved in a particular rivalry and the nature or cause of the rivalry in question. To construct this map, the following steps were used.

Step 1 Open a basic map of the world with the current national boundaries shown, as in Figure 2.4.

FIGURE 2.4   **World map**

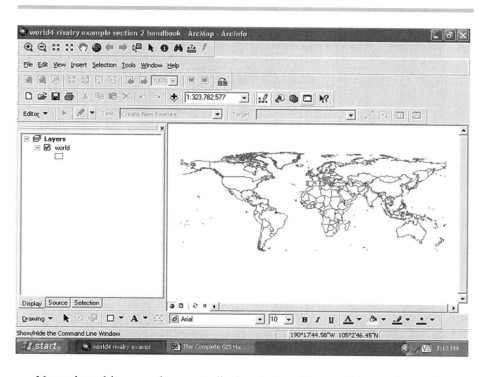

Note that this map does not display Antarctica; as this continent has no nations, it was excluded here; this can be done simply by opening the attribute table for the map, clicking on the editor, deleting the line in the table for Antarctica, and then saving the edits prior to closing the attribute table.

Step 2 Follow the procedures shown elsewhere in this book to add a field to the attribute table, and type in a 1 in the row for a nation that has been involved in a rivalry and a 0 for those nations that have not; again turn on the editor first, and remember to save your edits prior to closing the attribute table. The new attribute table will look something like the example in Figure 2.5.

FIGURE 2.5   **Rivalries among nations**

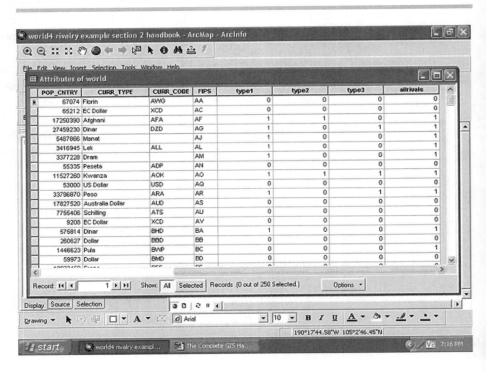

This table also contains fields for the three types of rivalries, although this is not necessary to produce the map shown in Figure 2.3.

Step 3 Create a thematic map with the field "allrivals" in the attribute table, and select blue and gray colors to show those countries that have not, and have, been involved in these conflicts. Do this using the Categories subfield on the Symbology tab, and select the Unique values. You have already been shown other ways to do this, but using this approach here will prove useful later in the process.

FIGURE 2.6   **Nations involved in rivalries, 1950–2003**

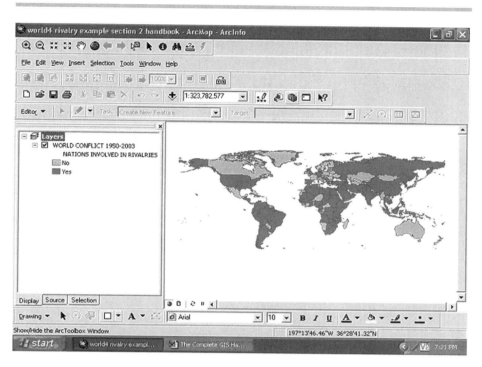

Step 4 At the bottom of the screen in ArcMap is the drawing tool bar, located on the lower right; click on the drawing style drop down, and select the new line command (see Figure 1.44).

Step 5 Further to the right on the bottom of the screen, select the line color object, and select a red for the first type of rivalry, that based on spatial or territorial disputes.

Step 6 When you move the cursor over the map, you will notice a crosshair mark has replaced the cursor. Using the data in the Microsoft Excel spreadsheet in Figure 2.7, look for the first two country pairs that have a Type 1 or spatial rivalry: Afghanistan and Pakistan.

FIGURE 2.7   **World rivalry data (Schulz, 2006)**

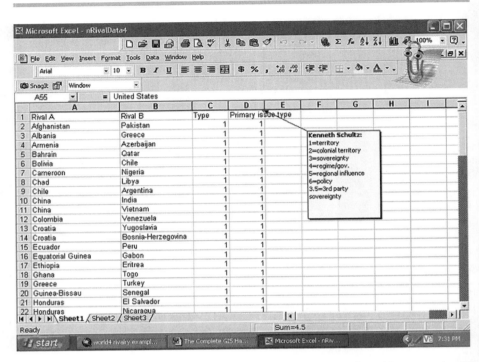

Step 7 Constructing this map will tax your knowledge of world geography. If you are not sure where Afghanistan and Pakistan are, remember you can use the Identify tool (the "i" in a dark circle) to point to potential countries for confirmation. It also helps to use the zoom in magnifying tool to show some of the detail in the map.

FIGURE 2.8   **Pakistan and Afghanistan, selected and outlined in light gray (blue) with gray background**

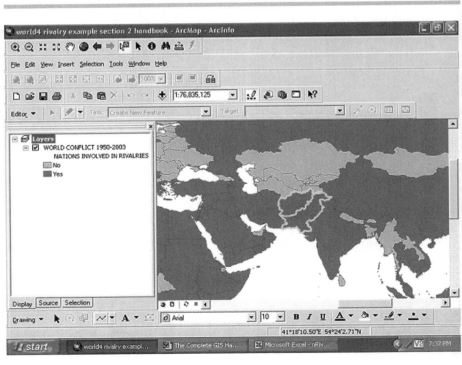

Step 8 Activate the drawing tool (by clicking on the new line symbol on the drawing tool bar), and move the crosshair mark over Afghanistan and right-click; move the crosshair into Pakistan, and double-click; a box outlines a black (red) diagonal line connecting the two rivals. Double-click inside the box and a Line Properties menu opens; adjust the thickness of the line to at least 2.0—the line will show on the whole world view more effectively.

Once the map looks like Figure 2.9, hit Escape and the box will disappear, and you will see the black line for a spatial or territorial rivalry. Continue in this manner until you have drawn all the necessary lines, as in Figure 2.3.

FIGURE 2.9   **The result of inserting a black (red) line between rivals**

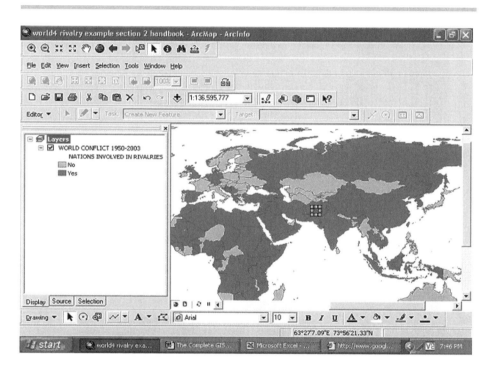

Step 9 Open the Layer Properties window and the Symbology tab. Here you can add information for the map key, which will eventually be added to the legend in the layout view. Do this by going to the Categories and Unique values menu you used to create the thematic map in Figure 2.6; hit Add Values, and then manually add values between 0 and 1 (0.3, 0.5, 0.7) so you can have three place holders in the map key. Then, use the approach used previously in this book to change what is displayed in the key to reflect what each color represents in terms of the three types of rivalries.

The lines collectively are essentially an overlay onto the thematic rivalry map in Figure 2.6; to see this, go back to Figure 2.3, and click the box next to the title of the layer; the result looks something like Figure 2.10.

FIGURE 2.10　**The three types of rivalries without the world background map**

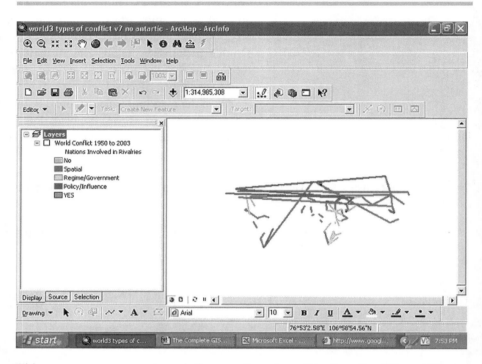

This means you can create variations on the color of the lines for different illustrative purposes. Suppose, for example, you wanted a map that just showed all the pairs of countries involved in rivalries, without first classifying them into types. You could do that here by selecting the arrow cursor, and drawing a box around all the lines. Click on the line color tool, select a gold color, for example, and all the lines will change to that color.

FIGURE 2.11　**Selecting and editing drawn lines**

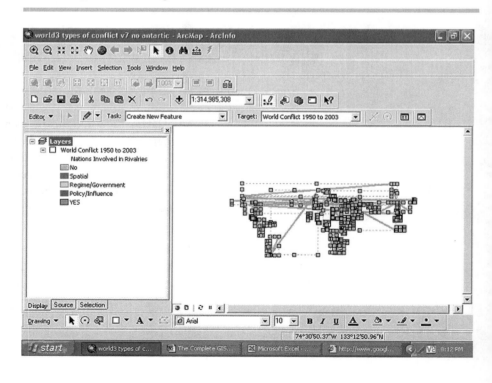

You can then turn the map itself back on by clicking on the box next to the title, and the map would look like that in Figure 2.12.

FIGURE 2.12   **All rivalries in world conflict, 1950–2003**

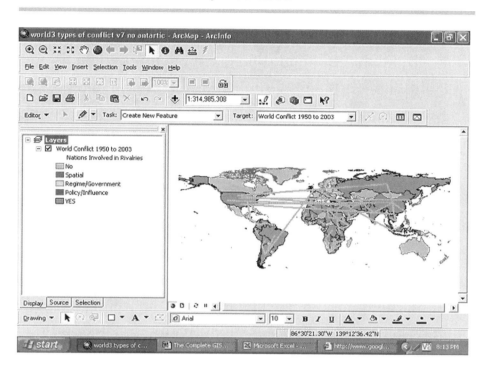

You should adjust the key if you were going to export this map for use in a presentation. The drawing tool gives you a powerful set of options to display additional information on any map. You have also seen how classifying your data into types that have distinctive characteristics is also a powerful tool for mapping and understanding your data.

Subsetting your data and creating a set of maps for decision making

As you can see from the world rivalries data and maps, classifying your data into distinctive subtypes is a powerful way to present information and to gain new understandings of the nature of the information you have. Sometimes looking further into the details of the data you are presenting reveals significant new information.

Example: Subsets of Youth Violence

In Section 1 you learned to geocode by using an example from law enforcement: youth violent incidents in Riverside, CA (see Figure 1.31). Criminologists might be interested in the number of contacts youths in this area have with police as a method of finding effective policy implications. In this example, we will create a map showing the rate of youth violent contacts with police. Using the population of the block groups as a normalization factor (expressed as per 1000 population), the thematic map in Figure 2.13 can be displayed showing how the rates of youth violence vary across the city.

FIGURE 2.13   **Rate of youth police contacts, Riverside**

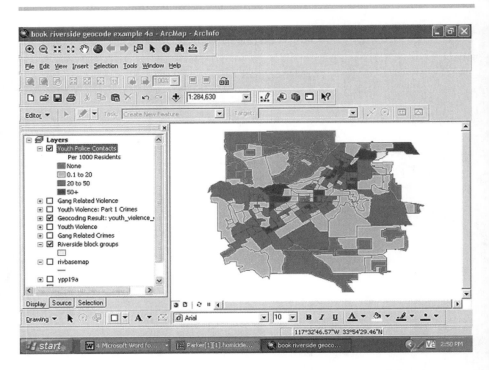

If you were working with the Riverside Police Department, you might want to use this map to decide how to allocate resources to combat youth violent criminal involvement by focusing your personnel, resources, and programs on the places with the highest rates (Figure 2.13). However, these data represent all the contacts and all types of violence that involve youth in the city. You might learn something different if you subset the data displayed here by different types of crime. Suppose, for example, that you are very concerned about youth gangs and their influence on youth violence in the city. These data contain information on whether or not the police contact was gang related or not. Subsetting the data on gang involvement and once again using the population per 1000 as a normalization factor yields the map in Figure 2.14.

FIGURE 2.14   **Gang-related violence, Riverside**

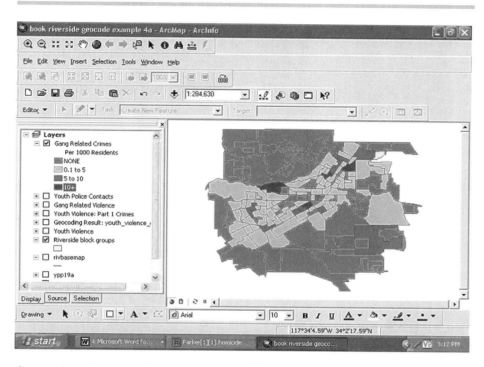

Comparing Figures 2.13 and 2.14, one difference is immediately apparent: the much lower rates of gang-related crimes compared to all youth crimes. In addition, different areas of the city have higher rates—there is some overlap, but notably an area in the lower right of the city seems to have a moderately high gang crime rate but a rather more modest overall youth crime rate. This would be an obvious target for enhanced prevention and enforcement activities targeted at gangs.

Some violent crimes are more serious than others. The FBI, the national internal police agency in the Federal government uses a system that classifies crimes into Part 1 and Part 2 crimes. Part 1 crimes are the most serious—in terms of violence, these include murder or homicide, robbery, rape, and aggravated assault. If we subset these data on these types of youth violence, the map of Riverside looks like that in Figure 2.15.

FIGURE 2.15   **Youth violence Part 1 crimes; block group outlined**

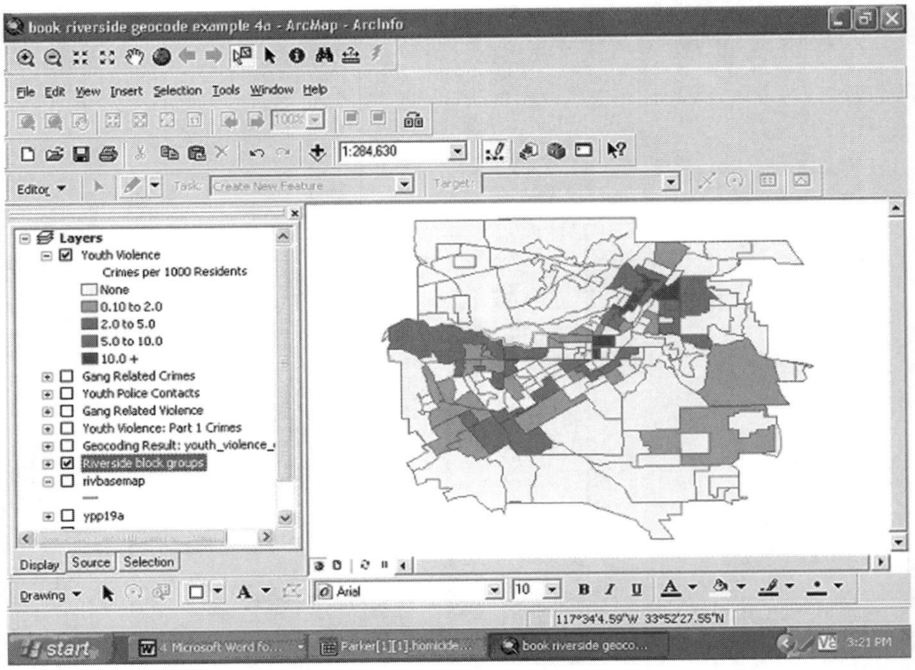

One block group is outlined to draw attention to it. If you compare this map with the previous two, you will note that in the overall map (Figure 2.13) and the gang-related incidents map (Figure 2.14) the block group highlighted in Figure 2.15 shows high rates in both overall and gang-related, but not in terms of Part 1, violence. It should be noted that Part 2 violence includes simple assaults, a crime that is often committed by gang members when they get in fights with other gang members; however, if your objective was to reduce Part 1 violence in the city, you would allocate resources and police officers differently than if you were focused on a different problem.

You can see from these examples the value of subsetting your data and examining the potentially different patterns that will emerge when you do so. In order to make informed decisions, you need to fully explore the different types of information available.

How do you subset data in ArcGIS? Beginning with the geocoding results from the overall youth violent incident data, the following steps will result in the subset maps shown in Figures 2.14 and 2.15.

Step 1 Open the attribute table of the geocoded data layer, as in Figure 2.16.

FIGURE 2.16   **Attribute table**

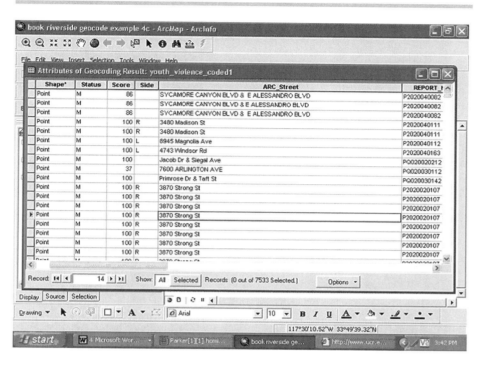

Step 2 Click on the Options button at the lower right to reveal a drop down
menu (Figure 2.17).

FIGURE 2.17   **The attribute table options drop down menu**

Step 3 Click on Select By Attributes, which brings up the window shown in Figure 2.18

FIGURE 2.18   **Select by Attributes submenu**

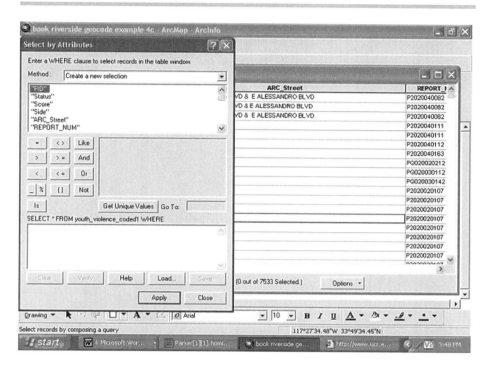

You will see that the fields from the attribute table are displayed in the selection submenu in the large window at the top.

Step 4 Select the field you want to choose a subcategory from, and double-click it. The name of that field will appear in the box below the phrase, "SELECT *FROM youth_violence_coded1 WHERE:" (youth_violence_coded1 is the layer name of the attribute table you opened above).

Step 5 Click on the button Get Unique Values; this will display all of the values that are in the field you have selected to subset in the box above this button, as in Figure 2.19.

FIGURE 2.19   **Building a selection formula**

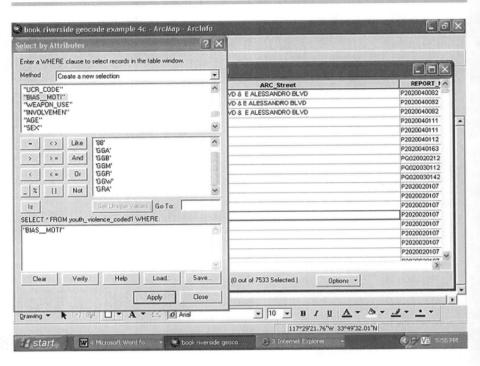

Step 6 Select an operator from those available in this submenu. In this case the values of the field are alphanumeric, that is letters and numbers are used as symbols for a category rather than using numbers mathematically (the latter are numeric fields), so that an equal sign is the appropriate operator; click on the equal sign above and it will appear in the Select *From box below.

Step 7 Now select the unique value you wish to subset your data on. Here we are interested in gang-related activity or GRA; select GRA, double-click, and it will appear to the right of the equal sign in the Select *From box below. You have now built a selection formula.

Step 8 Next you need to check if the formula is properly written according to the rules of logic that ArcMap uses. Click on Verify; if you have written the formula correctly, a box will appear telling you that the formula has been successfully verified, as in Figure 2.20.

FIGURE 2.20   **Selection formula verification**

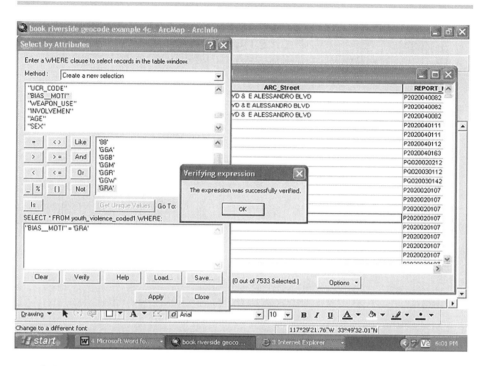

If the formula is not successfully verified, ArcMap does not give you a reason; but if you try to apply such a formula, you will not successfully subset your data. Go back to the formula and look for logical errors, a missing parenthesis (every open parenthesis needs a closed parenthesis), misplaced operators, and so on. Keep revising the formula until it verifies successfully. Remember that successful verification, while a necessary condition for a successful subsetting of your data, is not sufficient. The logic of the formula could be correct, but it might still fail to select anything, or fail to select what you wanted it to. Make sure you check the selected data to make sure the selection has operated the way you intend by opening the attribute table of the newly selected data and examining it closely, comparing it to the attribute table you selected from.

Step 9   Click OK on the verification window, and click on the Apply button; close the attribute window and you will see the map with the selected events highlighted over the original map.

FIGURE 2.21   **Results of selection on gang-related activities**

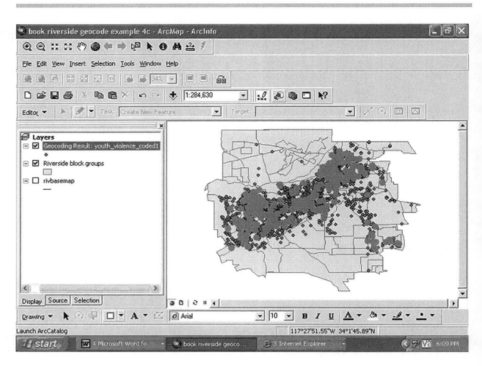

Step 10 To save the newly selected items into a new layer, left-click on the
original layer, click on Selection and bring up the selection submenu,
and click on Create Layer From Selected Features, as in Figure 2.22.

FIGURE 2.22   **Selection and Create Layer From Selected Features submenus**

The resulting new layer will appear in the table of contents
window, and will have the same name as the original layer but with
the word selected added to the end. Right-click twice on the name
and give the new layer a more informative name, like Gang-Related
Events, so as to keep track of the content of the new layer.

Step 11 Following the procedure in Section 1 for counting the number of
events inside spatial units (see Figure 1.90 and related instructions),
establish a count for gang-related activities in each block group, and
create a thematic map; this map is shown in Figure 2.14.

As an exercise, create a thematic map of the Riverside block groups using the percent of the population that is Asian and Pacific Islander in origin. Add the gang-related selection layer you just created in the previous example. Create the same map with the percent of the population that is White, African American, and Latino. Do you see any possible relationship between ethnicity and gang activity?

Once you have learned to subset your data, you can see that the possibilities are nearly unlimited for gaining greater understanding of the geography of your data, and the ability to inform decision making about resource allocation, shifting priorities, and effective response to problems is significant from this effort.

Planning and Projections: "What If" Multiple Variable Maps for Decision Making

We have displayed combinations of variables as rates, and subsets of data as additional maps, but for all intents and purposes the maps thus far have been focused on one set of information. Sometimes one set of information, even a rate, is not sufficient to tell us what the data have to say, and to properly support and inform decision making and planning for the allocation of resources and the planning of growth and change. Many cities have learned the hard way what happens if you do not plan adequately and anticipate the changes, both growth and decline, in the different sections of a city. So many resources that people need to be successful in an urban environment require large-scale capital investments and significant amounts of time to put into place, from schools to hospitals to roads and public transportation. The most effective communities are the ones in which urban and ecological planners use the information available to anticipate growth and change, and to plan the development of neighborhoods and resources in advance of such growth and change. Of course, not all possibilities can be imagined, but the more effort spent in this way the more sustainable the community will be in the long run. Mapping can be a very effective tool for these efforts, as it allows for the asking of "What if" questions. These are questions such as: What if the number of children of school age were to increase by 20 percent in some parts of the city and decline in others? This would have implications for the planning of educational facilities and parks in the various neighborhoods of the city. What if the areas where the younger families with school age children live changes over time in the city? New schools will have to be developed and perhaps some old schools will have to be closed to make effective use of the resources and to deliver the best education the city can muster for its residents. How can mapping help with these issues?

Example: Maps for School Planning

The map in Figure 2.23 shows the number of children by block group in Riverside based on the 2000 Census. The map shows some interesting patterns, such that

FIGURE 2.23   **Children aged 5–17, Riverside, 2000**

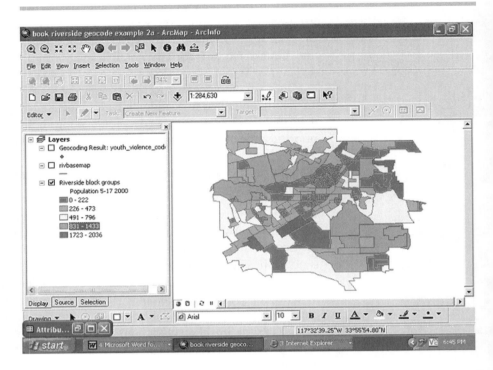

most of the areas that have the largest numbers of children are towards the edges of the city, in newer neighborhoods that were previously undeveloped for residential housing or were annexed to the city since the 1990 Census. In Figure 2.24, some of these areas, on the northwest side of the city, have been outlined.

FIGURE 2.24   **Outlying area of Riverside with larger numbers of children**

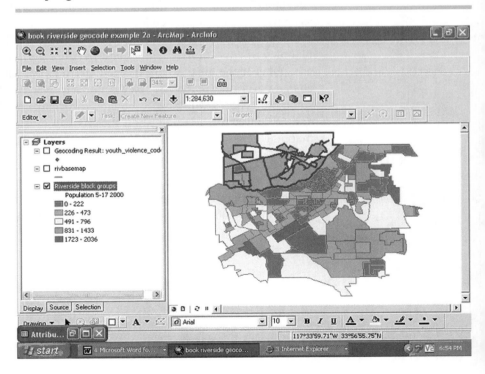

In fact, a very good question to ask would be how much growth and change was there between 1990 and 2000 in this statistic? If we put a symbol in each block group that grew or declined in the numbers of children between 1990 and 2000 by 25 percent or more this would give us some indication of the changing demand for schools and other child-oriented services (not to mention that such information could be very useful for child-oriented businesses planning where to locate new stores that cater to children and their parents), information that would be helpful for planning purposes.

FIGURE 2.25   **Areas of rapid growth (↑) or Decline (↓) in school age children, 1990–2000**

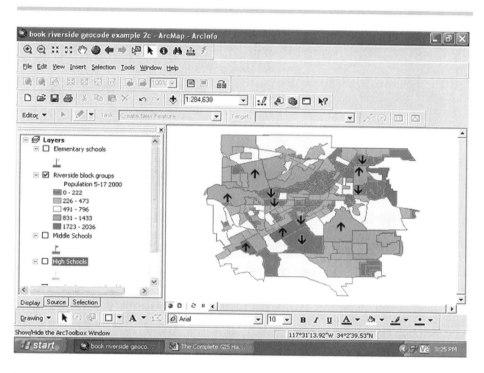

Now we have displayed two variables on the map, the number of school age children as a thematic map with the up and down arrows showing the second variable, focusing on where the rates of growth or decline have been 25 percent or more. It would be helpful to see where schools are located now to see if their locations are in sync with the decline and the growth of students in the various parts of the city.

Figure 2.26 shows the location of elementary schools. If we use the magnifying glass tool to focus in on parts of the city, we can begin to see the implications for future school planning of this information. For example, if we focus in on the area on the north of the map that we highlighted in Figure 2.24, we can see that a substantial number of elementary schools are there. If we were to research the dates these schools opened, we would see that many of them had been recently built and opened, as the growth of this section of Riverside was anticipated by the previous generation of school planners.

FIGURE 2.26 **Change in school age population and elementary school locations**

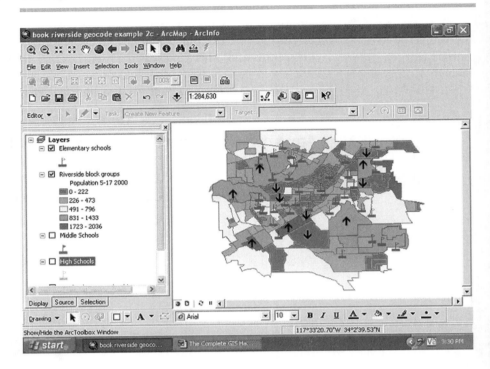

If we add middle and high schools, the situation is displayed in Figure 2.27. You can see in this detailed view that a number of elementary schools are in the areas of recent rapid growth. However, there are only two middle schools (in red, showing black here) and one high school (in green, very light here) in this general

FIGURE 2.27 **High, middle, and elementary schools in north Riverside**

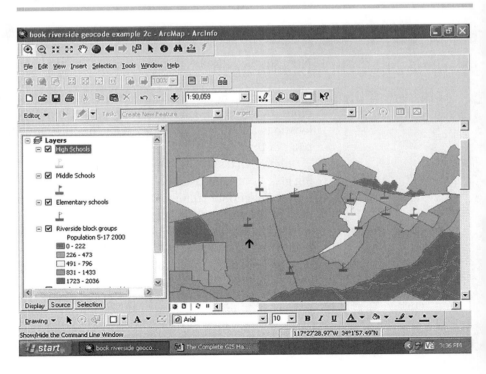

area, and these are located in the areas with fewer children and lower rates of growth. School planners might want to consider adding a middle and/or high school to the left or western side of this section given the rapid rates of growth in the past. This would especially be the case if those elementary schools in the black (red) areas are experiencing growing enrollment over the last few years.

On the other hand, the more central areas of the city have not been growing and have relatively small numbers of school children to begin with (mid-grays or green thematic color), but because of their location in the old downtown and near lying areas, these block groups have large numbers of schools. Given the relative lack of new children in these areas, officials may be faced soon with the need to close some of these schools, especially if their facilities are old and in need of upkeep or remodeling. This is evident in a close-up of the central portion of Riverside as shown in Figure 2.28.

FIGURE 2.28   **Slow growth and low populations of students, central Riverside**

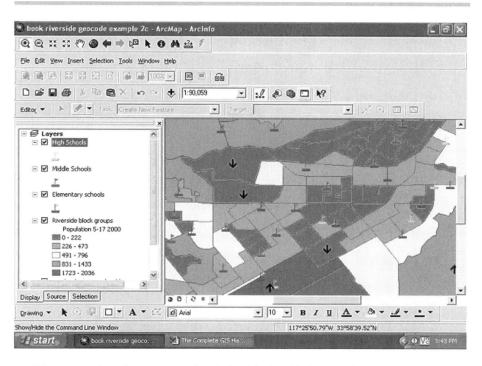

There are nine elementary schools in this detailed map of the area in mid-gray (green shaded) locations, plus three middle schools and three high schools (one middle school is at the same location as a high school, thus the body of the flag on top of the little school building is black (red) on one of the gray (green) high school symbols in the lower right section of the map). Some fast growing and large population areas are nearby, but some of these schools may be candidates for closure in the next few years.

Some of the areas that have large populations and higher growth rates seem to be underserved, and plans to construct schools in these locations should be accelerated if they are not already close to the construction stage. For example, the sections of large population and high growth to the far west of the city have very few schools, yet clearly a number of children live there now and more will be enrolling in school in the future. This can be seen in the close-up map in Figure 2.29.

FIGURE 2.29   **Large populations of children, growth, and few schools**

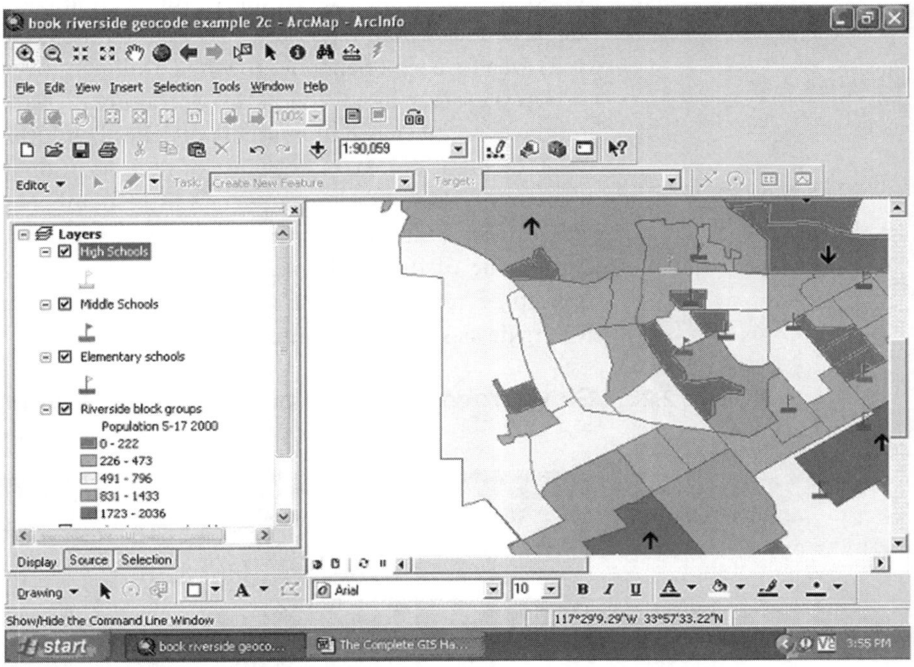

This example shows how you can use maps with multiple variables displayed to ask questions about the future and to plan for the future so that needs and important services can be provided for those who need them. Having adequate schools near where the children live is not only valued as a lifestyle and a safety issue, but it can help schools operate more efficiently by saving resources that would have had to be spent on transporting students from where they live to where the schools are. This in turn frees up scarce resources for instruction and extra curricular activities that enhance the quality of schooling and the experiences of the students.

Combining Map Types for Greater Understanding

To produce the map showing school planning information and school age population, maps of different types were combined and displayed together so that the common implications of multiple types of data can be more easily displayed, analyzed, and understood. To produce the map in Figure 2.26, the following procedures were used.

Step 1 Create a thematic map using the number of children aged 5–17 (as a pretty accurate proxy for school enrollment).

Step 2 Using the drawing tool (see Figure 2.8 and subsequent discussion), place a dot in each of the high growth and decline block groups; double-click on each dot, and use the change symbol button on the properties menu that is displayed to put either a down or an up arrow depending on the direction of change.

Step 3 Using MapQuest or another online or paper mapping source, locate the addresses of the public schools in Riverside, classifying them into elementary, middle, and high school; enter this information into a spreadsheet program such as Microsoft Excel, and save in dBase format. Figure 2.30 shows part of this spreadsheet.

FIGURE 2.30   **Spreadsheet for Riverside school addresses and type of school**

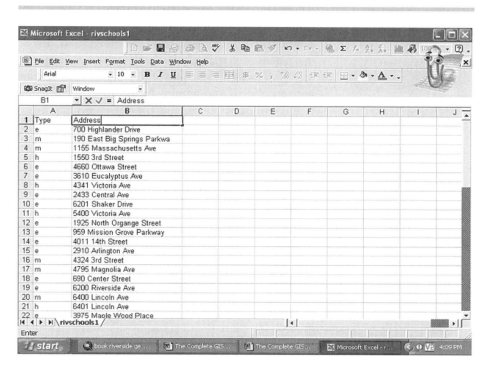

Step 4 Add these data to the map by using the Add Data tool (black cross on a light background) to add the dBase table to the display contents.

Step 5 Create an address locator using the toolbox to be used for geocoding the school locations (see Figure 1.15 and subsequent discussion). Geocode the addresses (following the procedures we outlined in Section 1; see Figure 1.21 and subsequent discussion).

Step 6 Using the procedures we have followed previously, subset the school data and create three layers—one for elementary, middle, and high schools, respectively. Right-click on the first school layer, and then select Properties. Click on the large "Symbol" button, and change the symbol to a school house, selecting a different color for each of the three layers, on the Symbol Selector submenu.

The resulting map is a combination of two pin maps (school locations and growth or decline) and a thematic map of the number of school age children. This is one of the basic ways you can combine multiple sources of data to produce more interesting and useful maps. However, you can also ask more fundamental questions about your data and the geographic patterns they display using the power of GIS to address your concerns and increase your knowledge.

What is the Proper Unit of Analysis in GIS?—Using Tessellations and Related Database Issues

In the maps we have discussed so far, the units within which data are displayed are defined by city boundaries, U.S. Census Bureau definitions of geography, such as tracts or block groups. There are many good reasons for using such geographic boundaries for geocoding and mapping. First, any address-based system of locating places in geography is based on the definitions each political system uses to identify places. Residences and business in the United States are grouped according to political and administrative units with defined boundaries, such as cities, towns, counties, states, and the national boundary as a whole. Our concepts of space are based on such divisions—when you meet someone, one of the first questions you ask is where are you from? The usual answer involves giving the name of a town, village, or city, and when the question is more specific, such as can I get your address so I can send you a package, the kinds of addresses you have used to geocode locations in this book are in this form. Further, when you started to construct thematic maps, the boundaries used to summarize the data came from the Census Bureau's definitions of space. All of these boundaries are arbitrary—some time in the past, somebody decided that the boundary of Riverside was going to be in this location, and then the Census Bureau officials used their rules for establishing the boundaries of census tracts and block groups, and so on. These constructions—the nature of which are independent of any consideration of what data you wish to study, understand, and use to inform decision making—were made in some cases many years ago and in a very arbitrary manner. Some of the spatial conflicts engaged in by nations we considered earlier came about because someone far away, and with little understanding of the geography and the social facts on the ground, drew an arbitrary line on a map.

However, the use of these arbitrary boundaries may be appropriate because they give us access to additional kinds of data that is useful for our research and our decision making. For example, in Figures 1.96 and 1.97, we saw how the number of divorces may have a relationship with the number of juvenile crimes in a block group—because we coded the juvenile crimes into block groups, this gave us access to Census Bureau data on the number of divorces, so we could ask the question, Is there a relationship? It makes sense to ask such a question, as one factor in juvenile delinquency may be the relationship a youth has with his or her parents, and in the case of divorce this relationship may be stressed and strained, particularly as a single parent usually has custody of a child after a divorce, and that parent may be working and commuting long hours, and is unable to supervise their child as much as in a two-parent household. The lack of supervision is the real factor that may result in higher rates of juvenile crime, but the number of divorced individuals in the area may be a proxy for the lack of supervision.

In general there are many possibilities to look for relationships among variables of interest and the more standard units are used, the more likely we are to have access to a number of potential indicators we are interested in. However, this is not the only way to group data together on a map. In some ways the arbitrary nature of these units creates difficulties for research into the geospatial relationships that are present in these types of data. This will become more apparent in Section 3, when we discuss the ins and outs of spatial statistical modeling and its uses. However, think about a street gang in a neighborhood, committing violent crime. These youths will hardly notice or even be aware of the fact that the route they usually walk from their homes to the local convenience store involves crossing a block group boundary—in fact they are likely to believe and act as if the entire area around their homes and the store are part of their "territory" and they may act on this feeling by assaulting any other youths who come into this area. The violent crimes that result would be geocoded into several block groups, and we will be splitting their behavior into discrete units when they are part of a larger whole. This fact can introduce bias into any analysis we want to do of these data and the relationships we want to examine. In Section 3 you will learn how to compensate for such features of geographic-based behavior in your analyses, but this example illustrates the problem of using artificial boundaries.

What is the alternative? It is possible to group data linked to physical space together in units that make sense given the distribution across space of the occurrences of the behavior of interest. So, for example, we could redraw the pin map in Figure 1.31 to reflect the distribution of juvenile violence without regard to the block group boundaries. The resulting type of groupings are called "**Tessellations**," referring to the tile-like pattern such units often display once they have been identified and mapped. Such techniques can be used to form units for analysis of spatially clustered databases on the physical location of events independent of the location of arbitrary census or political/administrative boundaries.

One of the disadvantages of using such an approach is the relative lack of data from other sources to relate the pattern of events found across the space being studied. Although some researchers have used algorithms to address this problem, producing weighted summaries of existing boundary-based data for the newly formed tessellations, these algorithms all contain untestable assumptions about the distribution of these other variables in the space, and thus cannot be recommended. However, some researchers believe that the advantages of constructing units based on the actual distribution in space of the events and their locations far outweigh any disadvantages in the measurement of other factors that might be related to these events and their spatial distribution.

Within the contexts of the types of maps and GIS techniques within the scope of this handbook, we can explore some of the implications of these boundary issues by using clustering techniques to modify our standard mapping approach. First, we will see what can be learned about our data and its distribution in space, and then we will demonstrate how these techniques can be used.

The data on youth violence and police contact we have used in several examples previously will be useful once again for this discussion. In Figure 2.31, a thematic map based on the number of youth violent events is displayed. Looking at this map in light of the discussion here, we can start to see ways in which the block groups, arbitrarily drawn from the point of view of our data on youth violence (but drawn according to U.S. Census Bureau algorithms for use in the Census of the Population), might be combined based on similarities in the distribution of events, that is the way events cluster in space. If we add the pin map to the thematic map, remembering that some of the points displayed on the pin map represent multiple events, this clustering becomes even more apparent (Figure 2.32.

FIGURE 2.31   **Number of youth violent incidents, Riverside**

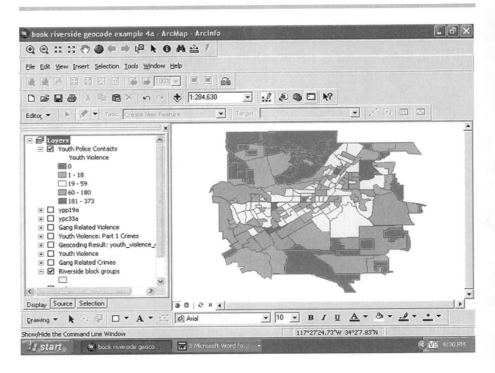

FIGURE 2.32   **Pin and thematic map number of youth violent incidents**

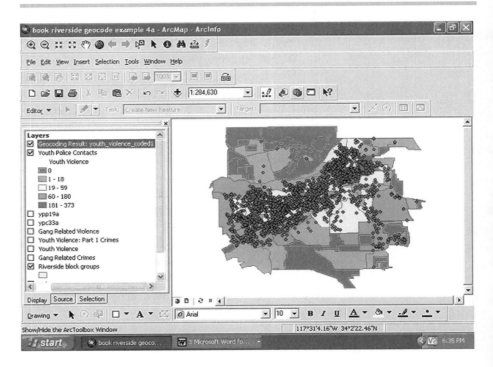

A detailed view of this map shows the potential for redrawing the boundaries of units with similar patterns of occurrence of these events in space that do not necessarily correspond to the block group boundaries. For example, there seem to be two relatively tight clusters of events in the detailed view shown in Figure 2.33

FIGURE 2.33   **Clustering of events across arbitrary boundaries**

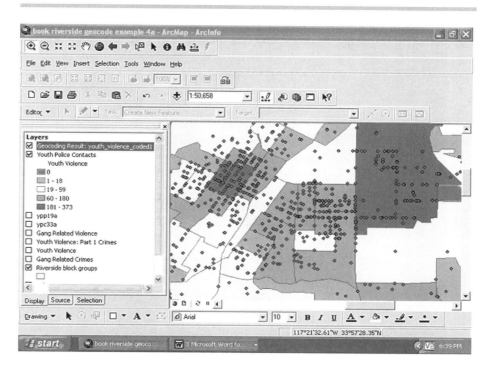

that cross several block group boundaries. The cluster of events in the middle of the map in the darker and light gray (orange and yellow) block groups form one cluster, tightly grouped, crossing several boundaries, but with some relatively blank space around the cluster. A similar pattern appears to the left of the map, in the group of block groups with a black (red) group in the center, surrounded by darker gray (orange) shaded units and some light gray (yellow) to the far left. You can also see the effect of boundaries, with lines of events strung out on the streets that are used in many cases to form the boundary of the block group. Is there a way to reconsider these units, or at least to combine block groups based on the similarity in the number and distribution of events?

One way to address this question is to use a clustering approach based on the spatial distribution of events within the block groups compared to that within the surrounding block groups. If the distribution and number of events in a block group is similar to that in a neighboring block group, it could be argued that the boundary between the two groups is arbitrary with regard to the events and where they happen. Thus it could make sense from this point of view to eliminate the boundary between the two units or block groups and form a larger "tessellation" of these two units. This process could be continued so that each block group or unit is linked with neighboring units that have similar patterns or clusters of events, such that large groups of units could be merged to make units that reflect the underlying distribution of these events.

Example: Tessellations and Youth Violence

ArcGIS has implemented Anselin's Local Moran I to analyze the clustering of events within and across unit boundaries (see Anselin, 1995). Although a topic to be discussed in detail in Section 3 of this book, Moran's I is the standard measure for the degree of spatial patterns or geographic similarity in the pattern of events in geographic locations. In group data like those being analyzed here, Moran's I provides a general measure of how much spatial correlation across units there is in these data arrayed as we find them on this map. The local Moran's I is a test of the degree to which the points in one unit are similarly distributed to the points in an adjacent unit. What is shown in Figure 2.34 is the significance of a Z test based on the values of the local Moran I for the block groups in Riverside with regard to youth violent incidents known to the police; black (red) indicates that there is highly similar distribution of points in units nearby that are also significant and thus black (red) in color. On the other hand, the darker gray (dark green) are places that show very different distribution from unit to unit as one crosses the boundaries from one unit to its neighboring units.

FIGURE 2.34   **Anselin's Local Moran I and clusters of youth violent incidents (Z scores)**

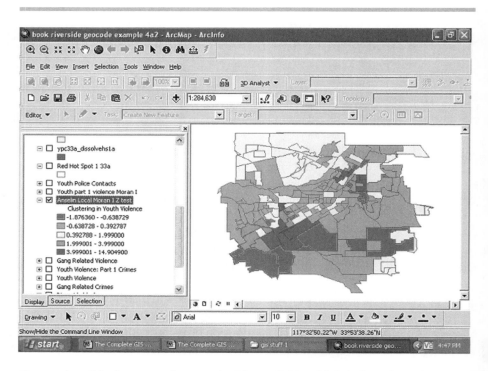

Comparing this figure to the map in Figure 2.31, which is based on the actual distribution of these events, shows a somewhat altered pattern, indicating that significant clustering has been detected in these data. For example, in the lower left portion of the map in Figure 2.31, there is one block group shaded black (red), indicating an area of a large number of violent events, and this area is surrounded by four block groups shaded in dark gray (orange), indicating a fewer number of incidents. In Figure 2.34, however, this unit is surrounded by four units that are similarly shaded black (red), indicating significant clustering among these units—as if they were not distinct areas but really part of a larger continuous area. This makes sense if we consider that the youth committing these violent acts have no idea that there are boundaries that divide up their neighborhood into the block groups that we analyze. The clustering test is telling us that these neighboring units show similar patterns of events inside each one, and this would be logical grounds for combining them into a single large unit that divides the space over which these events are distributed by the nature of the distribution of these events.

In the detailed view shown in Figure 2.35, the original hot spot in the lower left portion of the map is shown outlined (in blue) with the Local Moran Z tests plotted and the surrounding similarly clustered units shaded in black (red).

FIGURE 2.35   **Detailed view of clustering patterns**

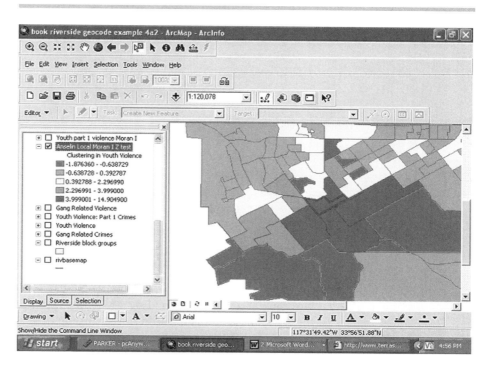

We can create a new unit which combines the events occurring in all four of the units shown in black (red) here to form a new tessellation based on the clustering the events we are mapping show, as seen in Figure 2.36.

FIGURE 2.36   **A tessellation based on the clustering of events in four block groups**

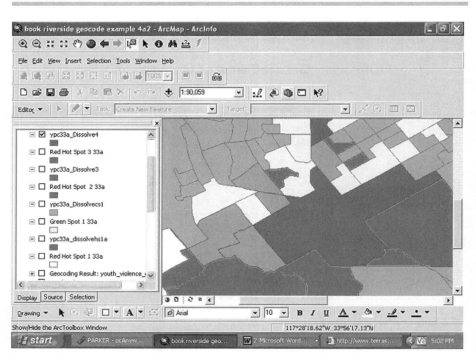

You can continue to build these new areas by combining block groups that have similar Z scores on the Local Moran's I, thus creating a map which divides the space these events occur in not according to arbitrary units devised for some other purpose, but on the basis of the events and their patterns across the space being studied. Several more such tessellations are shown in Figure 2.37.

FIGURE 2.37   **More tessellations based on clustering**

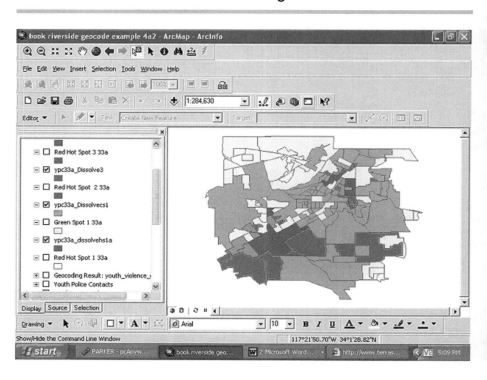

In this map, three areas of highly significant clusters have been joined, and two areas of gray (light green), areas of sparse occurrence of violent events, have also been joined, including a giant "super" tessellation combining 33 block groups in the middle right of the map. You can also see in Figure 2.37 that a light gray (yellow) super tessellation could be made in the upper left portion of the map involving 15 or more block groups; several other possibilities emerge from studying this map.

Now we are in a position to examine the problem raised earlier—How do we find population data, for example, to normalize the crime counts and create rates of youth violence in these newly created tessellations? Let's examine the details of one of the significant tessellations, within which the statistical analysis showed a hot spot, or dense clustering that was similar across several block groups. We can also display the pin map showing the actual locations of the events as shown in Figure 2.38.

FIGURE 2.38   **One hot spot of youth violence as a tessellation**

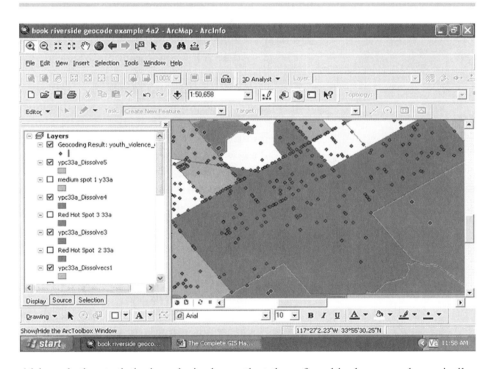

Although the statistical analysis shows that these four block groups have similar clustering in the events, you can see that the pattern is not evenly distributed across the space. For example, a large number of events cluster along the main streets that form the borders of the original block groups; in the lower right-hand portion of the black shaded area, there are almost no incidents. Suppose we just wanted to sum the population from these four original block groups to use for a denominator for population at risk in a rate—Would just summing across all four populations be a good estimate of the population at risk? Suppose you wanted to compute rates by ethnicity, to see if Latino involvement was higher or lower than Anglo involvement, and the vast majority of the Latinos lived in that lower right-hand section with almost no youth violent events. If that section of the area had a large Latino population, you might find a significant rate of Latino involvement if you simply took all the events in the tessellation and divided it by all the Latino population. You would be making an assumption that could be false—these youth violent events would have happened in places with few Latinos, yet the rate of Latino youth violence would seem to be large.

This example shows how when you create tessellations based on the clustering of one event, other characteristics of the space that may be related to the event in question may have different distributions—you cannot assume a uniform distribution across the space in one factor any more than you can in another, like these violent incidents. The best approach is to analyze geographic units as small as possible, in the same way that a raster image with smaller cells per unit of space is a better representation of a polygon or geographic shape. The smaller units bring you a more fine-grained picture to work with. As you will learn in Section 3, the use of these arbitrary units brings difficulties in the analysis of these data, but there are statistical models and corrections that can be used to overcome such problems. Ultimately there is no free lunch in geospatial analysis—the choices you make about how to conceptualize and map your data have an impact on the kinds of information you generate and the results you will get from any analysis. The best strategy may be tessellations in one case, and arbitrary but small units in another, depending on the nature of your data and the objectives of your map and analysis. One of the objectives here is to show you both sides of this important issue so that you know the implications for choices you make in your GIS work.

How were these maps produced? The same procedures already demonstrated in this book for the production of pin and thematic maps were used to construct the base maps for Figures 2.31 to 2.38. The two new wrinkles used to produce these maps were the use of Anselin's Local Moran I to plot statistically based hot spots and the use of a geoprocessing tool for "dissolving" the boundaries between similarly clustered block groups.

To compute and plot the Local Moran's I, the following steps were used.

Step 1 Open the toolbox by clicking on the toolbox icon in the main tool bar.

Step 2 Navigate down to the final line, Spatial Statistics Tools, and double-click; select the Cluster/Outlier Analysis with Rendering and double-click.

Step 3 The submenu appears; select the layer you wish to conduct the clustering analysis on.

Step 4 Select the field you wish to conduct the clustering analysis on.

Step 5 Create an output layer you wish to save the results of the clustering analysis in. Click on the browse folders button to the right to make sure you save the layer where you want to on your hard drive; when you type in the name and click on Save, the full path will be reflected on the submenu.

Step 6 Create a feature class to save the results of the clustering analysis in. The feature class will hold the combination of the data from the original attribute table and two new columns at the end of the new attribute table, for the Local Moran I and the Z test of its statistical significance; this map and associated attribute table will automatically be added to your display table of contents once the cluster analysis is complete. Your submenu should look like that in Figure 2.39.

FIGURE 2.39   **Setup for the cluster analysis**

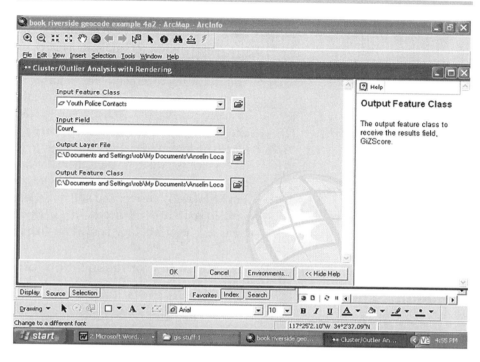

Step 7 Click OK and a box appears showing you the progress of the analysis; depending on the size of your data, this could take a few minutes.

Step 8 When the box shows that the analysis is completed, close it, and the new map will appear. Double-click on the new map and follow the steps shown in the previous section to make a thematic map of the Lmzinvdst variable which has been added as the last column in the attribute table, and your results should resemble Figure 2.40.

FIGURE 2.40   **Cluster analysis in progress**

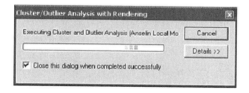

The other technique used in this example is using the Dissolve function to create the tessellations starting in Figures 2.36, 2.37, and 2.38. This can be accomplished with the following steps.

Step 1 Select the units you wish to combine into a tessellation. Start by opening the selection drop down from the main toolbar and open the Select by Attributes submenu.

Step 2 Select the layer you wish to use to make the selection from, and make sure the method box shows "Create a new selection."

Step 3 All the fields in the selected attribute table will appear in the box below method; navigate down until you see the field you want to select on. This field should have a unique identifier for each unit or block group.

Step 4 Double-click on the field, and if you are unsure of the exact id numbers or codes you need, click on the Get Unique Values box; all the possible values for the field will appear in the box to the right.

Step 5 Click on an operator next, usually the equal sign, and then find a value you want to select for and double-click on it; the operator and the value will appear below in the formula box.

Step 6 You can string together a large number of selection statements with the "OR" operator in between them, but they each must have the same structure: "FID_1" = 2 OR "FID_1" = 3 is correct; "FID_1" = 2 OR 3 and "FID_1" = 2 OR = 3 are *not* correct.

Step 7 Once you have all the units you want to select in the formula box, click on Verify; this will tell you if there are logical errors in your formula, but it will not tell you if you will select the proper units. A statement can be logically correct and still not select any units. When you have verified your formula successfully, click on OK to execute the selection. Your submenu will look something like Figure 2.41.

FIGURE 2.41 **Selection by attributes for tessellation formation**

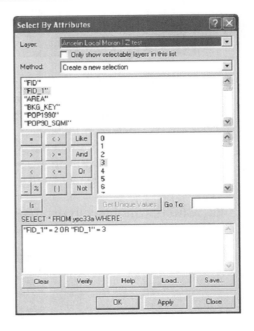

Step 8 When the window closes, left-click on the map you selected from, navigate to selection, then click on Create Layer from Selected Features; a new layer will be added to the display with the same name as the original layer with the word selection added at the end. Display this new layer on the map window to make sure you have selected the proper units.

Step 9 Open the toolbox and navigate to Data Management Tools; click on Generalization (not to be confused with General, above it in the list), and double-click on Dissolve.

Step 10 The Dissolve submenu opens. Select the new layer you just created with the selected units and select the field you want to dissolve; this will usually be the shape of the unit as you wish to dissolve the individual units into one larger shape. The submenu looks like that in Figure 2.42. Navigate down to the lower portion of the submenu. Here you can select a field that you wish to aggregate and have as an attribute of the new tessellation; this is an option, but in this case you might want to have the number of events aggregated from the individual units as an attribute of the new unit. You may also want to have the number of youth at risk for an event so you can calculate a rate for thematic display. You can add a number of fields here to be aggregated and select the type of aggregation you wish to perform.

FIGURE 2.42   **The upper portion of the Dissolve submenu**

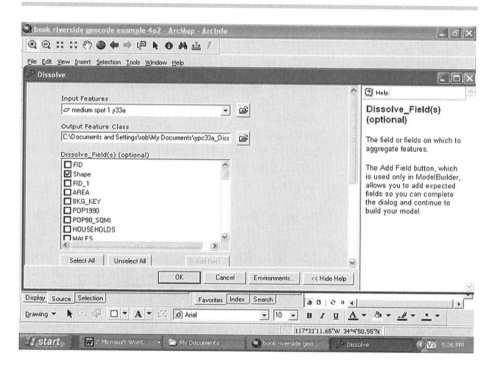

Step 11 Select any fields to aggregate and click on the "statistic type" box opposite each field you select to indicate the type of aggregation—in this case, you should select sum so that the number of events and the youth population can be aggregated and be attributes of your new tessellation.

Step 12 You are ready to dissolve the subunits and create your tessellation. Since we have already selected contiguous units, the multipart option is irrelevant for our purposes (under some circumstances you may create a new unit that is one unit but physically separated on the map—this is a multipart unit). Click OK and a new layer is added to the display, containing your new tessellation unit. You can show it over the original map and you will see the new unit displayed with the remaining old units as in Figures 2.36, 2.37, and 2.38.

Step 13 Continue to experiment with different groupings to form tessellations you see appropriate. When you have finished exploring, you can save your work and close the map.

Dynamic Maps: Showing Change over Time

One of the most powerful ways to use GIS techniques to show and understand how our world changes is to factor in the passage of time in our maps. As you probably recall, Hurricane Katrina had a devastating effect on the physical landscape of New Orleans, coastal Mississippi, and parts of Alabama in September 2005, but it was perhaps in the city of New Orleans itself where the devastation became best known to Americans elsewhere in the country and to the entire world. One of the tragedies of this hurricane and its aftermath was the way in which poverty, especially among African-American residents in New Orleans, left many people vulnerable and stranded. One question to ask about this is how did certain parts of the city end up being populated by poor people with few resources to deal with this disaster? Is this something that was always the case, and no one realized the problematic nature of the situation because New Orleans was very lucky during the past 40 years and had experienced no direct hits by such a power storm as Katrina? Did this situation develop recently, and therefore local residents and officials alike could not have anticipated the problems that might result? Issues like these are of dire importance to examine when planning for disaster relief. One way to examine this question is to map the rates of poverty among African-American residents in New Orleans over time and see if any patterns emerge that might illuminate the tragic situation and help New Orleans, other cities, and the Federal government plan more effectively for future storms hitting major urban centers.

Example: Rates of Poverty over Time in New Orleans

Using a specially prepared database, the Neighborhood Change Database, 1970–2000 (Geolytics, 2003), we can make valid over time comparisons possible because the census tracts have been standardized across the four census points (1970, 1980, 1990, and 2000). What was the extent of poverty among African-American residents of New Orleans in 1970?

The map in Figure 2.43 is focused on what we have all come to learn was the critical area of the city, between Lake Pontchartrain at the top of the map (the empty white space) and the Mississippi River curving through the city at the lower portion of the map (white curving lines); it was in the area where the river makes an ox-bow that many of the residents were stranded with no power, food, or means to evacuate after the storm hit and passed through the city. You can see that poverty was well established among this population in 1970. Was the situation constant over the next thirty years?

FIGURE 2.43   **African-American poverty rates, New Orleans, 1970**

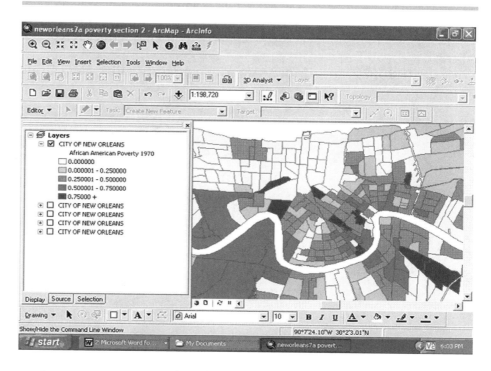

As you can see comparing Figure 2.44 to Figure 2.43, conditions in many census tracts of this area of New Orleans improved during the decade of the 1970s. Many more areas show light gray (yellow), the color used here to show no poverty among this population in the tract, and some significant changes towards

FIGURE 2.44   **African-American poverty rates, New Orleans, 1980**

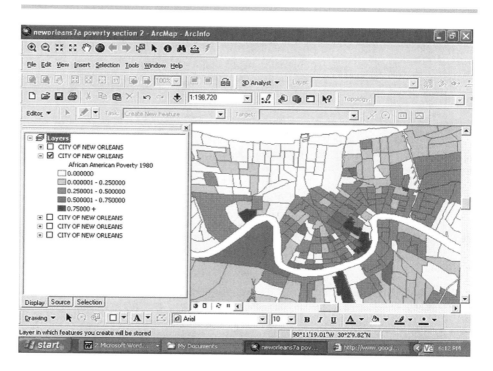

less poverty occur inside the ox-bow of the river. However, one section to the right where the river turns upward again seems to have become an area of concentrated poverty with several contiguous tracts with rates of 75 percent or more of the residents below the 1980 poverty line in terms of family income.

FIGURE 2.45   **African-American poverty rates, New Orleans, 1990**

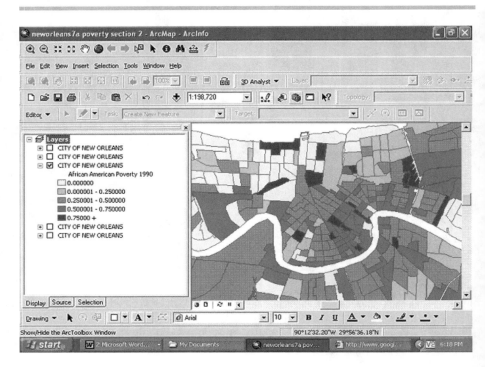

By the 1990 Census, the trend towards less poverty in many of these tracts had substantially reversed. Fewer tracts show light gray (yellow), and poverty is beginning to hit areas between the lake and the river on the right side of the map that had been consistently better off in 1970 and 1980. The area of concentrated poverty described in Figure 2.44 has improved somewhat, but now instead of 75 percent or more residents being poor in many of those tracts, now 50 percent to 75 percent are poor—an improvement, but not a great deal of improvement.

FIGURE 2.46   **African-American poverty rates, New Orleans, 2000**

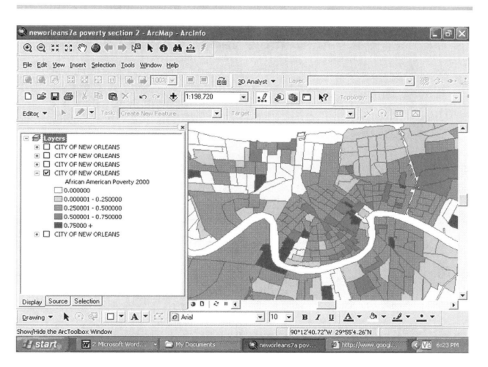

Between 1990 and 2000 there seems to have been little change in the pattern of overall poverty among African Americans in this part of New Orleans. A substantial number of census tracts show 50 percent or more at or below the poverty line in the critical area around the river and moving towards Lake Pontchartrain, the area that proved so prone to flooding with the storm and the collapse of the levy and canal system. Mapping this change or lack thereof over time can give the viewer a significant new perspective on the history of people and their economic and social situation in a community, and could have been used to help plan for the disaster that many expected to come to New Orleans sooner or later—it came sooner, before anyone had the foresight to use data like these to more effectively prepare for such a disaster.

Once the census tract map with the associated census data on poverty, displayed in an attribute table, is obtained, the procedures described elsewhere to construct thematic maps can be followed to make the 1970 map. Once this is in place, you can left-click on that layer, opening up the layer menu, and click on copy the layer. Left-click on the Layers indicator and click on Paste Layer(s); this will add a duplicate of the 1970 map. You can then double-click on the duplicate layer and construct the thematic map for poverty, 1980; repeat the process for 1990 and 2000 and you have the four maps needed for this example.

In Section 2 thus far, you have learned how to make maps a little more complicated, display different kinds of data, and to construct maps that tell us something about the situation of cities and their residents. These maps can inform planners for the future, anticipate needs and potential problems, and provide researchers with answers to questions of interest. The power of maps to show a great deal of information in a compact, convenient, and useful format has not been fully illustrated by any means in the examples so far. In the next examples we will attempt to demonstrate some of this ease of conveying complex information with multiple variables in ways that can be easily perceived by citizens, researchers, and policy makers alike.

Multiple Variable Maps

In a previous example (Figure 2.2), we displayed two variables as a combined rate on the map, so in a sense we were only, in the end, displaying one "variable." GIS allows for the display of multiple variables in different formats in order to convey more complex information. For example, Figure 2.47 shows a version of a map you may have seen in newspapers in the aftermath of Hurricane Katrina's impact on the city of New Orleans.

FIGURE 2.47   **New Orleans: persistence of poverty and flood depth from Hurricane Katrina**

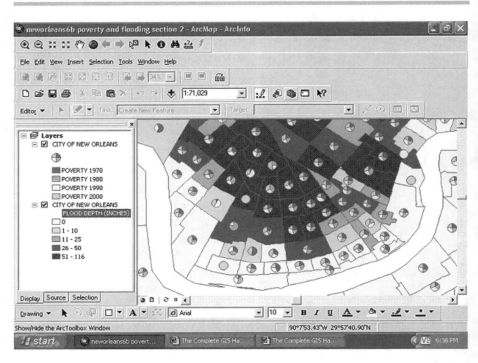

This map is focused on the city center of New Orleans, with the Mississippi River winding through the city at the bottom of the map, and out of sight just at the top of the map is Lake Pontchartrain, the source of much of the flooding that occurred in the aftermath of the storm. What you see is the result of seven variables being displayed simultaneously to show a relationship that only became apparent after the disaster, and it helps to explain why it was that so many poor people were unable to leave the city when they were asked to evacuate ahead of the storm, and hence the terrible scenes on the TV news about the Superdome, and all the people stranded in the city after the storm hit.

The pie graphs show the rate of African-American population living in each census tract (the units on this map) in each year of the Census that were poor, that is living in a household below the poverty line as defined at the time by the Federal government. Each color represents a proportion of the total summed over the four Census points. The graphs are constructed this way to show the stability or lack thereof in poverty rates for African Americans in New Orleans over this period. If the pie graph shows four equal slices in each color, it means that poverty among this population has been at the same rate over time—we do not know for certain that these are the same people, but given that most people in New Orleans have lived there most of their lives, it is likely that the same households that were poor in 1970 are also poor in 2000—suggesting long-term poverty in these areas. If the graph shows fewer than four slices or a lopsided set of slices, it means there has been significant change in the rate of African-American poverty in these areas over time.

The background display is a thematic map of the flood depth in the aftermath of Katrina, based on data gathered by C&C Technologies (www.cctechnol.com) as of September 19, 2005. The data show depth in inches, and these are approximations of the average depth over the area in question. What the map shows is that in the places with the heaviest flooding (darkest gray (blue) in the background), poverty among African Americans was a persistent condition across 30 years—the people living there just did not have the resources to evacuate on their own, as they were expected to do in the plan that the city had to work with. Being poor for that long means you have no access to a private car, you have no savings to draw out to sustain you in a new community; you have no knowledge of how to travel and where to go in such an emergency. Thus, the pictures and events involving people of color being abandoned and without help at the Superdome and elsewhere in the aftermath of this storm. This map also suggests that in planning for the next storm, or in other cities that face this kind of possibility, understanding the circumstances of the people in each area of the city will help to devise a better evacuation plan—What resources do residents have, and what do they lack?

How was this map constructed? First, we obtained data from the 1970, 1980, 1990, and 2000 Censuses on the poverty rates for African-American residents in each of the tracts; the tracts were adjusted for the fact that census tracts change over time so that a consistent definition of the tract was used across the four data points.

FIGURE 2.48 **Attribute table showing African-American poverty data, 1970, 1980, 1990, and 2000**

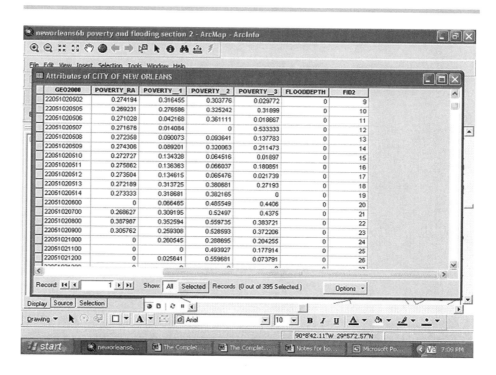

To construct the final map, the following steps were taken.

Step 1 Add a field to the attribute table for the flood depth data. Click on Options in the attribute table, to bring up the display shown in Figure 2.49.

FIGURE 2.49   **Attribute table Options menu**

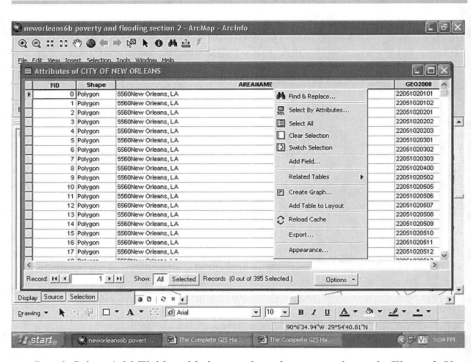

Step 2 Select Add Field and bring up the submenu as shown in Figure 2.50.

FIGURE 2.50   **Adding a new field to the attribute table**

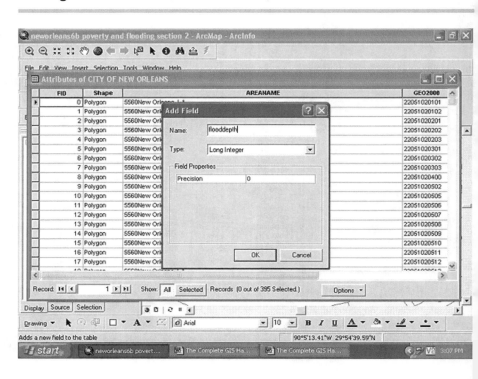

Type in the name for your field (flooddepth; 10 characters maximum), and select a precision for the new variable—in this case, you can leave it at zero, but if the new variable had decimal places to the right of the decimal, you would need to specify how many under precision. The new variable we want to add is in whole inches of water depth. Click OK and your new field will appear in the attribute table.

Step 3 On the main tool bar, click on Editor, and select Start Editing.

Step 4 Open the attribute table, go to the first unit you want to add new data for (not all census tracts in the city of New Orleans were under water after Katrina), and double-click on the cell in the attribute table.

Step 5 Type in the new data and move to the next cell.

When you are finished with all the additional data, minimize the attribute table and click on Editor again.

Step 6 Click on Save Edits, maximize the attribute table, and the flooddepth column will look like that in Figure 2.51.

FIGURE 2.51 **Attribute table with new data added for flood depth**

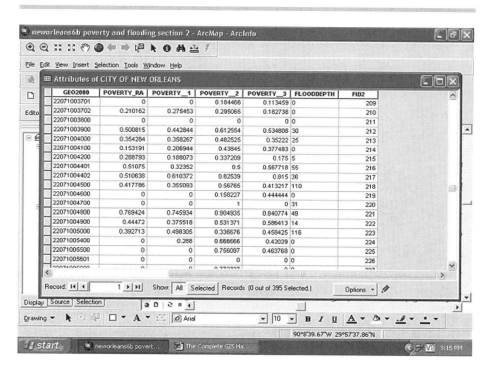

To construct the map in Figure 2.47, follow these steps:

Step 1 Open ArcMap and click on Add Data; click on the City of New Orleans layer to bring up the Census tract map as in Figure 2.52.

FIGURE 2.52   **Census tract map layer, New Orleans**

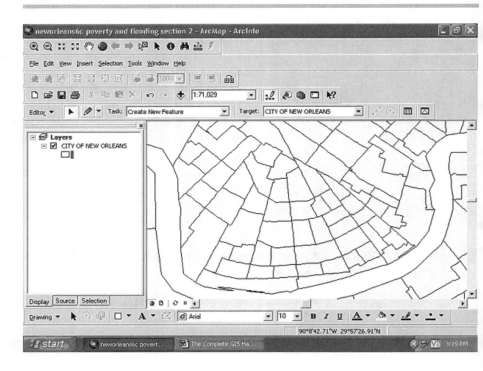

Step 2 Double-click on the Layer name to bring up the Layer Properties
window; click on Symbology.

Step 3 Select Charts, and a display will open up with the fields that can be
used in your data for a chart, as Figure 2.53.

FIGURE 2.53   **Charts submenu on Symbology tab**

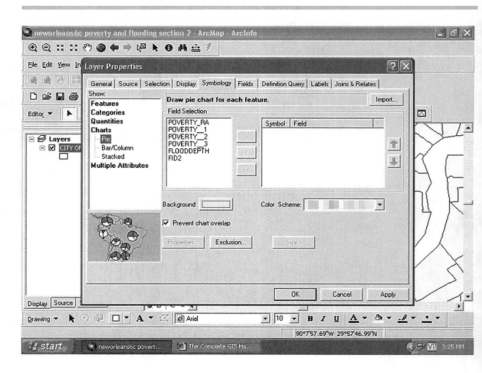

Step 4 Add each field you want to display in the chart, in this case the four poverty measures from 1970, 1980, 1990, and 2000 (they are in order from 1970 to 2000 in the window and in the attribute table), and adjust the color scheme by double-clicking on each color and selecting the one you want. When you have completed this, your screen will resemble that in Figure 2.54.

FIGURE 2.54   **Chart fields and color selection**

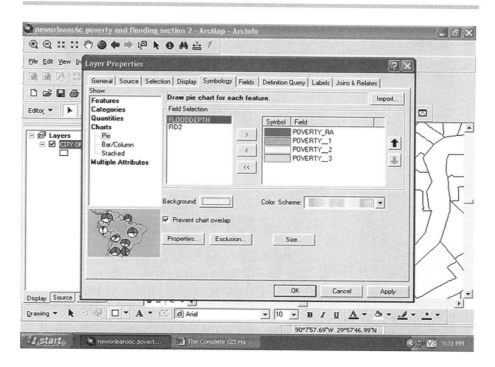

To complete the chart, you next should select attributes of the chart under properties and size.

Step 5 Select size, and reduce the size of the charts to be displayed to something manageable—in the example shown in Figure 2.55, 12 point.

FIGURE 2.55   **Chart size selection**

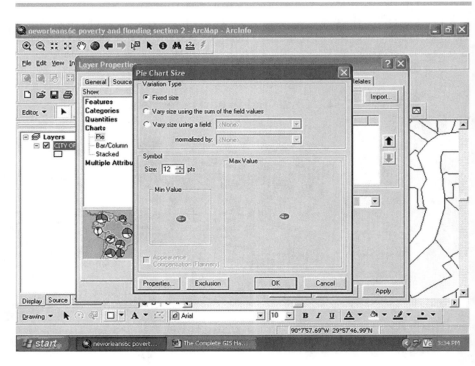

Step 6 Click on Properties, and in this case we clicked off leader lines (lines that connect a chart to the geographic unit it refers to if the drawing of the chart would overlap too much with other features), click off 3D (in this case we do not need it, but in other cases it will be useful), and we selected so-called geographic orientation for the pies as this preserves the time order of the field in a clockwise fashion, making the pies easier to interpret. Unclick the "Prevent chart overlap" box (again, the utility of this feature will vary), and click on Apply, click OK to close the Layer Properties window and each census tract will have a pie displayed within it on the map, as in Figure 2.56.

FIGURE 2.56   **Poverty from 1970 to 2000, African Americans, New Orleans**

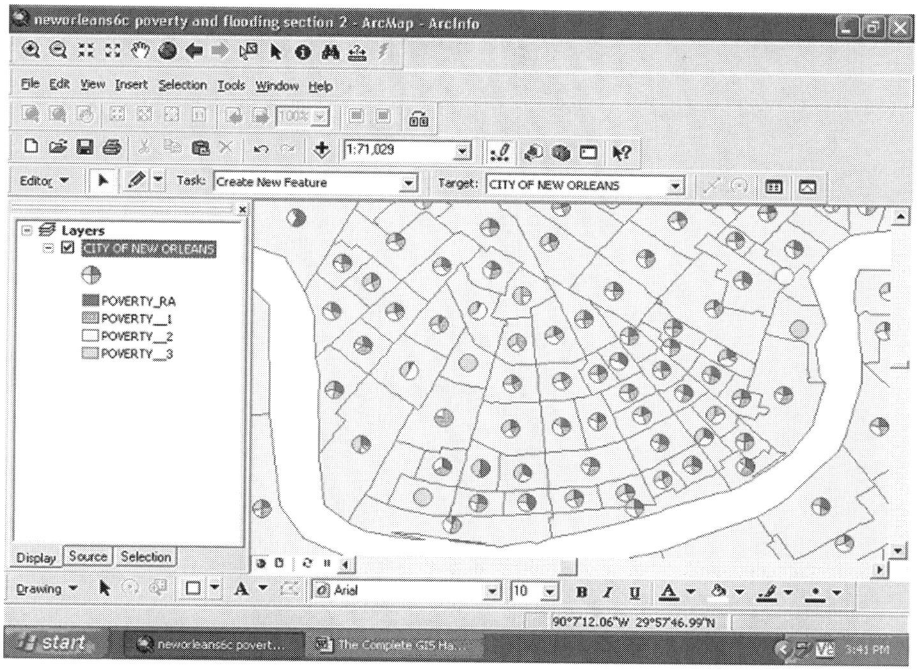

If you want to adjust the title for each field, right-click on each one twice (not a double-click, but two distinct clicks) and type a label you would prefer; this new name will show on the legend when you add it in the layout window (as shown in Figure 1.68). Before moving on to the next step, take some time to play with the options such as adding leader lines, and displaying the symbols in 3D. It is important to know what these options do in case you need to use them in the future.

Step 7 Click on Add Data again to add another copy of the New Orleans census tract map to the window.

Step 8 Double-click the layer name on this new copy to bring up the Layer Properties window and click on Symbology.

Step 9 Create a basic thematic map with the field Flooddepth with five categories, using yellow for the 0 or no flood waters in the tract, with a series of light to dark blue for the next four categories of flood depth. The map will now look very much like the map in Figure 2.47.

Another Way to Show Multiple Variables on the Map

Example: Patterns of Residency by Ethnicity

Pie charts are not the only graphic form which can display a lot of information in a compact form on the map. Figure 2.57 shows an example of the often complex pattern observed in American cities in the relationship between residential living patterns by ethnicity and the availability of economic resources.

FIGURE 2.57   **Ethnicity and median rent, Santa Ana, California, 2000**

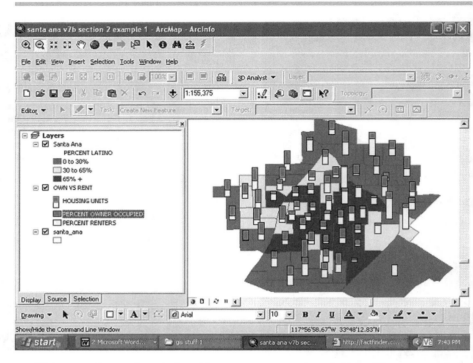

This map shows the relationships among several variables of interest to those who want to understand issues of residential settlement patterns, segregation by ethnicity, and the impact of economic resources like income and subsequently the ability to own or the need to rent housing on these relationships. The stacked bar graphs in each census tract in Santa Ana, a city in Southern California of about 340,000 residents located south of Los Angeles, represent the percent of residents in the census tract that either rented (in light gray (yellow) on the bottom of the bar) or owned (in darker gray (green) at the top of the bar) the residence they live in. The thematic background gives the percent Latino in each tract; the city as a whole was 76.1 percent Latino in 2000.

A number of patterns emerge from an examination of Figure 2.57. First, notice that the areas with the highest concentration of Latinos are all in the center of the city—from what we all have experienced about city centers in America, you realize that these areas are likely to be poorer, with less desirable housing, more multi-unit apartments and duplexes, and fewer single-family home-style neighborhoods. Likewise, the outskirts of the city are characterized by a medium tone in the thematic map, with fewer Latinos—remember that Santa Ana is 76 percent Latino. So the distribution of residential settlement is closely linked to ethnicity in this city, as it is in many American communities.

The bar graphs tell us something about the type of housing in each tract—the places in the center of the city are more likely to have the bottom (yellow) portion of the bar greater than the top (green) portion, indicating a majority of renters in the tract. This is especially true in the upper portion of the map and to the right of the map in the black (red) thematic areas where there are fewer Latinos and more Anglos. This is also the case in some of the light gray (green) areas to the right of the center of the city and the black (red) areas at the top right of the city. These are areas with fewer Latinos than Anglos, but they still show a majority are renters rather than owners.

The opposite is the case on the left side of the center of Santa Ana. In the light and medium, and even some of the dark areas, where Latinos are in the majority, home ownership is higher than renting—but the map overall shows that in a city with a large Latino majority, most areas are dominated by renters versus owners. Obviously income is part of the issue, and many more Latinos are poor than are Anglos in this city as in most places in the United States. The map in Figure 2.57 suggests that economic resources are not the full explanation, however, as the patterns displayed there seem to suggest that some kind of segregation between these two groups had operated to produce the link between ethnicity and home ownership. Census data show that overall in Santa Ana in 2000, about 18 percent of Anglos were poor, whereas about 23 percent of Latinos were poor, according to the U.S. Government definition of an income below the poverty line for a family of four, about $18,500. Although this is an important difference, it is not so great as to fully explain the differences in Figure 2.57. If you were concerned about the fact that fewer Latinos own their homes in Santa Ana, you might start looking at lending practices (Do banks tend to lend money for apartment complexes in some neighborhoods and single family housing in others, and does this correspond to the dominant ethnicity in the area?), or you might want to start and/or strengthen existing programs to assist first-time home buyers, especially those who are Latino and/or Spanish-speaking. You can see how maps can give you ideas for policies and practices that you would not have known were needed until you see the information the maps convey.

To produce the map in Figure 2.57, start with a map of the city of Santa Ana, as shown in Figure 2.58; these maps can be downloaded from the US Census Bureau's website (www.census.gov) in a format ready to open in ArcMap.

FIGURE 2.58   **The city of Santa Ana, California, 2000**

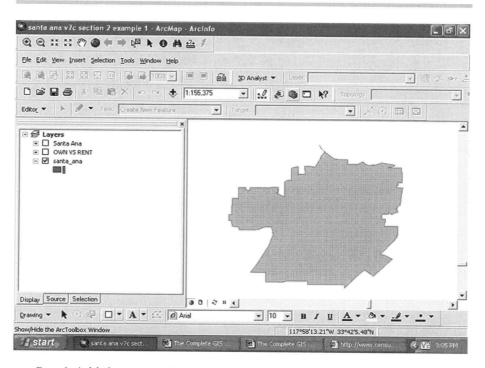

Step 1 Add the map and layer for California census tracts from the ArcGIS database; this map is a detailed map of the entire state of California

(Figure 2.59) and the accompanying attribute table has the basic census data needed to build the thematic map and the stacked bar graphs in Figure 2.57.

FIGURE 2.59   **California Census Tracts, 2000**

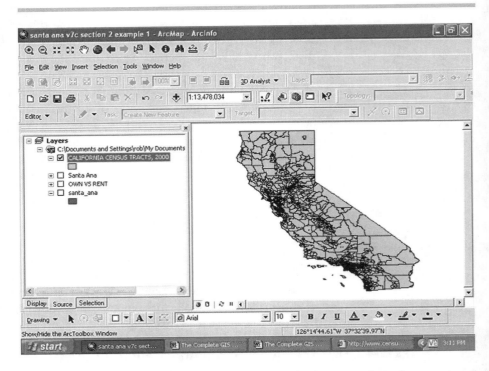

The city of Santa Ana is lost in the density of a large number of census tracts in Southern California around Los Angeles. Use the Santa Ana city map to cut out of the state tract map a selection that has all the tracts that are either in part or completely inside the city limits.

Step 2 Open the Selection tool from the main tool bar, and click on Select by Location.

Step 3 Make sure the first box reads "select features from," and check the California Census Tracts, 2000 layer as the location you want to select from.

Step 4 In the box under "that:" select the method for this selection, "intersect"; this will give you all the tracts within the city and those that are partially within the city that intersect the boundary.

Step 5 Under "the features in this layer" make sure that the Santa Ana city layer is visible; your submenu should look like that in Figure 2.60.

FIGURE 2.60   **Select by Location submenu**

Step 6 Once you click on apply, the selection will be made and highlighted on
the census tract map of the state; left-click on the census tract map
layer in the display contents, and click on Selection, and click on Zoom
to: Selection; your map should like Figure 2.61.

FIGURE 2.61   **Selected tracts for Santa Ana from California**

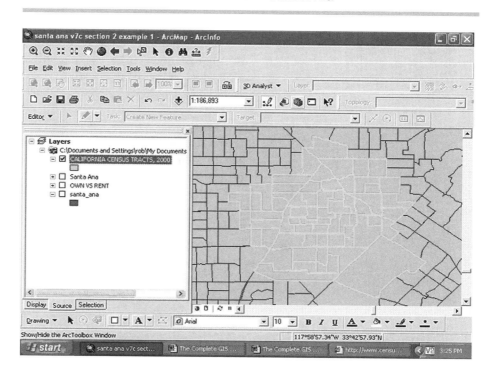

Step 7 Left-click on the original layer again, click on Selection, and click on "Create layer from selected features," and the new layer will be added to the display contents under the same name as the original layer with the word, "selection" added to the end of the title, as in Figure 2.62.

FIGURE 2.62   **Census tracts for Santa Ana, California, 2000**

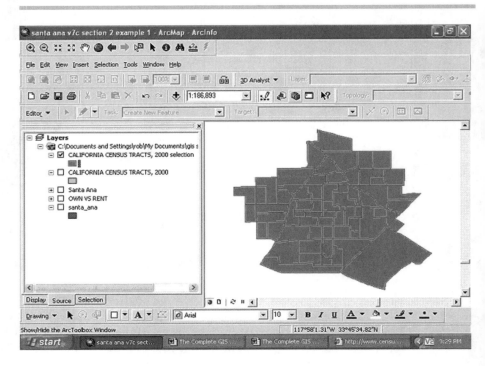

Use the procedures described previously to produce the thematic map for the percent Latino population. To produce the stacked bar graphs, use the following steps.

Step 1 Copy the thematic layer and paste into the display contents as a new layer; change the name to prevent confusion. Double-click on the new layer and select the Symbology tab.

Step 2 Select charts from the Show box, and click on stacked from the submenu.

Step 3 Select the two fields to display in the bar graph and click them into the box on the right.

Step 4 Click on each symbol to select the color scheme you want to use to represent each field in the bar.

Step 5 Unclick the box labeled "Prevent chart overlap" and click on the Properties button; turn off the 3D option and unclick the box for "show leader lines."

Step 6 Click on OK to get back to the main Layer Properties menu, and your screen should look like that in Figure 2.63; click on Apply and OK.

FIGURE 2.63   **Building stacked bar graphs to display over a thematic map**

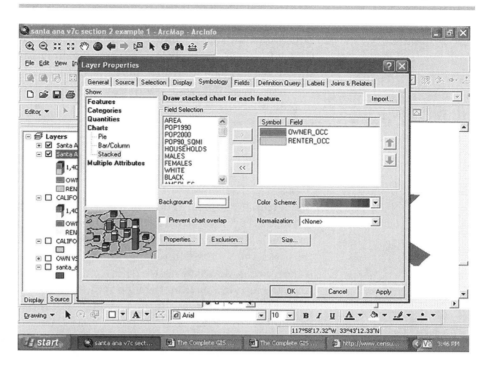

your map should look like the one in Figure 2.57 (make sure the display order lists the thematic layer above the stacked bar graph layer).

In these last two examples, you have learned how to add graphic elements to your map to represent additional information, thus expanding the way in which multiple sources of data can be mapped and more complex relationships made clear, especially the way these relationships have a geographic aspect. This is only one way of displaying more complex information; the next examples show how underlying models of geospatial data can be mapped and displayed in very powerful and imaginative ways using some of the more advanced features of ArcGIS.

Understanding Dynamic Data

In the New Orleans examples described previously, we were able to use information over time to gain insight into how the changes that occur over time can help us to better understand our current problems and needs. In this example, we examine a more formal mathematical approach to change over time, in this case concerning the spread of innovation in public policy and organizations among American states.

Example: Diffusion of Innovation in the United States (3D map)

The establishment of colleges to train teachers, called normal schools in nineteenth-century America, or the date by which a state required school age children to attend school are examples of the kind of innovation that organizational researchers study (Jensen, 2004). Using data from a study by Walker (1973), Jensen (2004: 3) examines a number of hypotheses that might explain the overall path of diffusion across 27 different types of organizational and policy innovation including the two educational-oriented adoptions we will examine. One of the interesting features of data on diffusion is that measures of diffusion combine both time and space. Diffusion happens across these two dimensions, and the degree to which one process dominates the other can impact the process of diffusion and the adaptation of innovative forms and policies. Imagine a situation where two relatively small political units share a common border and the reaches of both areas are well within a day's travel time. If one unit adopts a new organization or a new practice that is reasonably visible and judged by the people in the unit to be successful and to contribute to the greater good, people who reside in the other unit traveling back and forth will begin to wonder if this innovation would be good for them to adopt as well. So innovation can spread via diffusion over space. The length of time may vary by how far away the innovation is from the potential adopters and by how much communication, travel, contact, and so on there is between them as well as by how fast such activities occur. If we were to map such a process, we would see a small area where the innovation begins, and then over time we would see a gradual seeping out from that center, almost like water flowing downhill, faster (shorter time frame) or slower depending on how steep the terrain was from the high spot (first place the form was adopted).

On the other hand, diffusion can also skip the surrounding areas and appear to jump across space in a relatively short time. Suppose one of the influential founders of the innovation were to relocate several units away; this innovator may convince new fellow residents to adopt the innovation quickly, even though many of the new units' residents have not seen the new form in action as in the first example. Either way, mapping the adoption of these new forms and practices can help us to understand the process, the factors that might influence it, and the differences to be seen when comparing one innovation to another.

One way to proceed is to construct a thematic map of the places that adopt the innovation and the time frame involved. In the case of the opening of teacher training colleges, Figure 2.64 shows the time frames in which U.S. states adopted this organizational innovation.

FIGURE 2.64   **The adoption of teaching colleges among the U.S. states, 1839–1911**

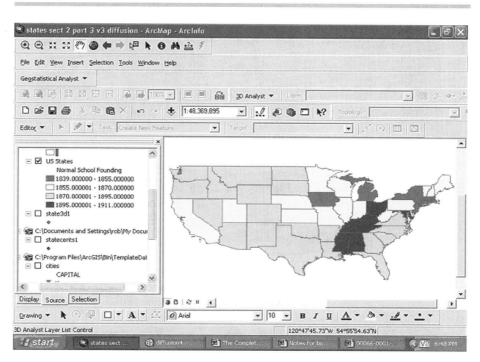

Several interesting patterns jump out from the map. These colleges were founded initially in the Northeastern states, such as New York, New Jersey, Connecticut, Massachusetts, and a couple of innovative Midwestern states, Iowa and Michigan. A second wave of adoptions seems to have occurred in a spatial diffusion pattern starting from New York and Massachusetts going north to Upper New England and south to Pennsylvania and Delaware; West Virginia only became a state during the Civil War but seems to have immediately adopted this innovation. A second wave of spatial diffusion emanates from Iowa, reaching most of the states that border on Iowa by 1870; a couple of distant western states also adopt in this period. Most of the Western U.S. states, along with Louisiana and Arkansas, founded these colleges in the period from 1871 to 1895, but there is a curious band of holdouts from Ohio to Kentucky, Tennessee, Alabama, and Mississippi that are the last, along with Maryland, to adopt this organizational form. Mapping these data show the patterns of diffusion clearly and suggest many possible explanations. For example, the southern states that resisted so long may have had problems with poverty and racial inequality that held back the adoption of teacher training colleges in the post–Civil War period.

Another way to look at these data is to take a more formal approach to the diffusion process. Walker (1973) calculates an innovation score for each of the 27 forms or policies his data cover to relate how each state's adoption of the innovation related to the entire process of adoption across all the states. Walker gave a score of 0 on this measure to the first state that adopted, and then gave subsequent states a score proportional to the length of time after the initial adoption that it took for later adapters to create the new form or organization or policy innovation. If Massachusetts adopted the first teacher training school in 1839, and Mississippi was the last state to do so in 1910, the latter gets a score of 1 and the former 0. If Indiana adopts this organization in 1865, the score for innovation is the time since the first one divided by the entire time it takes for all states to adopt, or 1865–1839/1910–1839, or 26/71, for a score of 0.3661. This measure is a kind of reverse innovation score, as the lower the score the more "innovative" the state is on this measure.

Although flat maps like the ones we have used thus far in this book can be very informative, the recently enhanced power of software and hardware available to the everyday GIS practitioner has meant that a powerful visual alternative, three-dimensional or 3D maps can now be constructed using software such as ArcGIS. Using height or elevation as a metaphor in the case of innovation and diffusion research is a potentially powerful tool for gaining new insight into these processes and the factors that influence new policy practices and organizational forms.

Constructing a 3D map of the reverse innovation score for the adoption of teacher training colleges reveals some very interesting new information, as shown in Figure 2.65. You can immediately see the differences in innovation and diffusion in the different regions of the country in the 3D display: the valleys of light gray (blue) where teachers colleges first were organized, the light gray (blue) of the first wave of diffusion spreading north into New England and south to Pennsylvania, and the spherical pattern of diffusion around Iowa, with distant western imitators California and Utah. Finally, the dark gray (red) mountain range of holdout states in the middle of the country, from Ohio to Mississippi and Alabama, are seen clearly in the 3D representation.

FIGURE 2.65   **3D map of innovation index, teacher training colleges, U.S. states, 1839–1911**

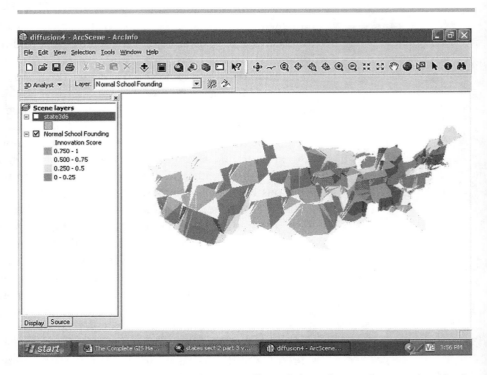

Making 3D maps is somewhat complicated, but the results may justify the difficulties. First, your license for ArcGIS must include the 3D Analyst extension (go to www.esri.com for further information on extensions). Second, you need to activate the extension by clicking on Tools on the main tool bar and clicking on Extensions; this will bring up the Extensions submenu, as in Figure 2.66.

FIGURE 2.66   **Extensions submenu**

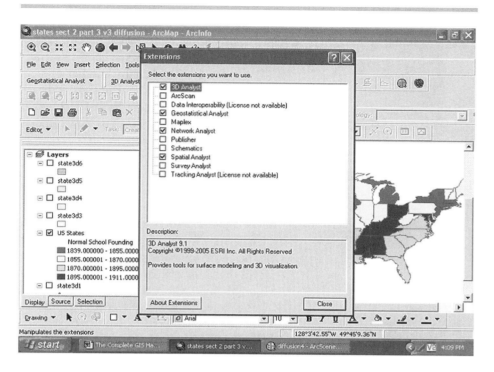

Usually if the extension is licensed, it will already be checked, but if it is licensed and not activated, simply check the box and click close to activate. Next you need to activate the 3D Analyst tool bar, by clicking on View, toolbars, 3D Analyst. You can drag the tool bar around the screen to place it in a convenient location.

To get a standard map ready for conversion to a 3D map, you need to add two fields to the attribute table of the map, one for the X coordinate and the other for the Y coordinate. In a geographic-based map like those used in the book, the X and Y coordinates are the familiar latitude and longitude. If you run your cursor across a map like the one in Figure 2.65, at the bottom of the ArcMap screen you will see the X and Y coordinates displayed; all these maps are based on these coordinates. Although the coordinates are in that sense built in to these maps, the 3D functions of ArcGIS need to have those coordinates listed for each point or polygon you use in your mapping process. For a 3D map, you need a third dimension, of course, but here is where you can use height or elevation as a metaphor, to be based on a variable of interest to you. In this case, we can look at the reverse innovation score as providing the source of the elevation data for the 3D representation. To get started on the process, first add the coordinates to the attribute table.

Step 1 Open the attribute table of the map you wish to convert to 3D by right-clicking on the layer and selecting Open Attribute Table from the popup menu.

Step 2 Click on Options, and select Add Field; if you have been editing, Add Field will not be selectable, so be sure to save any previous edits and stop editing before proceeding further.

Step 3 Create two new fields in this way called "Point_X" and "Point_Y"; select double as the precision for these fields.

Step 4 Minimize the attribute table, and click on Edit, and click on Start Editing. This is necessary for the next step of actually calculating the X and Y coordinates.

Step 5 Highlight the name field at the top of the column for "Point_X" and right-click to bring up the field submenu; click on Calculate Values to open the Field Calculator submenu.

Step 6 Check the Advanced box in the middle of the menu; this will bring up the label on the bottom box to become "Pre-Logic VBA Script Code," and move the Point_X = box down to new location at the bottom of the Field Calculator submenu.

Step 7 Click on Help. This will bring up a window that contains some very useful information about Pre-Logic VBA Script codes, and some examples you can use for the task at hand. What you want to do is to create an XY coordinate for the centroid or center point of a polygon and add that to the attribute table. Find the example labeled, "To add the X coordinate of Polygon Centroids," highlight the entire four-line script, press and hold the control key (Ctrl) and hit the letter c while holding the control key to copy what you have highlighted. Close the Help dialog box, move the cursor into the Pre-Logic VBA Script Code box, and paste the text from the Help dialog into the box.

Step 8 Type pArea.Centriod.X in the box under Point_X = so that the result of your calculation gets assigned to your coordinate field; make sure that the field in your original attribute table that describes the shape of the units you are using, usually polygon, is called Shape. If not, type the name of that field into the third line of the script where the word Shape appears between brackets. Your submenu should look like that in Figure 2.67.

FIGURE 2.67   **Calculate fields submenu for XY coordinates in polygons**

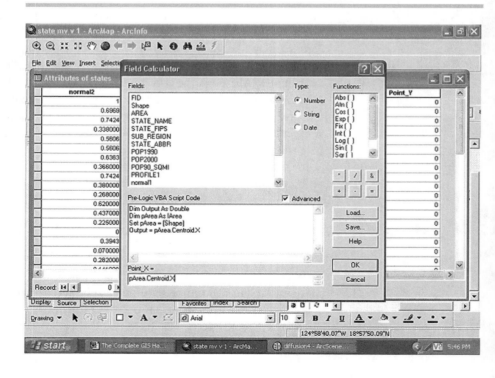

Step 9 Click OK, and the X coordinates should appear in the attribute table.

Step 10 Open the Field Calculator submenu for Point_Y and the submenu reappears with the Pre-Logic VBA Script Code box and the code as it was in Figure 2.67; change the X to Y in the fourth line of the script and in the box now labeled Point_Y = and click OK; coordinates for the Point_Y now appear in the attribute table.

Step 11 Minimize the attribute table, click on the Editor button, click on Save edits, and click on Stop editing. Now you can close the attribute table.

Now you are ready to convert your two-dimensional map to a three-dimensional map using an attribute at height or elevation, and the XY coordinates you have already added to create the 3D effects. To do this, follow these steps.

Step 1 Click on the 3D Analyst tool bar, select Convert, and select Features to 3D, as in Figure 2.68.

FIGURE 2.68   **3D Analyst and submenus**

Step 2 The Features to 3D submenu appears as in Figure 2.69; select the layer name for the map you want to convert, and select Input feature attribute as the source of heights. Select the field you wish to use—here we are looking at the reverse innovation measure for normal schools, which is called normal2 in this table. Under output features, type a name for the 3D layer file; click OK.

FIGURE 2.69   **Features to 3D conversion submenu**

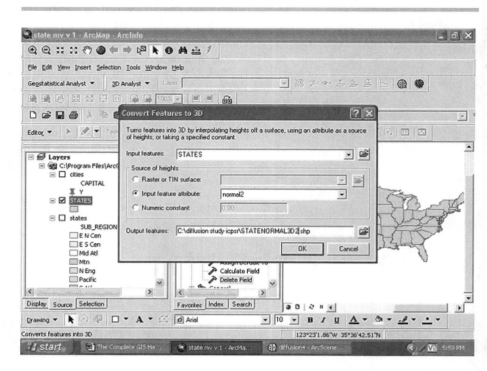

The new layer will appear in the display contents at the top and will be displayed on the map. Do not be alarmed that the map does not look any different; you are still viewing it in the two-dimensional world of ArcMap. To see the new features, you need to move the map into the 3D viewer that comes with ArcGIS, ArcScene, which can be activated by pressing the ArcScene button on the 3D Analyst tool bar. This will open the ArcScene window, as in Figure 2.70. The ArcScene window is very similar to the ArcMap window with many of the same commands, although it has additional commands and tool bars to handle the 3D viewing capabilities.

FIGURE 2.70   **ArcScene window**

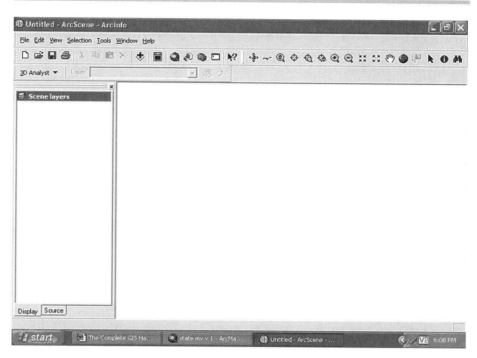

To fully convert your map to 3D, follow these steps.

Step 1 Return to the ArcMap window and right-click on the new 3D layer;
click on Copy when the popup menu appears.

Step 2 Return to the ArcScene window, and right-click on Scene layers in the
Display contents window. Click on Paste layers, and your new map will
appear in the window, as shown in Figure 2.71. The map now gives

FIGURE 2.71   **Newly converted 3D map**

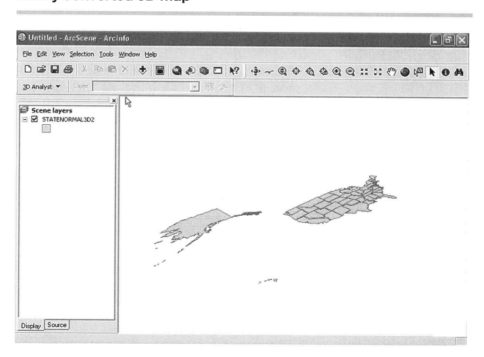

hints of having some elevation, but again do not be concerned that the 3D aspect is not very visible. More steps are required to give the proper aspect to the map for 3D viewing.

Step 3 Right-click on the Scene layers line again; this time select Scene Properties as in Figure 2.72. Under the General tab, click on the button labeled, Calculate From Extent. This feature provides a scaling of the 3D heights you have provided that makes it possible to see the three-dimensional structure of the map. Click on Apply and then OK, and the map will start to appear to have a third dimension. However, this is still hard to see. More steps will enhance and show the full potential of this approach to mapping.

FIGURE 2.72   **Scene Properties submenu**

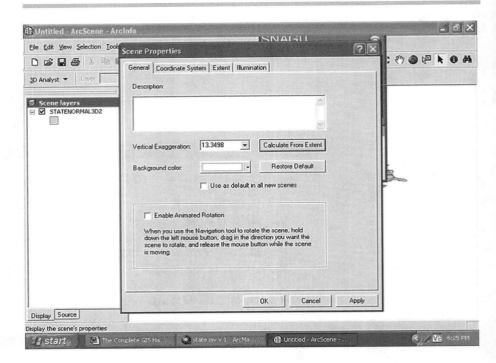

To really visualize the third dimension, you need to give your map some more realistic 3D characteristics, like depth and shadow, as if the sun were shining on this map from a particular angle. You realize through this process that a great deal of what we see when we view the three-dimensional world is the product of depth and shadow/light as well as the actual width, height, and length of objects we view.

Step 4 Click on the 3D Analyst tool, select Create/Modify TIN and select Create TIN From Features as shown in Figure 2.73.

FIGURE 2.73   **Creating a TIN (triangulated irregular network)**

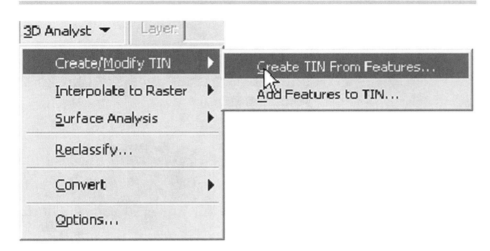

A triangulated irregular network (TIN) is basically a representation of a three-dimensional feature using a series of interconnected vertices of triangles to model the physical aspects of the feature—its height, the slope up or down to the height of the adjacent features, the shadows and valleys that are created by the ups and downs of the terrain, and so on. Figure 2.74 shows some of the aspects of a TIN taken from the ArcGIS help file.

FIGURE 2.74   **The structure of a TIN surface**

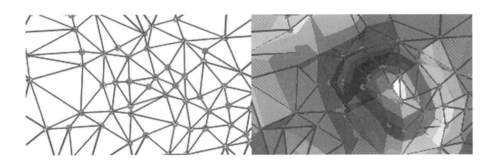

The mountain on the right is built from a series of intersecting triangles that interpret or model what the actual surface might look like given the three coordinates that describe the mountain peak and the surrounding areas as the mountain declines down to the valley surrounding it. In the map we are using, the states are each represented by three dimensions, and the TIN structure models what the surfaces connecting each state look like given that each state has an elevation based on the attribute of interest, in this case the reverse innovation score. The TIN creates depth and shadow more realistically to represent a three-dimensional surface and thus highlight the trends, differences, and similarities exhibited by the states on the attribute providing the elevation or height to the map.

Clicking on the final command in Figure 2.73 creates the TIN structure, as seen in Figure 2.75. You can now really start to see some of the three-dimensional aspects. For example, notice how the California coast seems to be very low and

FIGURE 2.75   **Initial view of TIN map**

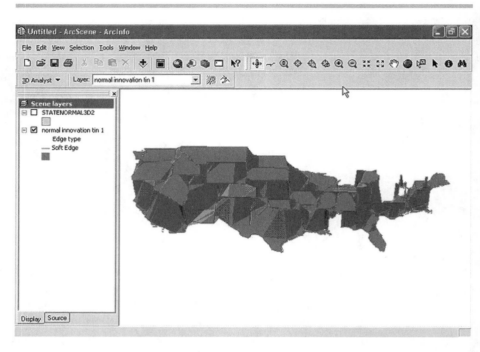

dramatically rise up to the next set of states—Nevada and Oregon, which form the beginning of a high plateau. This plateau goes up even higher as we pass into Idaho and Montana. These differences reflect the reverse innovation scores, but they are still not too clearly visible.

   Step 5 Open the Layer Properties submenu (Figure 2.76), and click on the Symbology tab. You will see in the left-hand side two boxes checked next to the words, "Edge Types" and "Faces." Uncheck the Faces box, and click Add right below this area of the menu. A popup menu with a list of choices will appear (the Add Renderer submenu): select "Face elevation with graduated color ramp." Click on Add and then Dismiss to close the window.

FIGURE 2.76   **Layer Properties menu and the Add Renderer submenu**

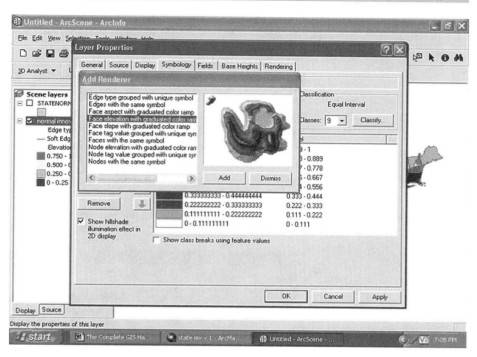

Step 6 Since the innovation score varies between 0 and 1, drop the number of classifications down to 4, and select an appropriate color ramp; change the colors if you wish to. The result will start to look much more interesting; you can manipulate the 3D image—rotate it, tilt it, even look upside down at it, with the tool on the ArcScene tool bar. Interesting perspectives can be gained in this manner, as Figure 2.77 demonstrates.

FIGURE 2.77   **3D map of normal school innovation score, U.S. states, 1839–1911**

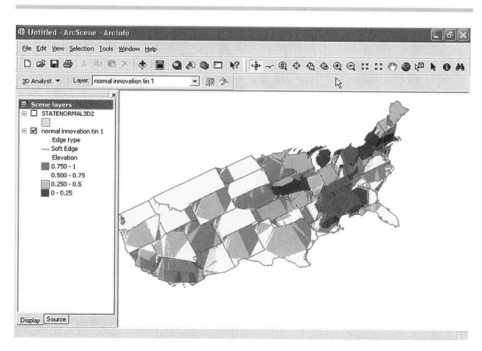

Now you can start to see the peaks and valleys that represent the diffusion of this innovation, and the possibilities for close-ups and magnification and different angles of view are potentially limitless. These kinds of manipulations and the insights that can be found in them are only possible with the power of the three-dimensional approach to GIS.

Another of the technical aspects of this example involves the power of Arc-Map's database management. To bring together the basic map data for the U.S. states and the data from Walker's (1973) study of innovation, some database manipulations had to be conducted to put the data from both sources into one attribute table so it could be mapped in the 2D and 3D forms. After saving the Walker data in a .dbf format file using Microsoft Excel, we had to add a field to the Walker data that would be a match to a field in the attribute table for the U.S. states map, as shown in Figure 2.78.

FIGURE 2.78   **Attribute table for the U.S. states layer**

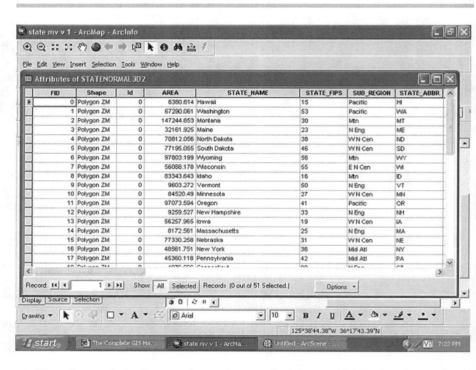

There is a code in the very first column called FID, which is simply a numeric identification code that ArcMap places into attribute tables. Since the states in the Walker file were in a different order than the states in the map layer, entering the FID code from the Attribute table of the map layer for each state in the Walker file would also allow us to sort the Walker file so that the states would be in the same order for joining with the map attribute table. This was done in Microsoft Excel as well and saved into a .dbf format. Using the Add data command in ArcMap, the Walker data were than added to the display contents (Figure 2.79).

FIGURE 2.79   **File "state2" diffusion study (Walker, 1973) added to the display contents**

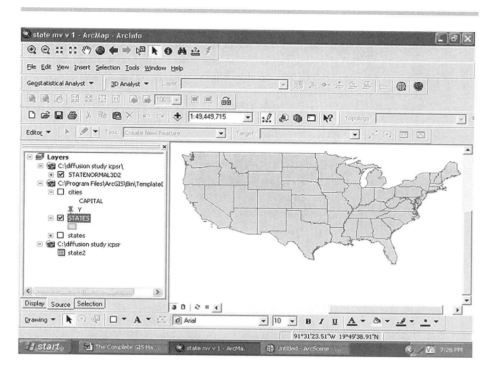

Opening the attribute table of state2 shows the variables and the common field, FID1, as shown in Figure 2.80.

FIGURE 2.80   **Attribute table for state2, diffusion data file with FID1 field**

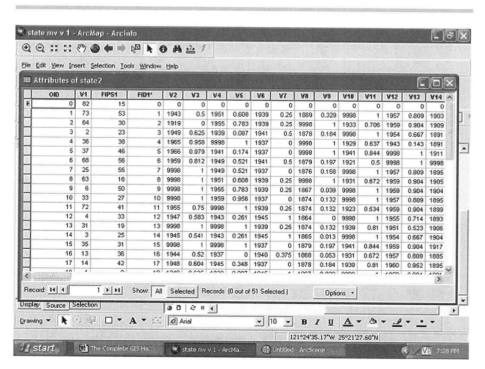

Step 1 To join the two tables, right-click on the map layer and select Joins and Relates; from the submenu select Join.

Step 2 Indicate the field in the map layer you want to base the join on, that is, the field that the other table also contains, in this case FID.

Step 3 Select the Table to join to the map layer, in this case state2.

Step 4 Select the field in the second table, state2, to base the join on, in this case FID1; your Join submenu should look like that in Figure 2.81.

FIGURE 2.81   **Join submenu**

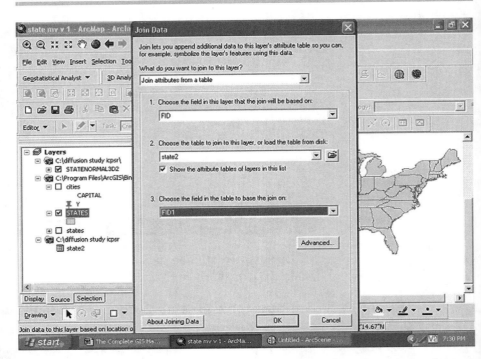

Step 5 Click OK and the join will occur. Open the attribute table for the map layer, and you will notice that all the new variables from state2 are now part of the table, with variables names like "state2.fid1" showing that they came from the state2 file originally. The variables in the map attribute table are also newly labeled as "state.fid" to show their origin. Now the Walker study variables are available to map and visualize in three dimensions.

Using Three Dimensions to Show Socioeconomic Conditions

Although the economic system of the United States, based on capitalism and free enterprise, has been very successful at creating prosperity and economic status that is the envy of many of the world's nations and individuals, the system is also very good at creating inequality and poverty, especially when compared to other advanced industrial nations. There are many and complex reasons for this, but one of the ways to increase understanding of these issues is to use the power of 3D GIS to visualize these differences and to reveal new and different aspects of them. In this example, data on average rents in the city of Riverside will be shown in a 3D visualization that might help prospective residents of the city decide where to look for housing and how to match their search to their budget but still understand all the options available to them in different parts of the city.

Example: Socioeconomic Conditions in 3D

Figure 2.82 shows a 2D map of the median rent in each block group in the city of Riverside in 2000. There is a great deal of information in this map and it is somewhat hard to interpret. Again, the power of the 3D visualization can help; if we make median rent in the block group the height or elevation on the map, the picture is somewhat clearer, as we see in Figure 2.83

FIGURE 2.82   **Median rents by block groups, Riverside, 2000**

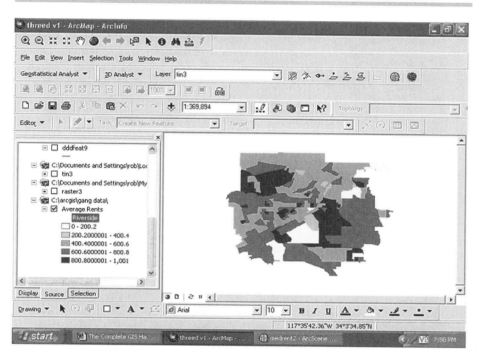

FIGURE 2.83   **TIN map of median rent, Riverside, 2000**

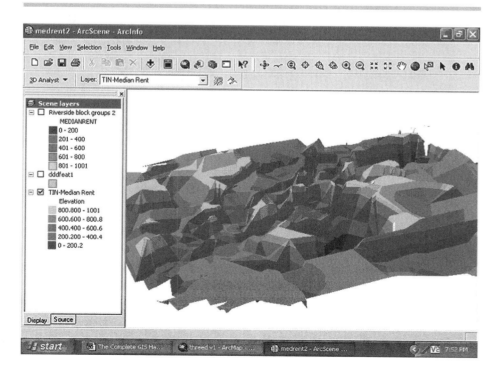

There are clearly areas of high and low rents that are very near to one another, given all the dramatic valleys and mountains in the TIN representation. Perhaps we can use the block group boundaries and a feature of the 3D system in ArcScene to help interpret this information.

Suppose we could impose another map of the block groups that was elevated all at the same height, that height being the median rental value for the entire city of Riverside. This would allow us to see the places with below median rents, and with the above median rents rising above, as it were, a level plain set at the overall median value of the city's rental units.

Using the same color scheme and number of categories, this layer is imposed on the TIN map in Figure 2.84. Now we can see much more clearly the differences in rents across the neighborhoods of the city: where the high points are, and the areas of more modest rent nearby, and, in the valley floor, the places of very low rents (shown in blue and purple). Some of these areas may have a low value because very little rental property exists or because they are really awful places to live, places with factories and warehouses, utility and railroad yards, but some of the places with median rents or just above that are near areas of very high rents and may be very nice places to live. Such a map could help city housing officials plan their programs and activities, as well as help prospective renters decide how to narrow their search given their budget.

FIGURE 2.84   **Floor of "valley" set at median rent for city, $623.00, 2000**

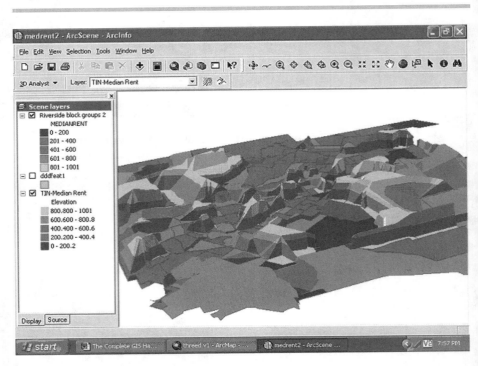

To construct this map, the same techniques as in the previous 3D example were used. Once the 3D TIN map was constructed, the 2D map of the median rents was copied from ArcMap to ArcScene, and the following steps were used to create the median rent floor effect.

Step 1 Calculate the approximate median rent for the city by averaging the median rents for the 210 block groups in the map. Open the attribute table and right-click on the field name of Median rent; select Statistics from the popup menu, and a summary appears; the mean is given at $623.41. The histogram also shows that the median should lie somewhere near this value (see Figure 2.85).

FIGURE 2.85   **Median rent calculation**

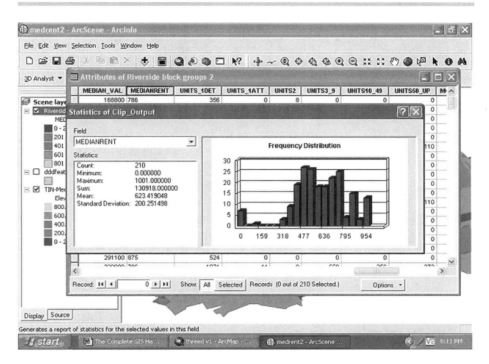

Step 2 Open the Layer Properties submenu for the 2D layer; because this is ArcScene, there are more options showing on the tabs. Select Base heights.

Step 3 At the bottom of this tab is a box labeled, "Add an offset using a constant or an expression"; type in 623 and click OK.

Step 4 Click this layer on in the display contents and the valley floor will show, and using the same color scheme for the symbology as the TIN map will preserve the information about rents below or at the median value, while allowing the higher rent areas to become clearly visible, as in Figure 2.84.

We have seen the power of multiple variables, graphics and charts, and finally 3D visualization for conveying complex information in a powerful and insightful way. In the next and final part of Section 2, we will take you through some specific illustrations of how many of the techniques you have learned thus far can be used in specific policy-related areas of great concern to cities, countries, governments, and citizens alike to inform and facilitate planning and decision making. Communities and their leaders are faced with many difficult and vexing problems, and always with limited resources; GIS can be harnessed to help these leaders make better decisions and use resources more effectively in a variety of policy areas.

Using Complex Maps to Simplify and Support Better Decision Making

In this final section, we will take you through a number of examples of specific policy relevant data and circumstances using a variety of data, from law enforcement and criminal justice, to public health and disaster relief, to education and substance abuse. All of these are areas which local communities, regional authorities, national governments, and world bodies like the World Health Organization are faced with each and every day; you will see how a greater use of the power of GIS will enhance the ability of these groups and leaders to make better decisions for all concerned.

Policies and Planning

Mapping and GIS have become powerful and useful tools in law enforcement and policing. Basic maps like the pin and thematic maps you learned to make in Section 1 were used in a pioneering way by the New York City Police Department starting in the mid-1990s—each precinct was able to map the crimes that occurred in the previous week and discover hot spots, patterns by time of day and day of the week, and by types of crime, and to use the geographic patterns to plan enforcement patterns, patrols, and personnel allocation to more effectively control and reduce crime (see Bratton, 1998). Today, about half of the police departments in the United States do some kind of mapping and spatial analysis to support their planning and personnel allocation. Here we will take you through two examples of GIS applied to crime analysis and planning to demonstrate the potential for safer neighborhoods and streets by harnessing the power of GIS.

Regional and Local Patterns in Homicide

Regional differences have been a source of fascination to researchers and individuals alike since at least the beginning of the American Republic, when Southern delegates to the Constitutional Convention differed with Northern delegates about the treatment of slaves in the U.S. Constitution. The American Civil War was fought because regional differences over slavery and economic policy had become so pronounced as to be irreconcilable by any other means. Today, many agencies and programs for data collection and reporting use regions as a way to organize their reports, and researchers often find that regional differences still persist in many social and economic areas of interest. In the study of crime and violence, regional differences have been a major source of debate (see Dewees and Parker, 2003, for a discussion of this and related issues).

Example: Homicide Patterns

In fact, the FBI uses such a division to report on the annual crime statistics in the country. Identifying differential crime rates by region can assist policy makers and law enforcement agencies in decision making about how to best handle crime in each particular area of the country. It may also assist in identifying other characteristics particular to a certain geographic region that make it more conducive to a specific type of crime. The map in Figure 2.86 displays data from the Uniform Crime Report (UCR), the annual report issued by the FBI on crime statistics. This data is from the 2004 UCR, the most recent UCR available. The map shows the differences in murder between regions in the United States; each dot in the map represents 100 murders, and the thematic colors represent the four Census Bureau regions, Northeast, South, Midwest, and West.

FIGURE 2.86   **Regional variation in U.S. murder density, 2004**

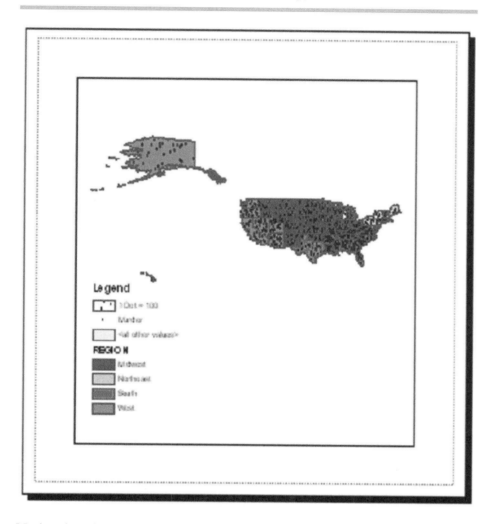

Notice that the concentration of murders appears to be highest in the region designated as South. The second highest concentration of murders appears to be in the region designated as Northeast. If the Federal government were to decide on a new program to aid local law enforcement in fighting crime, a map like this could be used to help decide how to allocate resources in the program to the different regions. For example, if murder rates are highest in the South, the Federal program to hire 100,000 new police officers might decide to allocate 40,000 of those to the southern region in order to address the higher homicide rates in that region.

By this point in the text you have enough knowledge to re-create much of this example on your own. Refer to previous examples if you need to refresh your memory about how to perform a particular step.

Step 1   Open ArcMap and add the States_Region shapefile.

Step 2   Scroll through the attribute table of States_Region to see what attributes are available in the data set. Note that in addition to data on the number of murders, data are also available on the number of robberies, and the number of aggravated assaults for each region. There are many more variables offered in the UCR, this subset was chosen for the purposes of this example. When you have finished exploring the attribute table, close it.

Step 3 Open the Symbology tab of the Layer Properties dialog.

Step 4 Choose Categories > Unique values. Specify the Region field and select a color scheme of your choice. Click on Add All Values. Your Symbology tab should appear similar to that in Figure 2.87.

FIGURE 2.87 **Symbology submenu**

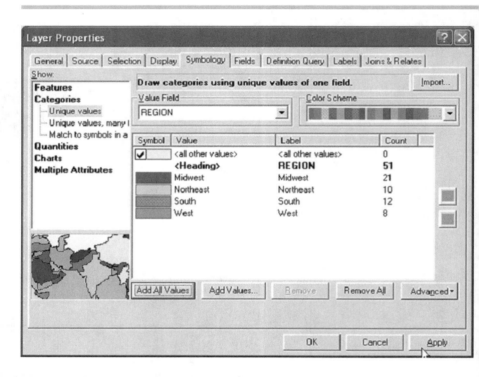

Step 5 After verifying that your Symbology tab is similar to the example, click Apply. Click OK to close the Layer Properties dialog.

Your map of the United States should now be displayed showing four distinct colors, each color representing a particular region as noted in the table of contents.

Next, you will add the data regarding murder to your map.

Step 6 Add the States _Region shapefile to your map for a second time.

Step 7 Use the General tab of the Layer Properties dialog to change the name of the newly added States_Region layer to Murder_Density.

Step 8 Go to the Symbology tab of the Layer Properties dialog.

Step 9 Select Quantities > Dot density. Use the arrows to move the Murder field from the Field Selection box to the Symbol field box.

Step 10 Specify a dot value of 100. This means that each dot on the screen will represent 100 murders in the region. Change the symbol color to black. Your symbology tab should look similar to the example in Figure 2.88.

FIGURE 2.88   **Dot density submenu**

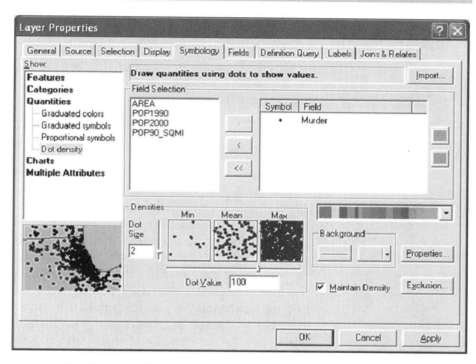

Step 11 After verifying that your symbology tab looks similar to the example, click Apply. Click OK to close the Layer Properties dialog.
Your map should look similar to the example in Figure 2.89.

FIGURE 2.89   **Murder density and regional variation, data view**

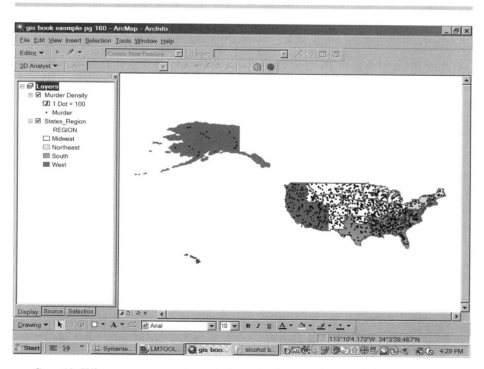

Step 12 When you are ready, switch to the layout view and give your map an appropriate title and legend. Once you have finished, save your map to a location for retrieval at a later time.

On your own time, you can experiment with different types of symbology for displaying regional variation in robberies and aggravated assaults to create maps for these crimes. If you want to experiment even further, go to the FBI's website at http://www.fbi.gov/ucr/cius_04 and manually add the statistics for other types of crime included in the UCR data that you can then include in a regional map. It might also be useful to explore the differences in population in these regions, as well as the number of rural versus urban areas within each region, and any other potential characteristics that may help account for the observed differences in crime.

Alcohol Availability and Youth Violence

Another area of concern for researchers and law enforcement agencies has been the relationship between alcohol availability and alcohol consumption and youth violence. A number of studies have shown a link between consumption of alcohol and youth violence (see Greenblatt, 2000) and between the availability of alcohol and rates of youth violence (see Alaniz et al., 1998). Although it is difficult for communities to regulate how much individuals drink, communities can regulate the density and number of outlets that sell alcohol, and some of the practices that those outlets engage in with regard to sales to underage youth. GIS can be used to help us understand this relationship, how it varies across a community, and to drive policy discussions, planning, and policy interventions to reduce violence through a reduction in access to alcohol by youth (Parker et al., forthcoming).

Example: Alcohol Availability and Youth Violence, Perris

The community in this example is a small city in Southern California, Perris. This is a community that has had a long history of difficulties and scarce resources, although it has begun to experience economic growth and influx of new residents as the expanding commuting zones from Los Angeles, Riverside, and Orange County make Perris an increasingly desirable bedroom community. Figure 2.90 shows the relationship between youth violence and alcohol outlet density.

FIGURE 2.90   **Alcohol outlet density and youth violence in Perris, California**

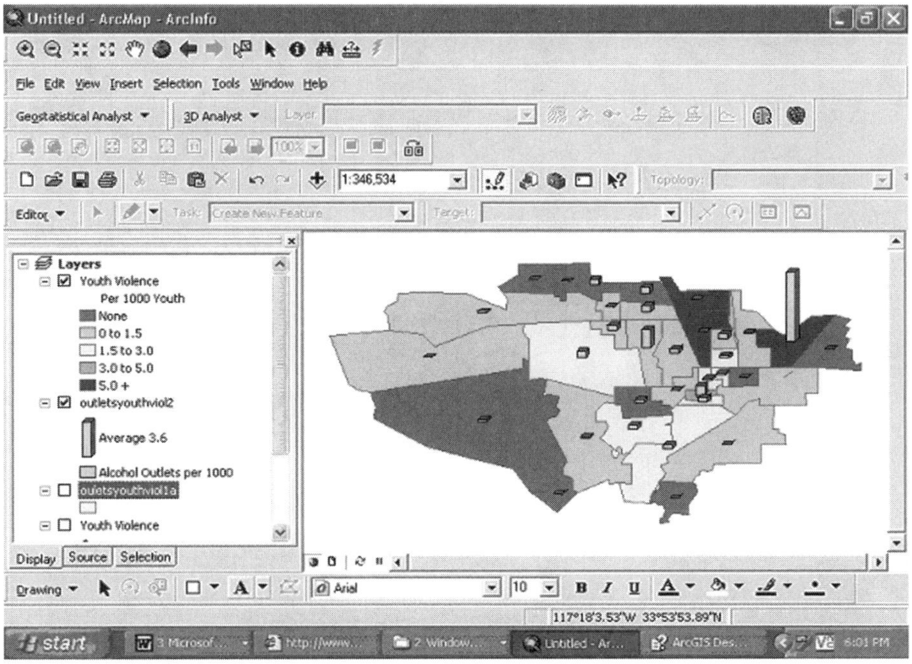

As you can see from the map, there is a fairly strong relationship between these two measures, consistent with many studies from across the country. Specifically, the Perris Police Department should be very interested in the fact that one of the census tracts that has among the highest rate of youth violence also has by far the greatest density of alcohol outlets. This area, in the upper right-hand portion of the map, would be ideal for an underage buy sting, in which the police authorize underage youth to enter the alcohol outlet and attempt to buy alcohol without a proper or legal identification. If the outlet sells to a minor without checking for ID, the outlet can be cited, fined, and eventually lose the ability to sell alcohol. Another focus might be on extra patrols and personnel in this area to make some arrests and try to discourage youth from drinking and engaging in violence.

The City Planning Commission would also be interested in knowing where the links are between these two measures. The tract we have just noted should not be allowed to open any more alcohol outlets, and perhaps one or two other areas where the relationship is strong should be scrutinized very carefully when and if an application comes in for a new outlet.

These examples show on a local and a national level the way GIS can be used to plan policies to reduce crime and violence and to develop multiple strategies for breaking the link between youth violence and substance abuse.

To produce the map in Figure 2.90, follow the instructions given previously for the Santa Ana rents and ethnicity map, shown in Figure 2.57. A difference to note in this case is that when you are using the Symbology submenu to add the bar graph to the map, you can normalize the number of outlets by using the population of the tract, as shown in Figure 2.91.

FIGURE 2.91   **Normalizing outlet density (Count_2) with population (P001001), bar graph submenu**

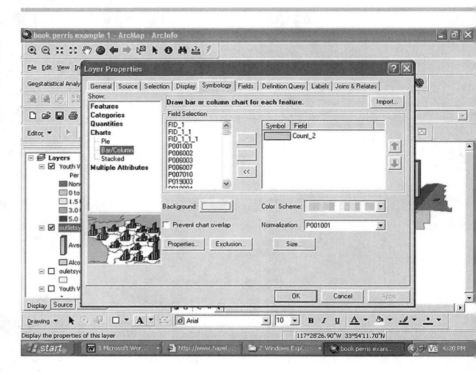

Education and Planning for Disasters

Recently, Hurricane Katrina in the United States caused great social upheaval for the areas immediately affected as well as the rest of the country. Hurricane Katrina took place in August 2005 and directly impacted the states of Alabama, Louisiana, and Mississippi. Media images of the affected areas demonstrated the catastrophic damages to these areas, which resulted in approximately 1800 deaths. In addition to the death toll, the destruction caused by Hurricane Katrina left tens of thousands of Americans homeless as well as jobless. These effects impact not only the states directly hit by the hurricane, but the entire country as well.

While much of the media and government reports focus on the rise in unemployment rates brought about by the hurricane, there is less consideration of the impact on the education of children who were victims of Hurricane Katrina. Students of all ages from pre-school to college were greatly affected by the hurricane. Many schools were closed down due to physical damage and inaccessibility. Further, schools in areas where Katrina evacuees were forced to relocate became overcrowded due to the influx of these new students. It is important for policy makers as well as the general public to be aware of the vast numbers of students affected by this natural disaster in order to determine the most effective ways to provide assistance for students such that the disruption to their education does not bring about negative ramifications for the future.

Example: Hurricane Katrina's Impact on Children and Schools

The map in Figure 2.92 displays the number of students at various stages of education that lived in the counties directly affected by Hurricane Katrina in the

FIGURE 2.92   **School children impacted by Hurricane Katrina in Louisiana, Alabama, and Mississippi**

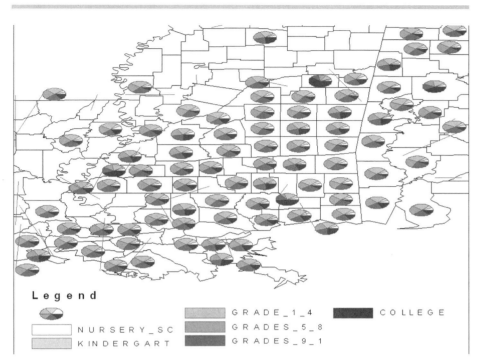

Legend

NURSERY_SC
KINDERGART

GRADE_1_4
GRADES_5_8
GRADES_9_1

COLLEGE

states of Louisiana, Alabama, and Mississippi. These three states have been identified as the most highly impacted by Hurricane Katrina. The data contained in the map are based upon information from the United States Census 2000.

Hurricane Katrina occurred too recently to assess any outcome effects on students in the affected counties. However, this type of assessment can be used in the future to examine the long-term impact of Hurricane Katrina on school age children. As the data show, there are many children in grades K-12 who were forced to relocate as a result of Katrina, some permanently. Many parents of these children were not able to return to their homes or obtain new homes due to loss of employment. Potential long-term effects of this include higher rate of high school dropouts, higher instances of property crime, higher rates of drug use, lower income, as well as other consequences of disrupted schooling. Future analyses can build from such data as are included in this map to examine whether these students suffer any of these negative ramifications.

Now, you will re-create the map of students in Katrina-affected counties presented in the example using the following steps.

Step 1 Add the counties.shp layer file from the ArcGIS sample data located in the TemplateData folder.

Step 2 Open the attribute table and use the Select by Attributes option to select only counties within the states of Alabama, Louisiana, and Mississippi as shown.

FIGURE 2.93 **Selecting the states for analysis**

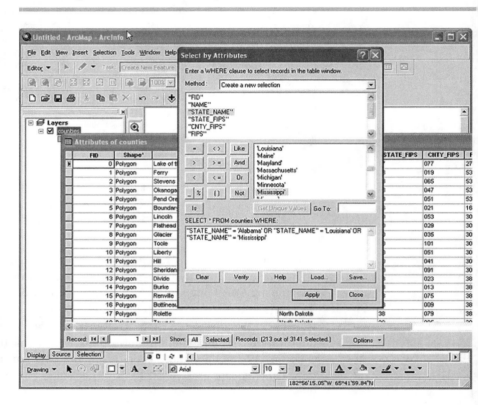

The results of the selection should show that 213 records are selected from the table, as in Figure 2.93.

Step 3 Close the selection dialog and the attribute table. Your map should look similar to that in Figure 2.94.

FIGURE 2.94   **Results of the selection of Alabama, Louisiana, and Mississippi**

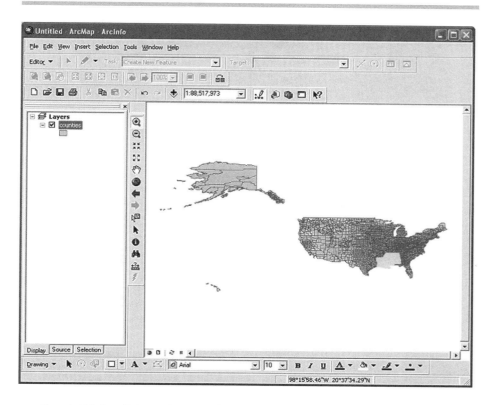

Step 6 Right-click on the counties layer name and choose Selection > Create Layer from Selected Features to create a new layer that contains only the states of Alabama, Louisiana, and Mississippi. Your new layer will automatically be added to the map.

Step 7 Right-click on the counties layer name and remove it from the map.

Step 8 Set the map scale to 1:6,950,000.

Step 9 Use the Layer Properties dialog to change the counties_selection layer name to "Katrina_Counties" and save it as a new layer file. The Katrina _Counties layer should look like the picture shown in Figure 2.95.

FIGURE 2.95   **Selected map of counties in three states impacted by Katrina**

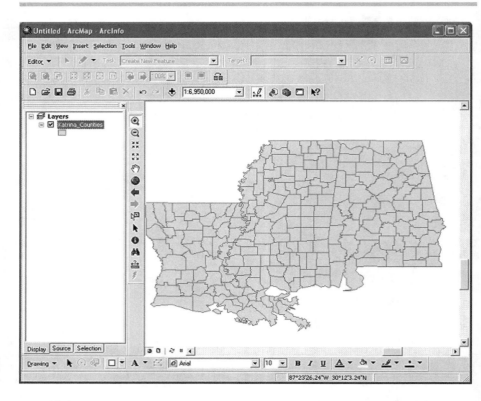

This is your base map. Now we will join the census data regarding the number of students at various stages of education in these counties during Hurricane Katrina to the basemap data.

Step 10   Right-click on the Katrina_Counties layer name and select Joins and Relates > Joins.

Step 11   Instruct ArcGIS to join the Katrina_Rev.dbf file to the Katrina_Counties attribute table based upon the fields where the county name is stored. When you have finished specifying the conditions of the join, your join dialog box should look like that in Figure 2.96.

FIGURE 2.96   **Join submenu**

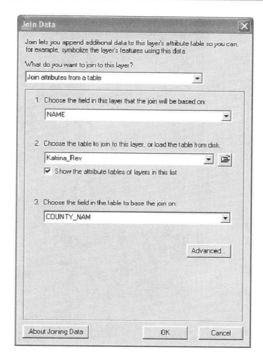

Step 12 After insuring your dialog box looks the same as the example, click OK.

Step 13 Open up the attribute table and scroll through the fields to see that the fields from Katrina_Rev.dbf now appear at the end of the Katrina_Counties attributes. Close the attribute table after verifying this.

Step 14 Right-click on the Katrina_Counties layer and select Data > Export Data in order to save the file with the joined data about students in Katrina-affected counties as a new layer. In the export dialog, browse to an appropriate location for saving and call the new layer Katrina_Students. The new layer will appear in ArcMap after you click OK.

Step 15 Remove the Katrina_Counties layer from ArcMap.

Next, we will symbolize the categories of students for each of the counties that were directly affected by Hurricane Katrina.

Step 16 Go to the Symbology tab of the Layer Properties dialog.

Step 17 Select Charts > Pie in the Show dialog.

Step 18 Add the fields of interest to the Symbol Field box (Nursery_School, Kindergarten, Grades 1–4, Grades 5–8, Grades 9–11, and College), and select a desirable color scheme for the symbology. Your symbology dialog should look similar to that in Figure 2.97.

FIGURE 2.97   **Pie chart submenu, Symbology tab**

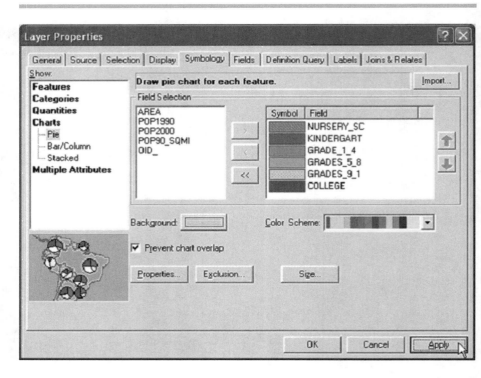

Step 19 After insuring that your Symbology tab is similar to the example, click Apply. Click OK.

Your map should now display the pie chart symbols showing the different numbers of students in each category specified in the counties affected by Hurricane Katrina as in Figure 2.98.

FIGURE 2.98   **Educational enrollment in Katrina-impacted counties**

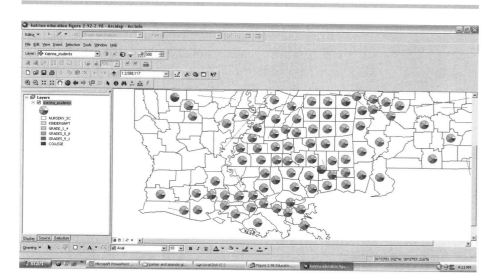

Don't forget to use the Identify tool to see specific attributes of counties you select with it, as in Figure 2.99.

FIGURE 2.99   **Choctaw County, Alabama**

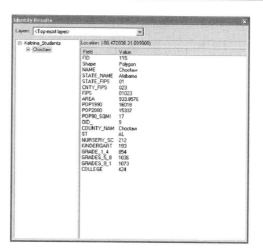

Step 20   Using your knowledge from previous examples, switch over to the layout view and give your map an appropriate title and legend. Once you have finished this, save your map for convenient retrieval at a later time.

Health and World Affairs

Example: HIV and Armed National Rivalries

In the first example in this section we looked at armed conflicts or rivalries between countries, and one of the findings was that there were several hot spots of these conflicts in Africa, mostly about territory and borders. Africa is also the continent which has a serious problem with HIV infections. One possibility is that there is a relationship between these two, that a high rate of HIV infection might create political and social instability, and governments might want to try to deflect their people from such difficult problems by being aggressive towards their neighbors. Figure 2.100 examines this relationship.

FIGURE 2.100   **HIV infection rate (% adults infected) and armed national rivalries in Africa**

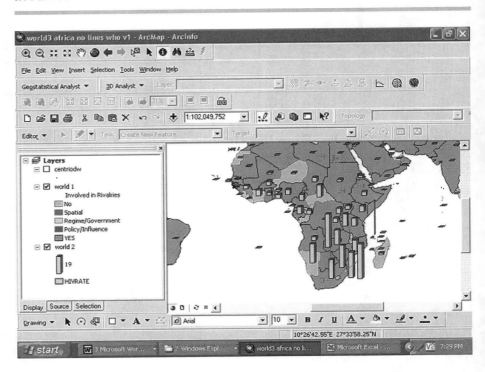

Although some of the countries that have very high rates of HIV infection have been involved in rivalries (South Africa, Botswana, Zimbabwe), so have a number of countries with very low rates (Sudan, Libya, Ethiopia). In addition, there are some countries with very high rates of infection that have not been involved in conflicts at all, like Malawi and the Central African Republic. The numbers superimposed on the map show the countries most involved in these events, and the pattern here is revealing: four of the five countries most involved, that is in three or more rivalries, have very low rates of HIV infection. Only South Africa is contrary to this trend, and all of its rivalries were conducted when it was rogue nation prior to the fall of the Apartheid regime in 1994.

Sometimes the power of GIS can tell you what is not true, what is not useful for planning purposes—those hoping to combat HIV as a way to reduce world conflicts may not find this strategy useful. In fact, these data suggest an alternative hypothesis, that nations disrupted socially by a very high rate of HIV infection may be unable to organize aggression towards their neighbors. This is not a reason to stop fighting the spread of HIV, but simply demonstrates how GIS can show planners and researchers what is and is not supported by the data. In other words, mapping can show the wrong direction to go as well as the right direction.

The same approach that was used in the example concerning outlet density and youth violence (Figure 2.90) was used here to make the map shown in Figure 2.100, building on the earlier world rivalries map and data (Figure 2.3). The lines showing the partners involved in the rivalries and by color what type of conflict, were removed by selecting all the lines drawn on the previous map and cutting them out using the edit tool on the main tool bar. The symbol 3+ was then added to the appropriate countries by using the text tool, used previously in this section.

Immigration and Economic Conditions

An ongoing debate in the United States is how to best handle the influx of immigrants both legal and illegal from other countries. Policy makers consider the options of implementing tighter controls at the U.S. borders to deter illegal immigrants, and imposing more restrictions on those who are allowed to legally immigrate to the United States as means of controlling high levels of immigration. While these solutions may offer plausible answers for more controlled levels of immigration in the future, they raise another issue, one that is more complicated to resolve: How does the United States deal with the huge numbers of legal and illegal immigrants currently residing in the United States?

Example: Immigration and Unemployment in the United States

Some argue that the United States should force all illegal immigrants to leave the country, and stop new immigration (both legal and illegal) into the United States due to the toll of immigration on unemployment. Individuals with this perspective suggest that the U.S. unemployment rate is high due to the fact that immigrants are occupying so many jobs that U.S.-born citizens are not able to find employment for themselves. The flipside of this argument is that legal immigrants have as much right to work in the United States as U.S.-born citizens. Unemployment in the United States thus affects both immigrants and U.S.-born citizens in similar manners. A more convincing argument however is that unemployment in the United States is not correlated with immigration. The GIS map in Figure 2.101 shows the levels of immigration and unemployment in the United States for the year 1994 on the same map.

FIGURE 2.101   **Immigration and unemployment in the United States, 1994**

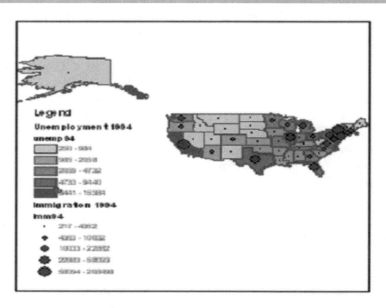

As documented in the map's legend, the graduated shades of light to dark indicate the unemployment level, and the graduated size of the dots (from small to large) indicates the immigration level. The map shows that for 1994 states such as California, Texas, and New York had high levels of both immigration and unemployment. Based upon this map alone, one might conclude that immigration and unemployment are correlated. However, if we look at the next map in Figure 2.102, showing a GIS of the immigration and unemployment in the United States for the year 2004, a different picture is revealed.

FIGURE 2.102   **Immigration and unemployment in the United States, 2004**

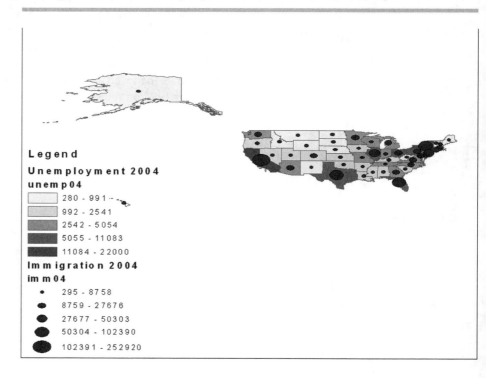

The 2004 map shows unemployment to be high in states with high levels of immigration such as California, Texas, and New York as did the 1994 map. However, it also shows that states in which unemployment increased between 1994 and 2004 such as Nevada and Utah did not experience such an increase in immigration levels. Further, the maps show that the immigration level for states such as Washington, Oregon, Illinois, and Wisconsin declined between 1994 and 2004 despite a steady level of unemployment between these years. These findings indicate that the correlation between immigration and unemployment shown in these maps may be due to a spurious variable.

There are many potential sources of such a relationship between the unemployment rate and immigration. It is possible that the cause of the rise in the unemployment is entirely unrelated to the immigration. For example, massive layoff occurrences throughout the United States would cause an increase in unemployment, but has nothing to do with the number of legal and illegal immigrants in the country. Data regarding massive layoff events (layoffs affecting 50 or more employees) in the United States for 1994 and 2004 were obtained from the Bureau of Labor Statistics to examine the relationships between unemployment, immigration, and the massive layoff events. The data regarding layoffs were included in the GIS to create the map of the United States in 1994 shown in Figure 2.103.

FIGURE 2.103   **Immigration, unemployment, and layoffs in the United States, 1994**

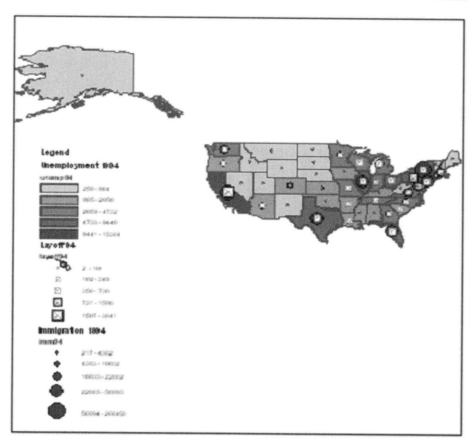

This 1994 map shows all of the states with the lowest unemployment also have the lowest number of massive layoffs, indicating a potential correlation between these two variables. States with larger populations such as California and Texas have higher levels of all three variables. States such as these that have more people tend to have more businesses, and therefore more jobs available that may attract immigrants. Because these states tend to support more and larger businesses than smaller states, they may be more prone to massive layoffs than smaller states.

The same map for 2004 appears in Figure 2.104.

FIGURE 2.104   **Immigration, unemployment, and layoffs in the United States, 2004**

The 2004 map shows an increase in massive layoffs in Nevada and Utah from that in 1994. Recall that immigration levels did not change in these states between 1994 and 2004, but unemployment increased during this period. Based upon the addition of the massive layoff data, it appears that the unemployment rise is more likely correlated with the massive layoff events than with immigration. However, there are other states such as Georgia in which the number of massive layoffs increased between 1994 and 2004, but the unemployment rate did not change. This indicates that there may be still other variables outside of the current model that account for the spurious relationship between unemployment and immigration. In the interest of time and space, we will not explore the effects of any additional variables here. Instead, we will go through the steps used to create the current maps so that you can re-create them on your own and add further variables as you see fit to test what may account for the spurious correlation between unemployment and immigration.

Step 1 Gather data for GIS analysis.

Collecting the data you need for a GIS can be a matter of actually going out into the field and gathering data as you would for any research project. Alternatively, it may be a matter of finding the right existing data set to look at the phenomena you wish to study. In this case, all of the data used to create the maps showing the rates of unemployment, immigration, and massive layoffs in 1994 and 2004 are from existing data sets. The unemployment and massive layoff data came from the U.S. Bureau of Labor Statistics, and the data regarding immigration were obtained from the U.S. Department of Homeland Security.

Step 2 Prepare the basemap file.

As in Section 1, you will need to have a basemap file which the GIS application will use for a reference as to where items in your data set are geographically located. In the case of the United States base map, not much preparation is needed. ESRI provides a sample data file that contains the United States base map.

Step 3 Open the United States sample data map.

    a. Start ArcMap and open with a New Empty Map
    b. Use the Add Data button and browse to
       \ProgramFiles\ArcGIS\Bin\TemplateData\USA and add the file
       called states.shp to ArcMap.

A map of the United States should appear in your ArcMap data view window as shown in Figure 2.105.

FIGURE 2.105   **Base map, U.S. states**

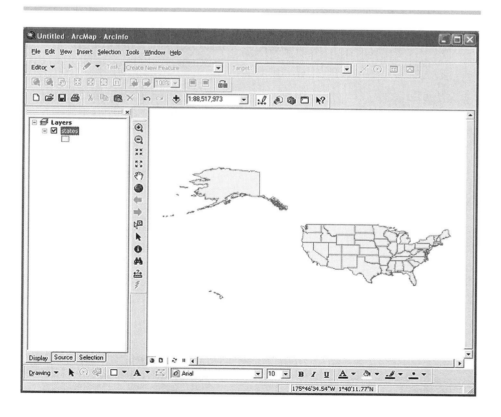

For demonstration purposes, the immigration, unemployment and massive layoff data used to create the example maps have already been added to the states.shp data file for you. The following steps were used to add this data into the existing states.shp file:

Subsetp 1   Right-click on the states layer name and open the attribute table.

Subsetp 2   Using the options pulldown menu, select Add Field as shown in Figure 2.106.

FIGURE 2.106   **Attribute table and options submenu**

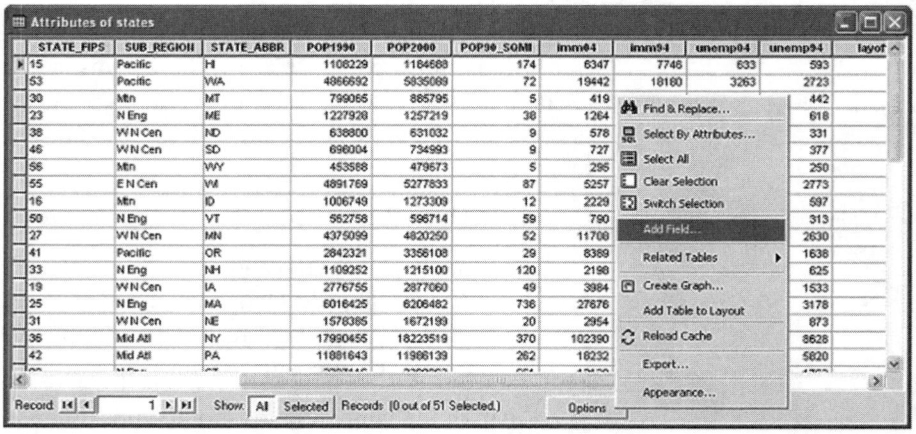

Substep 3   Name the field "Test," and use the pulldown menu to select the appropriate field type for your data. You will also need to set the appropriate precision for your particular data. In this case, we used the Long Integer type and specified a precision of 12 to be sure that we could handle any potential cell values.

Substep 4   Click OK. A new field called "Test" will appear appended to the end of the attribute table with no values in the cell. Use your mouse to verify that the field appears.

Now, you can add values from other data sets into the states.shp file for analysis.

Substep 5   Use the ArcMap Editor pulldown menu to select Start Editing as shown in Figure 2.107.

FIGURE 2.107   **Attribute table and the edit tool drop down**

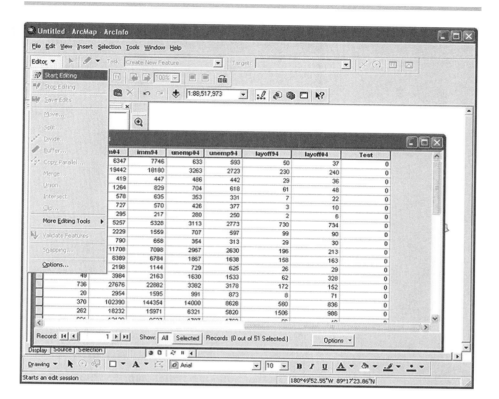

This feature allows you to input information from other sources directly into the shapefile while in ArcMap. Use your mouse to click in any of the cells in the test field and add some values just for testing purposes. This method was used to add the values in the fields imm04, imm94, unemp04, unemp94, layoff94, and layoff 04. If you decide to examine the effects of other variables outside of the model used in this example on your own, you can use this method to add the data directly into the shapefile.

Substep 6   Use the Editor pulldown to select Stop Editing. DO NOT SAVE YOUR EDITS.

Substep 7   Select the newly created Test field with the left mouse button until it appears highlighted. Use the right mouse button to select Delete Field (Figure 2.108).

FIGURE 2.108   **Attribute table and the Calculate Values popup menu**

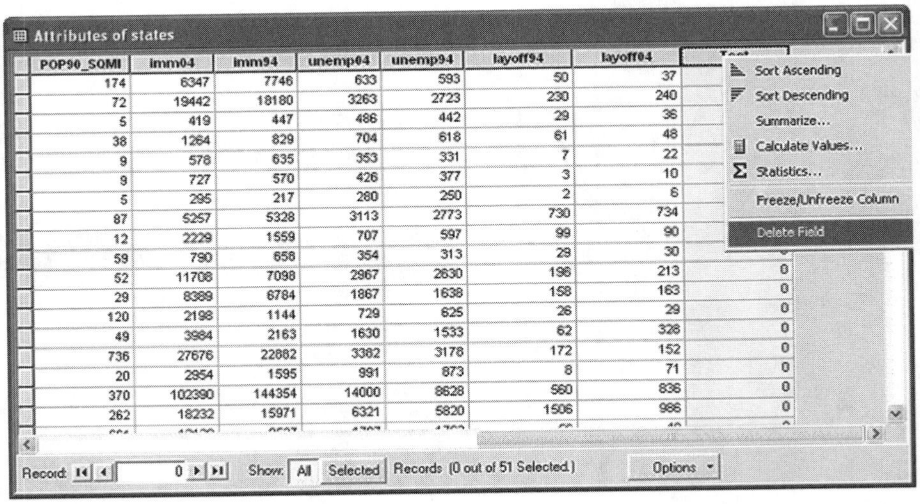

It is good practice to delete fields that do not have values. Empty fields sometimes cause difficulty in the processing of computer software applications. Select Yes when ArcMap asks if you are sure you want to delete this field. Scroll through the table to insure that the Test field is removed.

Now that you know what steps to take to add data into existing shapefiles, we will continue with the steps to re-create the maps used in this example. First, we will create a map depicting just the unemployment rates in the United States for 1994.

Step 4   Right-click on the States layer name and open the Properties window. Select the General tab and change the layer name from States to "Unemployment 1994." Click Apply. You will notice that the layer name behind the Properties window is refreshed to read "Unemployment 1994" instead of States, as in Figure 2.109.

FIGURE 2.109   **Layer Properties menu**

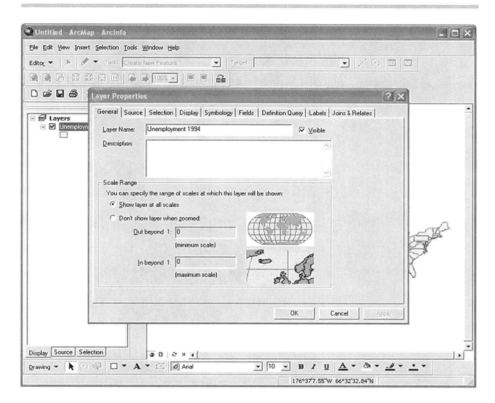

Step 5 Select the Symbology tab. Select the Quantities option in the categories window. By default, graduated colors will be selected. Specify unemp94 in the values pulldown. The symbol range will populate with the default values. For the purposes of this example the default values will be sufficient. Recall from Section 1 that these values can be changed manually as well as by using a different pre-defined classification system in ArcGIS. Click Apply, then click OK. You have created a map showing the unemployment rate for the United States in 1994.

FIGURE 2.110   **Thematic map, unemployment in the United States, 1994**

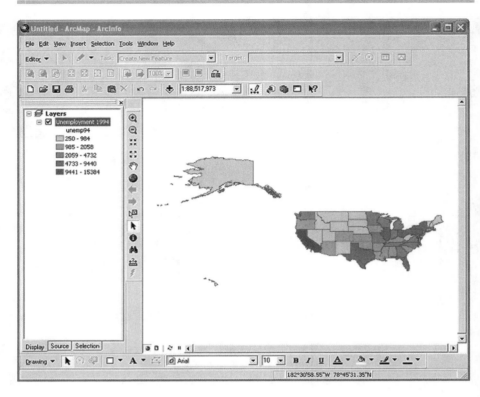

Since we are examining the relationship between the unemployment rate and the immigration rate we will now need to map the immigration rate onto the same map for comparison.

Step 6 Use the Add Data button and browse to the location where States.shp is stored. Add the States.shp file to ArcMap a second time.

Step 7 Use the Layer Properties > General tab to change the layer name from States.shp to "Immigration 1994" as in step 5.

Step 8 Switch to the Symbology tab of the Layer Properties window. Select Quantities in the categories window. Select graduated symbols instead of graduated colors. Specify the "imm94" field from the values pulldown. Click on the template symbol button to launch the symbol selector window, as shown in Figure 2.111.

FIGURE 2.111   **Symbol Selector submenu**

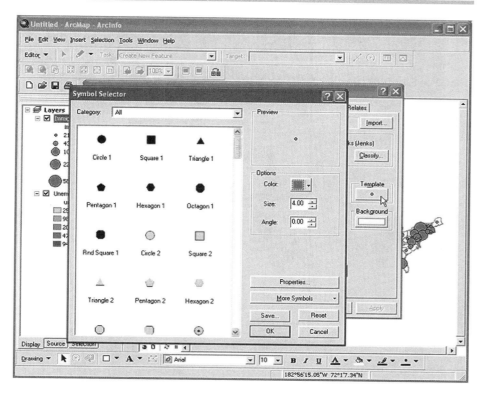

Step 9   Use the Color pulldown to select the color called "Tuscan Red."
Click OK. Click Apply, Click OK.

The graduated symbols representing the immigration rate for
1994 will appear on the United States base map as in Figure 2.112.

FIGURE 2.112 **Immigration in the United States, 1994**

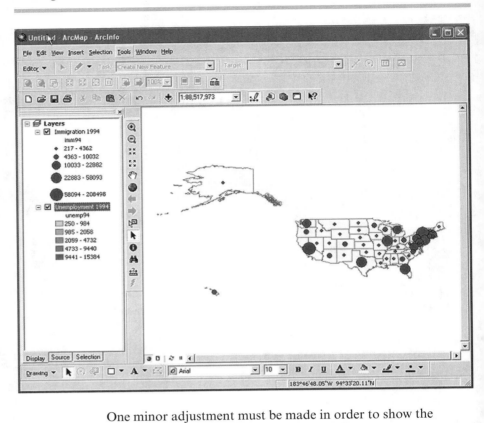

One minor adjustment must be made in order to show the unemployment and immigration layers on the same map.

Step 10 Use the left mouse button to select the Unemployment 1994 layer in the ArcMap table of contents and drag the layer until it is on top of the Immigration 1994 layer. This tells ArcMap that it needs to symbolize the Unemployment 1994 layer before the Immigration 1994 layer allowing for the symbology for both layers to appear in the same map as shown in Figure 2.113.

FIGURE 2.113   **Changing the order to layers in the display contents**

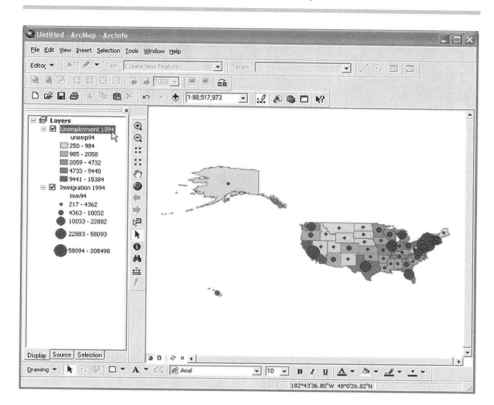

Now your map shows both the rate of unemployment and the rate of immigration in the United States for 1994.

Step 11 Using your knowledge from Section 1, switch to the layout view to add a title and legend that adequately represents the map. Save the resulting .mxd file to a location where it can be retrieved for later use if needed.

Next, you will use the same steps used to create the map of immigration and unemployment in the United States for 1994 to create maps of immigration and unemployment in the United States for 2004 on your own. Just refer to the steps listed above for guidance, and remember to symbolize using the imm04 and unemp04 fields instead of imm94 and unemp94 to be sure that the data for 2004 is included in this map instead of the data for 1994. After adding your title and legend for the 2004 map, save it to an appropriate location for retrieval at a later time.

To complete your replication of the maps presented, you will need to add the data regarding the massive layoff events to assess the potential spurious relationship between immigration and unemployment. This can be added in to the existing maps you just created for immigration and unemployment in 1994 and 2004.

Step 1 Browse to the location where the map of immigration and unemployment for 1994 is saved, and open the file in ArcMap. By default ArcMap will display your .mxd file in the layout view.

Step 2 Switch to the data view using the globe symbol.

Step 3 Use the Add Data button to add another instance of the states.shp file into your map.

Step 4   Use the Layer Properties to change the layer name from "States" to "Layoffs 1994." Click Apply.

Step 5   Using the Symbology tab of the Layer Properties dialog, tell ArcGIS to symbolize the field "layoff94" using graduated symbols.

Step 6   Click on the symbol template to launch the Symbol Selector dialog.

Step 7   Select the symbol called "square 11," and the color called "solar yellow." These properties will help to more easily distinguish the massive layoff symbols from the symbols already on the map.

Step 8   Click OK. Click Apply. Click OK.

Notice that the map display in the ArcMap window now shows the symbology for the massive layoff events and for immigration, but we can no longer see the symbology for the unemployment data. The symbology for the unemployment layer is in the map, it is hidden underneath the symbology for the unemployment and immigration layers. Recall from the previous example that the layer on the top of the table of contents will display on top of the other layers.

Step 9   Click and drag the Layoff 1994 layer to the position in between the Unemployment 1994 layer and the Immigration 1994. The map will now display the Layoff data underneath the unemployment data, but on top of the immigration data, allowing for a comparison between all three variables.

Step 10   Compare your final product to the example in Figure 2.103 to check for consistency.

Step 11   Once you have verified that your map looks the same as the example map, give it an appropriate title and legend, then save it.

Now, follow the same steps you just used to create the map for 1994 to create a map showing immigration, unemployment, and massive layoff events in the United States for 2004. Refer to the steps above for guidance, and save your map once you have completed it.

On your own time, try adding some additional variables of interest to the states layer to see how they relate to immigration, unemployment, and massive layoff events in the United States for 1994 and 2004. The variables you choose to look into should be guided by theory, as well as data structure, as with any other type of data analyses. This is a great way to get a handle on how to use your own data in a GIS that is prefabricated for you.

Educational Policy and Educational Outcomes

Example: California Education System

The state of California recently implemented a system of mandatory exit examinations for high school students. The logic behind the mandatory exams is accountability on the part of school administrators and teachers as well as students in the public school system. Students are given several opportunities to take these exams throughout their high school career. The exams are separated into sections based upon subject matter such as English, Math, and Science. Once a student passes one section of the exam they are not required to take that particular section again. However, if a student does not pass a particular section by the time of graduation they will not be permitted to graduate from high school. Depending upon the status of the student, several alternatives are offered. These include: staying an additional year at high school (if the student will remain under the age of 18 during that additional year), taking the General Educational Development (GED) exam for a high school equivalency certificate, as well as attending adult education courses to complete a high school diploma.

While many in the community advocate the mandatory exam system, there are many others who feel that the system allows for an unfair advantage for students in some schools over students in other schools. For example, schools that are considered socioeconomically disadvantaged may not have the same kinds and amounts of resources to dedicate to exam preparation as schools that are not considered to be socioeconomically disadvantaged. Additionally, some schools may be more crowded than others, requiring them to hire teachers that have emergency credentials instead of full credentials in order to accommodate the large number of students. Emergency credentialed teachers may not be as fully prepared as teachers as those who are fully accredited. The number of fully accredited teachers in a particular area may be correlated with the socioeconomic status of the area.

The map in Figure 2.114 uses data obtained from the California Department of Education regarding the number of socioeconomically disadvantaged schools (SD_API), number of fully accredited teachers (FULL), and scores of students in grades in 9–11 on the English and Math portions of the mandatory high school exit exam (VCST_E911, VCST_M911). The map displays how these variables are correlated at the county level.

FIGURE 2.114   **High school exit exams, accredited teachers, and disadvantaged schools in California, 2005**

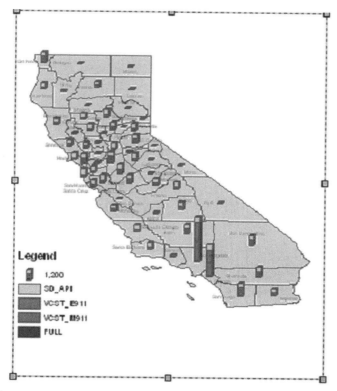

From the map symbols, we can see that the proportion of fully accredited teachers in all counties seems low. This could be due to recent influx of students in

California requiring many schools to accept emergency credentialed teachers. Despite the low number of fully accredited teachers, students in some counties such as Los Angeles County and Orange County have relatively high scores on both the English and Math portions of the exam. If you look at these two counties in particular, you will notice that the proportion of socioeconomically disadvantaged schools contained in these areas is relatively much lower than that of other counties showing much lower scores on the exam, such as San Luis Obispo, and Mendocino. This particular data analysis thus appears to indicate that socioeconomic disadvantage has more influence on students' scores on the mandatory high school exit exam in California than the influence of the number of fully accredited teachers has. The two independent variables do not appear correlated with one another.

Now, you will use the steps provided to reproduce this map shown in Figure 2.114.

Step 1 Open ArcMap.

Step 2 Use the Add Data button and browse to the location where the ArcGIS sample data is stored on your machine. By default, this is \ProgramFiles\ArcGIS\Bin\TemplateData. Add the file called "counties.shp." You will see a map display that shows the United States divided by county borders as shown in Figure 2.115.

FIGURE 2.115   **U.S. county base map**

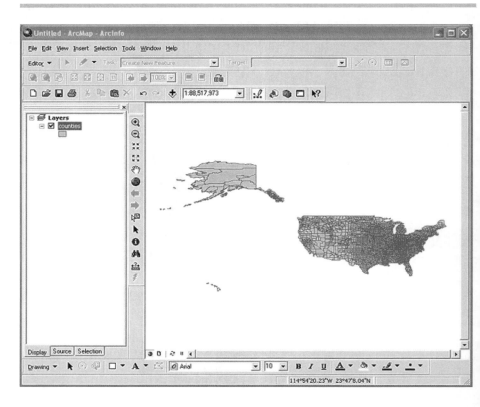

Since we are only interested in the counties contained in California for the purposes of our map, we will need to select a subset of counties from the United States map to create a base map of only the counties in California.

Substep 1   Open the attribute table of the counties layer.
Substep 2   Use options menu and choose Select by Attributes to launch the
             Select by Attributes dialog box, as in Figure 2.116.

FIGURE 2.116   **Select by Attributes submenu**

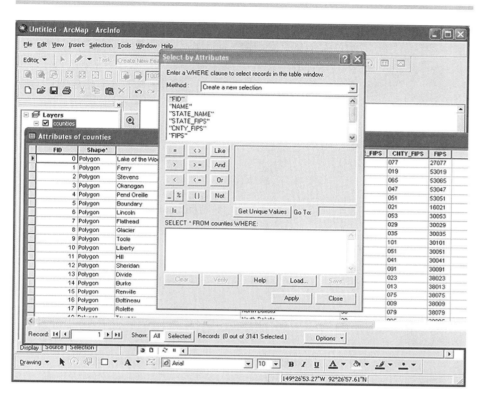

Substep 3   Populate the Select by Attributes dialog by telling ArcGIS to select
             only those counties that are contained in the state of California.
             You can use the mouse to double-click on the field names and
             arithmetic signs rather than manual entry so that the syntax will
             automatically be populated correctly for you. Note that if the
             values for the field selected do not appear automatically you will
             need to click on "Get Unique Values" after you populate the field
             from which ArcGIS should select records before selecting the
             record value you wish to select.
Substep 4   Once the box is populated as shown in Figure 2.117, click Apply,
             and close the attribute table. Note that the counties contained in
             California now appear highlighted on your map of the United
             States (in Figure 2.118). This indicates that these counties are
             currently selected by ArcMap.

FIGURE 2.117   **Select by Attributes submenu with populated box**

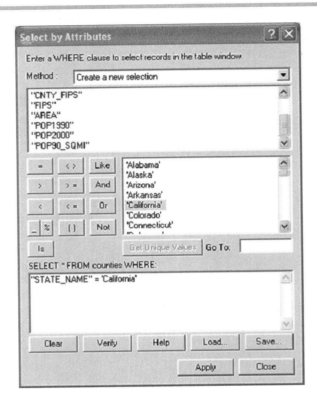

FIGURE 2.118   **Selection of California counties**

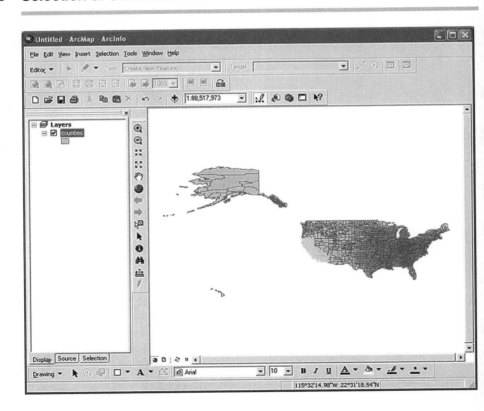

Next, you will create a new layer consisting of only the counties contained in California.

Substep 5 Right-click on the states layer name and choose Selection > Create Layer From Selected Features as shown in Figure 2.119.

FIGURE 2.119   **Creating a layer from selection results**

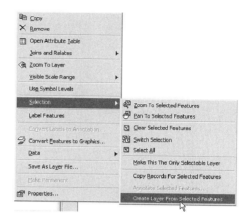

A new layer called "counties_selection" will automatically appear in the table of contents of your ArcMap window.

Substep 6 Use the Layer Properties dialog to change the counties_selection layer name to "California Counties." Click Apply and OK until the Layer Properties dialog is closed and the layer name reads California Counties in the table of contents.

Substep 7 Right-click on the California Counties layer name and choose Save As Layer File to save your newly created layer to an appropriate location.

You have now created the base map containing only the counties in the state of California and can proceed with the GIS analyses of the California high school exit exams.

Step 3 Right-click on the counties layer and remove this layer from your map. Only the counties in California should appear in your ArcMap window. Because the scale for this map was originally set so that the counties contained in the entire United States would be displayed, the display of the counties in California is much smaller than necessary. You will need to change the scale to get a better sized display.

Step 4 Use the mouse to click in the map scale window and manually change the scale to 1:10,500,000 as shown in Figure 2.120.

FIGURE 2.120   **California counties**

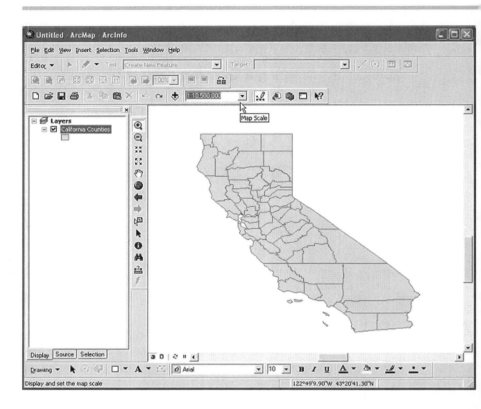

Now the counties contained in California are enlarged in your
ArcMap display window.

Next, we will need to add the data from the California Department of Education (CDE) regarding test scores, socioeconomically disadvantaged schools, and
fully accredited teachers. Since the CDE provides data on their website in .dbf
format, a format which is supported by ArcGIS, there is no need to manually add
the data to your ArcGIS layer as in the previous examples. Instead, we can use a
process called "join" to join the attributes of the CDE data to the attributes of the
California counties data contained in the base map.

As with the performance of any type of statistical analysis using computer
software, you will need to make sure that the data are prepared for use with the
computer application prior to performing any tasks within the software. Do not
assume that because the data are already in .dbf format the data will automatically be read into other programs that support the .dbf format. For example, with
the CDE data we discovered that the numeric values in the original .dbf file were
stored as text rather than string, or numeric values. In addition to the inability to
perform statistical procedures on text values, the warning message provided in the
.dbf file stating that numbers are stored as text is read into the .dbf file as a
leading note. ArcGIS cannot work with .dbf fields that contain leading notes,
spaces, or dashes. The software will automatically convert any fields with values
such as these to null values. Thus, this issue needed to be corrected prior to
working with the file in ArcGIS. The file provided for you to use in this example
has already had the values converted from text to string so that you do not have to
perform this task on your own. There are many different options for converting
data types. To find the most appropriate option for data you may be working with

in the future, refer to the help instructions of the particular database software you are using to prepare the data file.

The following steps explain how to join the CDE data to the basemap data for analysis.

> *Step 1* Right-click on the California Counties layer name and select Joins and Relates > Join as shown in Figure 2.121.

FIGURE 2.121 **Join and Relate submenu**

> Next, you will tell ArcGIS how to perform the join operation between the California counties data and the CDE data.
>
> *Step 2* Populate the join dialog as shown in Figure 2.122.

FIGURE 2.122 **Join submenu**

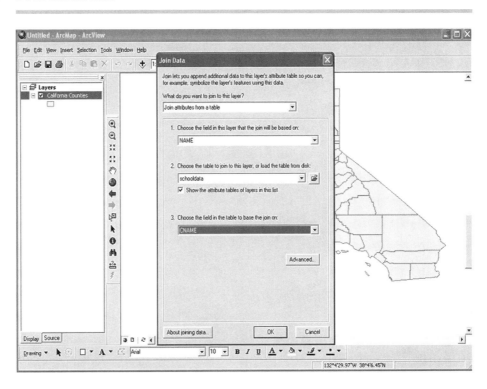

The values in the join dialog tell ArcGIS to match the county name field in the California Counties layer to the county name field in the schooldata.dbf file. A common field is required in order to match up attributes from two different tables in one table. The resulting table will retain the attributes of both tables as joined by the common field of county name.

Step 3 Click OK.

Step 4 Open the attribute table and scroll through the fields to see the fields from the school data table now included at the end of the table. In order for ArcGIS to use these fields for symbology, they must be made a permanent part of the file.

Step 5 Right-click on the California Counties layer and select Data > Export Data as shown in Figure 2.123.

FIGURE 2.123   **Export Data submenu**

Step 6 Browse to the location that you want to save the exported layer file to and name it School_County.shp. Click Save (Figure 2.124).

FIGURE 2.124 **Saving Data submenu**

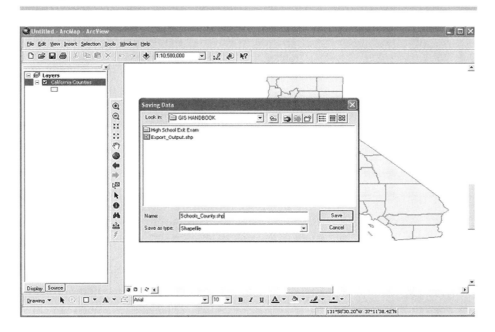

> *Step 7*   Specify that the export procedure should Use the same coordinate
>   system as the layer's data source, and click OK (Figure 2.125).

FIGURE 2.125 **Finalizing the Export Data command**

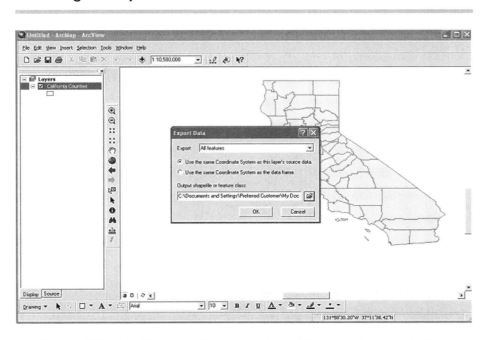

> *Step 8*   When ArcMap asks if you want to add the exported layer to the map,
>   select Yes.
> *Step 9*   Right-click on the California Counties layer, and remove it from the
>   table of contents.
> *Step 10*   Open the attribute table of the School_County layer and view the
>   attributes. Notice that all of the fields from both the California

Counties attribute table and the schooldata.dbf file are now contained in one layer. Close the attribute table.

Step 11 Right-click on the School_County layer name and choose label features so that the names of the counties display on the map.

Now that the data is ready you can proceed to making the map showing the relationship between students' scores on the mandatory high school exit exams in California, the number of fully accredited teachers at high schools in California, and socioeconomic disadvantage of high schools in California as in the example in Figure 2.114.

Step 12 Double-click on the County_School layer name to open up the layer properties window.

Step 13 Select the Symbology tab from the Layer Properties window.

Step 14 Choose the Charts > Stacked option from the show box of the symbol properties window. Use the arrows to populate the symbol field telling ArcGIS to symbolize the fields containing the data about the number of socioeconomically disadvantaged schools in the county (SD_API), scores of students in grades 9–11 on the English portion of the mandatory high school exit exam (VCST_E911), scores of students in grades 9–11 on the Math portion of the mandatory high school exit exam (VCST_M911), and the number of schools with fully accredited teachers in the county (FULL). Use the color scheme pulldown to choose a color scheme for the symbols. Your symbol properties window should appear as in Figure 2.126.

FIGURE 2.126   **Symbology tab and construction of stacked bar graph**

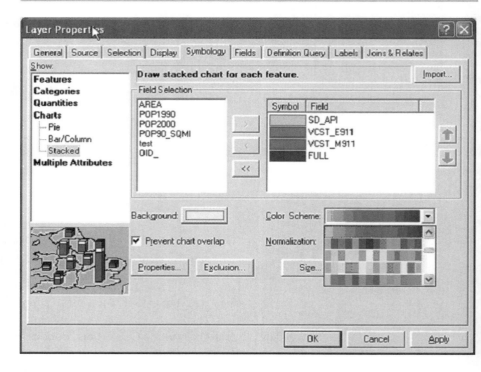

Step 15 After insuring that your properties are the same as the example, click Apply. Click OK. The map in Figure 2.127 should appear showing the stacked bar chart symbology for the variables of interest.

FIGURE 2.127   **California educational characteristics by county**

Step 16 Use the Identify tool to view the details about the different counties from the data contained in your map. The example in Figure 2.128 shows the Identity Results for Los Angeles county.

FIGURE 2.128   **Los Angeles county attributes**

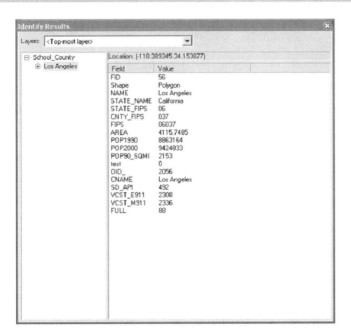

Step 17 Using your knowledge from previous examples, switch to the layout view and add a meaningful title and legend to your map for presentation. Once you have added these, your map is complete. Save the .mxd file to a location convenient for retrieval at a later time.

Conclusion

In this section you have learned a great deal about how to produce complex maps and to use those maps to support decision making, policy research, planning, and to increase understanding about how and why some of the events of import in the news have happened the way they did. You have seen that there is a great deal of information that can be conveyed clearly and powerfully in the GIS framework. You have even explored using the three-dimensional metaphor to understand social and economic phenomena from a GIS perspective. These examples have been illustrative of the kinds of maps you can produce; your knowledge, interests, and imagination are the only limits to your mapping.

Along the way you have learned a set of techniques and strategies that can be used to produce useful and informative maps in any subject area. We urge you to adapt what you have learned to your areas of interest and expertise, and to see what you can learn and show others. These maps are a form of communication, and with them you can communicate all kinds of complex and useful information in an easy to understand format. The more this approach comes into common practice in our community, in our industry, in our organization, or in our society, the better the decision making, and the better the quality of life will become.

One of the coming attractions in GIS is the power of animation. Animations used to take enormous computing power and could not be done except on mini-computers or $100,000 workstations with massive graphic support. The time is fast approaching when animations can be made and viewed on the standard PC computer available to most people at work and/or at home. Although beyond the scope of this book, such new tools will make the visual impact of the information conveyed in these maps even more powerful and more effective.

Section 3   Geospatial Modeling and GIS

This section is different in nature and purpose than the previous two, which were designed to introduce, at the most basic level especially in Section 1, social science students and researchers from sociology, criminology, political science, economics, public health, and other social and behavioral sciences to GIS and map making for dissemination, research, and policy decision making. This section takes on a much more advanced topic—spatial modeling—and our goal is to try and use the same philosophical approach that we took in Sections 1 and 2. We hope to explain this complex topic in an accessible manner and to provide examples and step-by-step instructions both to illustrate the workings of software to conduct spatial analysis and to demystify the process for the first-time user. However, as the topic is more complex, we expect that most undergraduate students will have difficultly moving directly on to this section. Spatial modeling is a topic that can be seen in one way as an extension of regression analysis, a mainstay of quantitative social science and policy research in many disciplines. A reader without a basic course in regression analysis and/or significant experience as a researcher using regression analyses would find it very difficult to take up this section, however gallant our effort to simplify and explicate this topic. So why include this topic here at all?

Spatial modeling is the next logical step from the end of Section 2, where we discuss making and using multivariate complex maps to support analytic thinking, test hypotheses and relationships in space and time, and support policy decision making in the complex realities that communities and people exist in. The maps you made in Section 2, as complex and interesting as they are, have limits, and the way to approach those limits and to overcome them is via spatial modeling. One of the last examples in Section 2, concerning immigration and unemployment in the United States, which examines the relationship between these variables, is charged with political, economic, and social controversy. Using maps and three variables, we were able to suggest that a common assumption that immigration leads to higher unemployment may be spurious and should not be used to make immigration policy. However, how many more variables could we explore using a map-based framework and be able to make any sense out of what we were seeing? This section on spatial modeling is included here for the students, researchers, scholars, or just plain readers of this book who want to go further, to take the next step to be able to explore social contexts and the spatial realities around them with the most appropriate tools and with the confidence that their inferences and decisions are the best they can be substantively and scientifically.

Before moving directly between Sections 2 and 3, the reader should have regression experience or be able to get through a text on basic multivariate regression such as Allison's *Multiple Regression* (1999) or Schroeder et al.'s *Understanding Regression Analysis* (1986).

Geospatial Modeling and GIS

So far in this book you have seen the way mapping information, even complex and multiple pieces of information, is possible and can be very effective at showing relationships and changes across time and space. Even these maps start to have their limits, however, and the conclusions drawn from them can be suspect, because the social, political, economic, and interpersonal worlds that our data are taken from are complex and multifaceted places. A number of processes are occurring simultaneously in the real world, and just because we can isolate a few of these on a map and show what appears to be a compelling story about, for example, a relationship between crime and alcohol availability, or the lack of a relationship between HIV infection rates and national rivalries, does not mean that we have fully explored the entire realm of possibilities. This is not to say that the maps are not a powerful means with which to support decision making, make policy, and test relationships, at least, that is, in all the examples we have discussed thus far. The realities we need to deal with to be effective at the tasks GIS can help us with call for a greater complexity to the approach we take to gain understanding about how these complexities operate. This section is about how to model the multivariate complexities of the geospatial realities we have already shown you how to construct using GIS. As such this section on spatial modeling is a natural extension of the previous section in which you learned to make complex and multifaceted maps to examine real world problems and relationships.

The situation with regard to GIS is similar to developments over the past 50 years in most social and behavioral science disciplines. In the 1950s, sociology was dominated by research that examined a few important factors at a time, for example looking at the link between education, income, and occupational prestige (Duncan, 1961). During the 1970s, sociologists began to use complex regression and log-linear models with 10 or 20 variables to model occupational prestige, income, and status attainment (see Sorenson, 1979). By the end of the twentieth century, sociologists were regularly using multilevel models and structural equation models, approaches that involve modeling systems of equations to more fully understand the complex sociological realities they study (Hagan et al., 1996; Wheaton and Clarke, 2003). This does not undermine the validity of qualitative research (see Burawoy, 2003) in any way, but simply reflects recognition of the complexity of sociological phenomena, and the desire on the part of sociologists who do quantitative modeling to have at their disposal the best models available for handling that complexity.

It has been argued that the maps we have discussed thus far in this book are the booby prize of GIS. By this we do not mean to suggest that the maps are unimportant or not worth the considerable efforts, as you have seen by following the examples, that it takes to plan, construct, and interpret them. However, the maps are limited in terms of their ability to test properly specified hypotheses, advance theoretical models, or evaluate interventions. Instead, this line of reasoning suggests that the real power of GIS is as a method for linking geographic and spatial data with non-spatial data that has geospatial roots or links, so that databases can be constructed that unify these often disparate sources and types of data. These more complex databases allow us to address more interesting, more realistic, and more complex questions, but this additional complexity means that we must go beyond the capacity of even the most strategically constructed multivariate map in order to model and understand what these complex databases can tell us about our world. Like the developments in methodology in many behavioral and social sciences, we therefore need to embrace the complexity our data can give us and use more complex analytic approaches to understand that complexity.

This argument also does not undermine the value of the maps we have discussed thus far in this book. The well-conceived and displayed map, as we have already seen, can be a powerful way to convey important and complex information. Suppose that together with the map, we were able to buttress the conclusions of the map with a complex, multivariate geospatial statistical model using the same data as on the map and additional data from the GIS database constructed for the purpose of making the map, a model that supported the conclusions implied by the map? This would be an ideal situation to be in, and is analogous to the way sociologists and other social science researchers will often present correlations or tables early in an analysis, and then use a multivariate model to see if the basic relationships of interest hold up in the face of additional controls and alternative hypotheses expressed in the statistical model; when the original and theoretically implied relationship holds up in the context of a complex model with the appropriate rival hypotheses and statistical controls accounted for, this is a very powerful endorsement of the theoretical model and the importance for understanding the phenomena under study of the observed and verified relationship. The same is true of GIS and mapping; if we can also use geospatial modeling techniques to verify what the map is saying, we are in a much stronger position to advocate for the conclusions the map suggests, the policy it recommends, or against the intervention the map shows to be ineffective or wrongheaded. However, this will not always be the case.

Consider the chart in Figure 3.1, which is based on a gang intervention program in Riverside, California. Project Bridge was one of the original sites in Irving Spergel's National Demonstration Project of the Comprehensive Model for Gang Prevention, Intervention, and Suppression, developed by Spergel based on his long experience as a gang interventionist and researcher (see Spergel, 1999

FIGURE 3.1   **Outcome results from Project Bridge, Riverside, CA, 1994–2000**

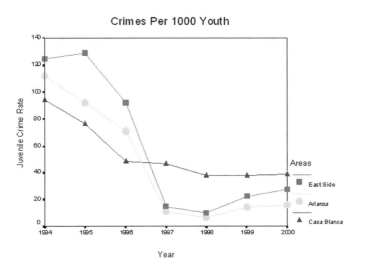

or Klein and Maxson, 2006). The interventions in each site were tailored to the local conditions, so that in Riverside the intervention involved targeting the intervention in two neighborhoods that the local people involved in the project believed to be the most seriously gang-encumbered areas in the city. A third area, also having significant gang involvement, was selected as a control area, where no interventions from the project were implemented. In this way, the researchers evaluating the intervention could compare its impact in two "treatment" areas, to use a public health-style term, and to also make the comparison between the two treatment areas and a "no treatment" area or a comparison neighborhood. This is a stronger design than just having one implementation and one no treatment area, as you have two additional comparisons to make; in a sense, these represent alternative trials of the intervention and its impact. You can now also compare the two intervention areas to each other, and if they differ in the outcome measure, in this case youth violence rates, you can study the differences in implementation and starting or background conditions to seek an explanation of the differences. In a way you have a replication of the intervention study within the same site. The replication is not independent, but provides an additional test of the impact of the intervention. In addition, you can compare both interventions to the control or no treatment area, together and independently.

Examining Figure 3.1, you can see that the intervention seems to have worked in both treatment areas, although the two areas, East Side (line with the squares), and Arlanza (line with circles), responded somewhat differently over the seven time points represented here. The Arlanza area seemed to have a more effective intervention sooner, and youth violence started to drop steeply in the first year of the implementation, 1995. The East Side had a less smooth start to the intervention, and rates actually increased before they started to drop. Both areas declined significantly (t statistic equals 3.17 and is significant, 0.05, in a comparison between each treatment area and the no treatment area (Casa Blanca, the line with triangles)), although the East Side began to increase somewhat in 1999 and 2000 (see Parker et al., 2004a).

The problem with these interpretations is that there may be other factors that could explain why these youth violence rates dropped the way they did over this time period in Riverside. For example, suppose that the three areas differ in terms of ethnic or racial composition, and that during this period one group had significant decreases in gang activity in one of the areas; then the intervention could have had nothing to do with this. Yet if we look at the graph in Figure 3.1, or the map in Figure 3.2, which gives the neighborhoods and their youth violence rates at the baseline year for Project Bridge, 1994, we risk making a mistake in our inference about why the results are coming out the way they did. Perhaps there were other changes in other variables that could explain the changes we see, and unless we can assess those factors, we cannot be certain that our conclusion about the success or failure of Project Bridge is correct. Perhaps these areas differ in terms of some other major predictors of youth violence, like poverty, family structure, or opportunity structure—all factors that have a long history of explaining changes in youth violence (see Parker et al., 2004a, for a review). So although the map can tell us a lot, we need more complex modeling techniques to fully understand the outcomes of an intervention like Project Bridge, which we will examine later in this section. If we were just shown a set of maps and a graph about Casa Blanca, we would conclude that an intervention must have caused the downturn in youth violence, but there was in fact no intervention there in this project. The fact that youth violence rates were declining across the country

FIGURE 3.2   **Youth violence in the three areas of Project Bridge, 1994**

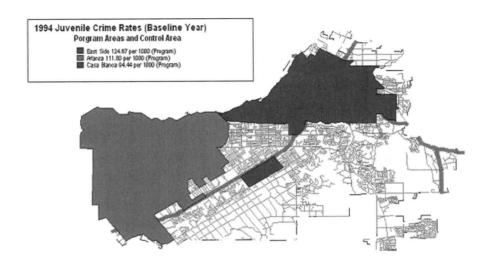

during this period (Bratton, 1998) helps us to understand the decline in Casa Blanca; knowing this makes the even sharper declines in the treatment areas all the more impressive, although we still do not know if we can attribute this to Project Bridge or not.

A second notion that underscores the importance of spatial modeling in GIS is the potential that such statistical models have for explaining why the relationships we see in the map are occurring the way they do. It is one thing to verify that the relationship suggested by the map is still true when we have controlled for all the other possible influences that might exist, but the question of why such a relationship exists in space across the community or the nation or the world is another, albeit extremely important, question. We need to know why things are the way they are if we can ever hope to successfully intervene to change some of the things we can observe with the maps. We have seen maps of potential racial profiling in traffic stops, and we have seen relationships between alcohol availability and crime, and these maps imply that we can intervene to reduce or prevent such negative outcomes as racial bias and discrimination, or gang-related youth violence. If we cannot bring some good evidence to bear on why these relationships exist in our community, we could intervene in such a way as to increase rather than decrease the likelihood that the problem will get worse rather than better. In addition, suppose we decide to try an intervention, the question then becomes, How can we tell if the intervention is having any impact? Once again we can map the intervention and the results over time to see if they appear to be connected, but if we can evaluate the intervention in terms of its impact on the outcome in a spatial model, we will not only be able to see if the intervention is effective but also to understand why it is effective. These arguments together show the importance of spatial modeling in the overall context of GIS as a research method and as a mechanism to support policy and decision making.

In this section we will introduce a basic approach to spatial modeling and demonstrate its utility with several examples; we will also discuss some of the software for doing spatial modeling and use one of the available packages that is particularly useful and easy to obtain and use. However, before we can proceed to show you how spatial models can be constructed and estimated, a discussion of the role of space in the causal modeling of social and behavioral processes is necessary to gain a full understanding of why spatial modeling is useful.

The Meaning of Space in Causal Modeling

There are two major conceptual ways to understand the impact of space on social and behavioral processes. The first is the idea that the nature of the space itself has a direct influence on the type, nature, scope, frequency, and repetitiveness of the behavior in question. This kind of argument has been advocated for sometime by the Crime Prevention Through Environmental Design movement in architecture and urban planning and a branch of the Routine Activity theoretical approach in criminology (see Felson, 1987; Cornish and Clarke, 1987; Gruenewald et al., 2006). Another branch of Routine Activity in criminology is focused on "hot spots," or places that seem to attract a great deal more crime and violence than areas nearby (Sherman et al., 1989) or on the notion that there are "Deviant Places" (Stark, 1987).

The various strands of this argument share in common the notion that the characteristics of the space itself—independent of the social activities that occur there—seem to contribute or attract certain kinds of behavior. The approach here is about crime, but it could easily be some other kind of attraction to a particular space—for example, certain neighborhoods may attract families with children, or certain shopping areas may attract a particular demographic of shoppers, or certain neighborhoods may attract a type of business or ethnic-related activity. The underlying theme in this approach is that the characteristics of the space itself have a causal or explanatory role in the type of behavior that is occurring at that place.

In a framework of spatial modeling, the causal role of the nature of the space and its characteristics can be taken directly into account. Studies have repeatedly shown that places with a greater density of bars or retail outlets for alcohol have higher rates of crime and violence net of other factors (Sherman et al., 1989; Alaniz et al., 1998; Gruenewald et al., 2006). Many urban centers have been attempting to replace mid-twentieth-century-style high-rise low income housing developments with smaller decentralized structures because the high-rise public housing structure has been seen time and time again to contribute to higher rates of crime and drug sales/use. Other cities create urban pedestrian zones to attract strolling potential shoppers to once deserted downtown areas. These are all examples where it is assumed that the nature of the space itself has a direct influence on the kind of behavior that is attracted there and that occurs there.

A second major notion of the role of space in causal or explanatory modeling is the idea that the way we typically administer space for the purposes of data collection creates artificial effects of space on data we wish to analyze with spatial models. This idea was already raised in Section 2 in the discussion of the proper units of analysis and the notion of creating units that respond to the density of events as we observe them rather than grouping them according to the artificial boundaries of Census Bureau or other political entities such as cities, towns, or school districts. In this approach, the role of space can create problems for the full understanding of the impact of these artificial collection units on the spatial modeling process. In this case, the way space impacts the models is as a nuisance factor, but a powerful one; as we shall discuss below, this impact of space has significant negative consequences for standard statistical modeling approaches and must be effectively dealt with in the spatial modeling context.

Measuring the Impact of Space and Spatial Relationships

The basic statistic used to measure relationships among variables in space is the same as that used in general to measure relationships—the familiar correlation coefficient, or Pearson's r—a statistic that varies between +1.0 and −1.0, which measures the degree of linear association between the distribution of cases on one variable and the distribution of another variable on the same set of observations. This statistic is the basis for all the models that are used in social and behavioral research—regression, structural equations, hierarchical models; the models that deal with nonlinear variable and alternative approaches like cox regression, logit models, event history or survival models, log-linear analysis are all alternative ways of measuring association between variables when the correlation coefficient cannot be calculated because the data are not continuous or take on only a few categorical values.

We can use the same basic approaches to spatial data that we do to regular data, but the problem in doing so is that the nature of spatial data creates conditions among the observations that violate fundamental assumptions required to insure the outcomes of these analyses are accurate and appropriate. For example, Pearson's r, regression, and most other similar models work properly if the observations are drawn from independent samples of the population you are studying. This would mean that the cases of youth violence we have been examining in this book would be taken from randomly distributed locations across the space we have been mapping—but we already know that this is not the case. We saw in Section 2 that these incidents cluster and are very dense in some parts of the map and quite sparse in other parts of the map. How do we measure how space is related to the variables we want to map and analyze?

In an earlier example we discussed the statistic called Anselin's Local Moran I, which was used as a measure to determine how similar the clustering of data was in a geographic unit and its neighboring units. High positive values of the Local Moran I suggested that the clustering was similar and that these units might be collapsed into a larger homogeneous unit referred to as a tessellation. Did you wonder at the time that if there was a Local Moran I, was there also a Global Moran I? Indeed there is, and Moran's I is the most prominent measure of spatial relationship that is used in the GIS literature (Moran, 1950). Moran's I is a correlation coefficient that measures the degree of association across space in a variable's distribution—that is how spatially clustered the observations are in this variable. The formula for the coefficient is, in a very simplified form:

$$\text{Moran's I} = \frac{\sum_{1}^{N} \sum_{1}^{N} Y_i Y_j}{\sum_{1}^{N} Y_i^2}$$

which means the product of a variable's observation in one spatial unit multiplied times the same variable's observation in another unit, indicated by the subcripts "i" and "j," summed over all the "i" and "j" pairs of units, divided by the summation across all the units of the observation squared. This formula takes the form of a product moment correlation like Pearson's r, and varies between −1.0 and +1.0, in that it is basically the covariance of the observations divided by the variance of the observations. Usually the variables have been mean standardized and this is the unweighted "raw" version of the coefficient.

If Moran's I is positive and closer to 1.0, it means that the data in the units are similar across space, and that there is a great deal of spatial clustering. If the value of Moran's I is close to zero, it means the data are randomly distributed across space, and if the value of Moran's I is negative and closer to −1.0, this means that the data are dissimilar from one spatial unit compared to another, and therefore there is little clustering of similar observations on this variable.

The purpose of spatial modeling is to explain the spatial pattern or relationships among the data, but as we saw earlier there are two ways in which the spatial nature of the data can impact these relationships. If the variable to be explained or predicted shows evidence of spatial patterning, or **autocorrelation** as this effect is called, it may be due to the effects of the observations on this variable in other spatial units, it may be due to the effects of the variables you think are related to the dependent variable, or it may be due to the errors introduced into the model because of the spatial nature of the data.

Let's consider the second scenario first. If the observed raw Moran's I measure of spatial autocorrelation is caused by the impact of one or more of the independent variables you include in your model based on theory and/or some applied knowledge of the behaviors and locations being studied, this is perhaps the ideal situation. If you can model directly the spatial relationships among the variables in the model and the non-spatial relations, you will be able to develop a very thorough understanding of the data and their meaning. This will be the case as long as you know all the correct variables to measure and you can include them on your map and in your model. What happens if you do not know or cannot measure all of the correct variables?

To ascertain if this is true or not, you can run a spatial model with all the variables you think are important to include, and calculate a new Moran's I statistic based on the residuals of the model instead of on the observations substituting the vector of the regression residuals for Y, as given in the equation above. However, you would also want to add to the equation another feature of the space you are analyzing that helps the model to understand its structure; this is called the **connection matrix**, and we will discuss its nature and importance below. For the sake of argument, however, suppose that your new Moran's I still revealed spatial autocorrelation in the residuals; this would indicate one of two possibilities. The first is that the spatial relationship within the dependent variable is very strong and remains significant even after the influence of the other variables in the model. The second possibility is that you have inadvertently left out one or more variables from the model that would in fact account for the spatial pattern in the dependent variable that remains important after the influence of other variables is accounted for. Either way, these latter two scenarios would indicate that the standard regression model is not appropriate for the spatially influenced data you are trying to analyze.

Statistical Issues in Spatial Modeling

The nature of spatial data makes it very likely that the spatial patterning in the dependent variable you are interested in will remain after the influence of the other variables has been accounted for. To understand why this is, recall the discussion in Section 2 about tessellations and spatial clustering, and the arbitrary nature of the way in which we usually divide up space into spatial units for analysis.

In Figure 3.3, the city of Santa Ana is shown in terms of its borders. You can see from this map that the boundaries are arbitrarily drawn—this explains the

FIGURE 3.3   **City boundaries of Santa Ana, California**

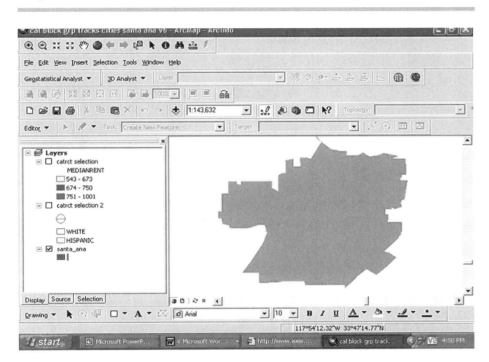

sharp turns and twists of the boundary line and the bulging section on the left-hand side of the map. However, when the Census Bureau draws its boundaries for the subunits it uses to collect data in, such as tracts or block groups, the boundaries are more and more arbitrary, as we can see in Figure 3.4. Would anyone believe that behaviors we might want to study and explain would be bound by or even notice these types of boundaries? These boundaries exist only on the maps that we use to analyze and categorize these data. No one behaving or interacting in this space will know about or be influenced by these borders, and yet when we construct databases, geocode data, and place objects in space on these maps, the observations on these variables are in fact divided up in this arbitrary fashion. This means that by definition there are going to be observations and data that are considered individual observations on a variable that are in fact right next to each other on the map and may in fact be due to the activities of the same population and the same events that created the observations. These observations are not independently drawn as all of the statistical models we use require that they be. Thus the very nature of the data and the way we process and collect data create statistical problems in the case of spatial modeling.

FIGURE 3.4   **2000 Census tracts, Santa Ana, California**

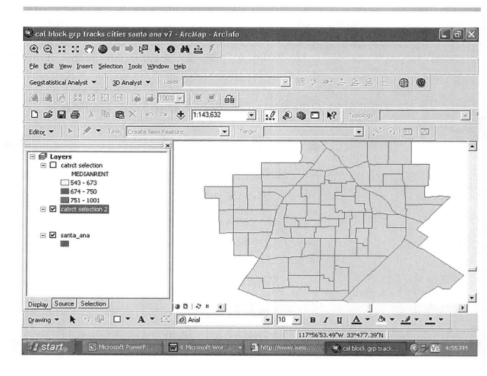

The structure of the space also has an impact. Consider in Figure 3.5 a detailed view of the map of Riverside after the tessellations we constructed in Section 2 were applied; the dots indicate the location of gang-related youth violence.

FIGURE 3.5   **Gang-related youth violence, Riverside, California**

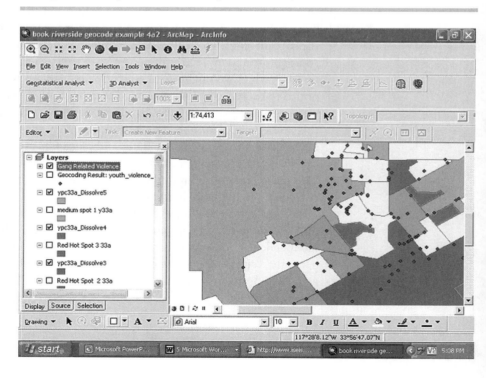

Here there are two very large units, created on the basis of the Anselin's Local Moran I cluster analysis, shown in gray (green) at the upper left and in black (red) on the lower right of the map. The units displayed on the rest of the map are block groups, relatively small units of analysis, especially when compared to the rather large tessellations shown here. On the one hand, it can be argued that smaller units are better as you get a better match between the observed behavior and the very local and specific aspects of the environment that this behavior occurs in. On the other hand, from a point of view of spatial autocorrelation, the more your space consists of very small arbitrarily placed units superimposed over patterns of behavior, the more spatial autocorrelation you are going to introduce. In Figure 3.6, we have drawn a circle around a set of points that seem to cluster and perhaps have something in common—perhaps they were all incidents involving a single gang.

FIGURE 3.6   **A set of gang-related incidents in the circle**

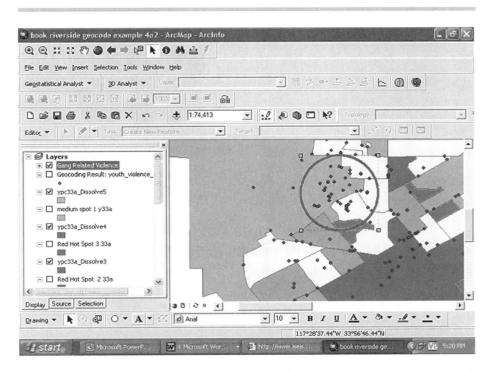

The tessellation exercise was somewhat successful at grouping most of these incidents together in one unit, but notice how the remaining incidents inside the circle are contained in three other units—if our assumption is true that these incidents are linked, we have created arbitrary divisions among this single cluster and thus introduced spatial autocorrelation into these data. It seems clear then that space that is made up of a few large units may be less subject to the introduction of spatial autocorrelations than space that is divided up into many small contiguous units.

The spatial modeling approach advocated here can take the structure of the space into account and in fact the adjusted Moran's I formula takes into account a set of weights that describe the structure of the space in addition to the covariance among the observations on the variable of interest, or in the case of a model, the residuals. This consideration of the structure makes for a more accurate assessment of the degree of spatial patterning in the data or residuals being analyzed. The simplest version of the weight matrix is referred to as a connection matrix, and it contains a row for each unit in the analysis and a column for each unit; in each row, column position is either a 1, if the two units share a common border, or a 0 if they do not. As with many such decision rules there can be complications; in Figure 3.6, the large black (red) unit to the bottom right "intersects" one of the orange units up and to its left only at a single point or vertex—is this a common boundary or not? One can include such boundaries (referred to as bishops points as in the movement pattern of a bishop in the game of chess) or not, as there are no hard-and-fast rules. Sometimes it is useful to experiment and construct a connection matrix both ways and see if the results differ. If they do not, then you are safe in making either choice; if they do, perhaps the more inclusive definition of common boundary is the best one to use. Figure 3.7 shows a connection matrix.

FIGURE 3.7   **A connection matrix for a six-unit spatial map**

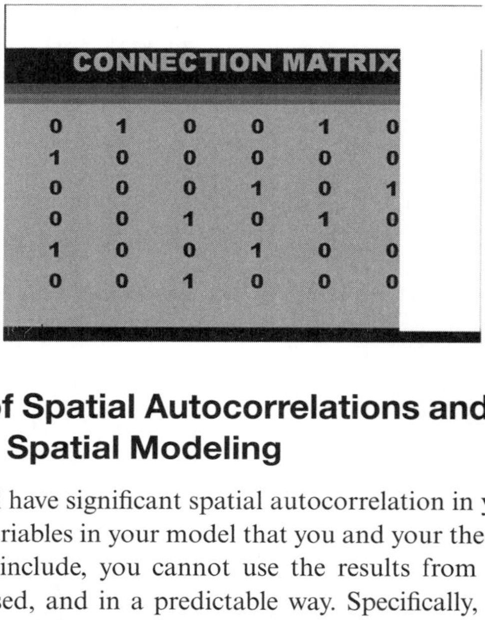

The Impact of Spatial Autocorrelations and Error Structures in Spatial Modeling

If you find you still have significant spatial autocorrelation in your residuals after including all the variables in your model that you and your theoretical framework think you should include, you cannot use the results from your model; these results will be biased, and in a predictable way. Specifically, in the presence of unaccounted for spatial autocorrelation, regression results are biased towards **false positives**, that is your results will be more likely to tell you a variable is a significant predictor or explanatory factor in understanding your dependent variable than is really the case. The false positive problem is the most dangerous problem in statistical modeling, because you would conclude something is true when it is not. Suppose you are doing analyses for a city and planning and zoning decisions are influenced by the results? Suppose you are doing policy-related research on health outcomes and legal regulation of products and behaviors is at stake? Your results might suggest a product should be banned from the public because of its harmful effects, when in fact the spatial nature of your data produced a false finding suggesting that this was the case.

It is easy to understand why spatial autocorrelation produces false positive findings. The significance test for whether a regression predictor is significant or not is based on the ratio of two quantities: the estimate of the size of the effect of the independent variable on the dependent variable, and the degree to which that estimate is accurate, which is referred to as the standard error of the estimate. This latter quantity is actually the square root of the variance of the estimate, which is understood to mean the degree to which, if we repeat this model with new data drawn from the same population we drew the original data from, this estimate is stable. A big variance and thus a large standard error suggests the estimate of the effect is not very stable, and thus not likely to be truly important. If the standard error is small, this suggests the estimate is pretty stable and you are likely to get the same or very similar estimates in replication after replication of the model with a new sample.

The standard error of the coefficient is itself based on the ratio of two quantities: the covariance among the residuals in the model and the product of the variance of the independent or predictor variable times one minus the multiple correlation of the independent variable with all the other independent variables in the model. In the situation of spatial autocorrelation, the first quantity will be inflated, because the spatial pattern created by the arbitrary similarity imposed on the dependent variable because it has been enclosed in neighboring spatial units will increase the similarity among the observations on the dependent variable and therefore inflate the covariance of the residuals. This in turn means that the standard error for the regression coefficient will be smaller than it should be in the absence of the inflationary effects of spatial autocorrelation. This means that you will be more likely to find significant coefficients than you should be.

Fortunately, there are extensions to the regression model that have been adapted to the spatial regression case (see Cliff and Ord, 1971; Loftin and Ward, 1983). The error structures implied by the two natures of the impact of space described previously are referred to as the nuisance model, in which the spatial autocorrelation is assumed to be the result of omitted variables that are unknown, and thus the way to correct for the biases introduced by such autocorrelation is to adjust the model for it. The second type of error structure is caused by the spatial autocorrelation within the dependent variable itself, above and beyond that accounted for by the independent variables in the model. The approach to solving this problem is to model the spatial process within the observations of the dependent variable and adjust the model for the magnitude of the effects on the dependent variable; this is referred to as the autoregressive model. In either case, the resulting adjusted model results are clear of the biases introduced by the presence of spatial autocorrelation; both of these models can be estimated in a Generalized Least Squares or GLS framework (see Hanushek and Jackson, 1977). A set of statistical tests can help you determine which model is appropriate for your particular results.

Statistical Modeling of Spatial Data

The basic model for the approach taken here to geospatial modeling is the spatial regression model. Figure 3.8 shows the three steps in the model. Equation 1 is the basic regression model. Equation 2 shows the way in which the spatial nature of our data is incorporated into the model. The error term vector of residuals in Equation 1, e, is divided into components that allow us to model the impact of autocorrelation and the structure of the space. The letter I stands for an identity matrix, a simple matrix which has 1s on all the diagonal elements and zero elsewhere—it is a device to help sort out the terms properly in Equation 2. The next term, r, refers to Moran's I, the measure of spatial autocorrelation in the residuals of the standard regression model. The next term, W, is the weight or connection

FIGURE 3.8   **The basic spatial regression model**

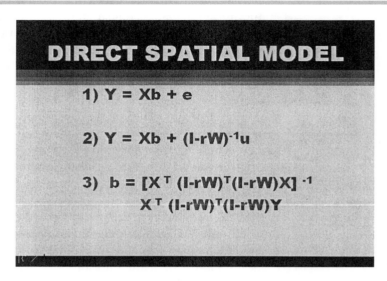

matrix, describing the structure of the space we are analyzing, and u is the new error term from which the spatial components have been removed.

Equation 3 simply rearranged the terms in Equation 2 so that we can solve the equation for b, the vector of regression coefficients. This shows you how the independent variables, represented by X, and the dependent variable, represented by Y, combine with the spatial autocorrelation and the connection or weight matrix to solve for the regression coefficients.

Figure 3.9 shows the rest of the model, including the GLS specification. We have already presented a simplified formula for Moran's I; Equation 4 in Figure 3.9 gives you the weighted formula used to calculate the degree of spatial autocorrelation in the regression residuals, represented here by U. The term W is the connection matrix and Moran (r) is the term from Figure 3.8 that is used to adjust the regression model for the degree of spatial autocorrelation. The final equation

FIGURE 3.9   **Computing the weighted Moran's I from the regression residuals and the maximum likelihood estimator for the GLS spatial model**

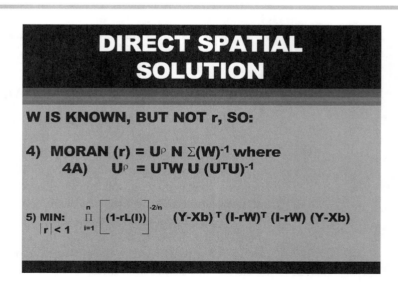

gives a general form for the GLS estimation of the spatial model. The nuisance and autoregressive error structures add additional complication to the equation and are not shown here (see Hanushek and Jackson, 1977). This is a maximum likelihood equation that requires an iterative solution because of the complications we have introduced. There is no direct solution, but we can estimate a start value for our estimate of r, the weighted Moran's I, and arrive at a solution over a number of iterations. This model is described here and in Figure 3.8 as a "direct" spatial model because there are alternative indirect models, although they are neither as complete or appropriate as the direct model described here (see Land and Deane, 1992).

The general procedure is as follows:

Step 1 After selecting a package program to estimate spatial models (we shall discuss some alternatives below and provide illustrations with a program called S³ (Ponicki and Gruenewald, 2005)) and preparing and reading your data into the selected package, estimate Moran's I on your dependent variable. Note the extent of spatial autocorrelation indicated.

For example, suppose you wanted to look only at youth violent incidents in which an arrest was made, as in Figure 3.10.

FIGURE 3.10 **Youth contacts with police that resulted in arrest: Riverside**

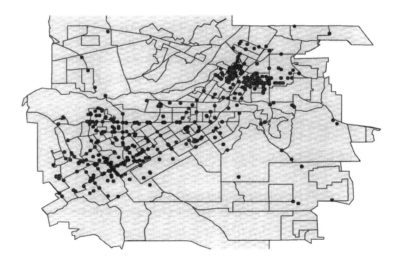

Using the software and procedures discussed below, you can calculate the Moran's I for these data, which in this case equals 0.231059, which is significant from zero with a probability of less than 0.01.

Step 2 Estimate a standard regression model using your spatial data; the package should provide you with diagnostics including Moran's I recalculated on the residuals, and the Anselin and Florax (1995) diagnostics, LM-ERR and LM-LAG. These tests help you determine which GLS model to estimate; if the LM-ERR is the more significant, it is likely that you should use the nuisance error structure model. If the LM-LAG is more significant, you should investigate using the autoregressive error structure model. In this example, we ran such a model (again the details are discussed below), and we included four independent variables: percent African Americans, percent Latinos, alcohol outlets per population, and percent young males (aged 16–24). The Moran's I on the residuals from this model was equal to 0.204384, still significant at probability less than 0.01. Although this is a significant reduction over the Moran's I for the raw dependent variable, the results indicate that significant spatial autocorrelation is still impacting this analysis. The LM tests indicated that the LM-ERR statistic was the larger one, with a value of 79.99, as opposed to the LM-LAG test statistic, equal to 78.85. We ran a nuisance error model next.

Step 3 Estimate a GLS model based on the results from Step 2. The results you get will be unbiased due to the influence of spatial autocorrelation. The results from this estimation yielded an estimate for spatial autocorrelation of 0.476, thus removing any impact of this possible source of false positive findings. For example, the impact of percent young male, found to be significant in the initial model, was found to be statistically insignificant, going from positive to negative in sign. In this case, spatial autocorrelation was not fully accounted for by the independent variables, and spatial autocorrelation had caused the estimate for young males to be inflated.

Types of Data Used in Spatial Models

There are two major types of data that can be used in a spatial model, and the type of data influences the variations that are available to the general procedures and models discussed above. The first is cross sectional spatial data, also referred to as a static spatial model; this is the usual case with most spatial data sets and is represented in most of the examples we have presented in this book. You have data on the rate of gang violence in a city, such as Riverside, and you are interested in finding out whether the number and density of alcohol outlets in the city has an influence on gang violence. You also know that gang violence may be related to a number of other variables, so you add U.S. Census data to your database for the block groups in Riverside, and you geocode the gang incidents and the alcohol outlets, and compute rates of each for the block groups. As this is the standard type of data, covering one point in time, you can use the procedure described here to estimate a spatial model; we will demonstrate this approach with such data below.

The second type of data is when you have spatial observations for a place, but you have not just one set of observations but repeated sets over a time period, observed at regular intervals. Perhaps you are studying a gang intervention program, and tracking over time how it impacts the rates of gang violence in a city such as Riverside. Another example might be that you are conducting a longitudinal study of a community and examining the alcohol outlet density and youth violence relationship, when the city you are observing decides to reduce its alcohol outlet density with a zoning change that forces a number of liquor outlets to close. Now you have what is often referred to as a "Natural Experiment," when in the second year of your three-year study, a major change in the density of outlets in some of the city's neighborhoods was effected and you can observe these units in space and time—before, during, and after the closing of the outlets (Parker, forthcoming). This situation is referred to as a **pooled cross**

sectional and time-series design, and we will illustrate a spatial model with such data below.

The procedure is slightly more complicated with a pooled design. There are additional options that should be investigated, so the following steps should be followed.

Step 1   After preparing and reading in your data (a task which is made more difficult by the pooled nature of the data), estimate the Moran I on your dependent variable.

Step 2   Estimate two non-spatial models: the standard regression model, and a model referred to as the Least Squares Dummy Variable model, or LSDV. This latter model is one in which a dummy variable for each cross sectional unit in your data is included in the model and estimated along with the standard regression coefficients. It may be that there are unique components to the variances in your data that can only be accounted for by including such terms for each unit. It turns out that you can compare the results of the LSDV and the standard Ordinary Least Squares or OLS model to help decide what kind of GLS model you wish to run. You may also have time serial autocorrelation in addition to spatial autocorrelation, and depending on the results at this stage you may be able to run a GLS spatial model with a lag structure to account for this type of error structure.

Step 3   Run a GLS model with a Cochrane Orcutt lag structure for the temporal autocorrelation. This is likely to be the best model if you have more time-series points than cross sections in your data, an unusual situation for most spatial models. If the LSDV model was not seen as appropriate during Step 2, you can run a more general Random Effects Model (REM), in which the unique impact of each cross section is assumed to be properly modeled as a unit specific error term, the distribution of which is expected to be random. This situation is analgous to the corrections for heteroscedasticity that have become widespread in GLS modeling with non-spatial data (see Hanushek and Jackson, 1977). This is a more general model than the LSDV, and does not stress the estimation by the inclusion of all those dummy variables, one for each unit. Including those dummy variables may help with the unique contribution of each unit to the model, but including so many variables in the model may undermine your ability to get good estimates of the effects of the other substantively important variables you have included.

Choosing Software to Estimate Spatial Models

Although GIS software can be expensive (a basic stand-alone license for ArcGIS is $1,500.00 as of mid-2006, and updates and downloads may add to the cost after the first year of use; academic and non-profit discounts may also be available— see the website for this book at www.routledge.com and www. presleycrimeandjusticecenter.ucr.edu for more information), the good news with regard to software to estimate spatial models is that there are several free packages available that are excellent and comprehensive. A number of freeware and licensed software are summarized at: http://info.wlu.ca/~wwwgeog/facstaff/ BBoots/software.pdf.

GeoDa is a freeware product produced by Luc Anselin, one of the leading researchers on spatial modeling in the world today (Anselin et al., 2005). It is relatively easy to use, has full spatial regression capability with standard regression models and spatial diagnostics as well as GLS models with spatial lags, and has some mapping and database features that are attractive—such as producing connection matrices. Some of these capabilities were added in the release of GeoDa 0.9.5-I, available in 2004. Experience suggests that it is memory intensive—on a Dell Dimension 2400 with 384MB of memory and a Pentium 4 2.5 GHz, a problem with 209 spatial units was unable to proceed due to inadequate memory (increasing the memory to 640 MB solved this problem). This is a very popular software, such that more than 10,000 downloads of the software have occurred since 2003, when the original version was released (www.geoda.uiuc.edu to download the program and documentation).

A second freeware package called SAGE—Statistical Analysis in a GIS Environment, was written by a group at the University of Sheffield (Ma et al., 1997) and available at: www.shef.ac.uk/~scgisa/newscgisa/research.htm #methodology.

It has a number of GIS-related capabilities, as well as estimating regression models with spatial diagnostics and GLS spatial models, and it has the great advantage that it was written to operate in tandem with ArcInfo, part of the ArcGIS software family. This link makes it possible to manage and build GIS databases in ArcGIS and link them directly to SAGE for spatial modeling. The disadvantage is that SAGE is written to operate only on Sun workstations running the Solaris operating system; a number of Intel-based PC desktops can run the Solaris operating system as of 2006, but there are no indications on the SAGE websites that these machines could run SAGE.

The third package we will discuss here is S[3]—Spatial Statistical Systems, a freeware package that runs under a commercially available package called Mathematica (available from: www.wolfram.com; stand-alone license $1,800.00; many universities and other organizations have site licenses available as well). S[3] itself is available from the Spatial Systems Group of the Pacific Institute for Research and Evaluation (www.pire.org/PRC/SSG/S3.htm; to inquire about obtaining S[3], go to www.prev.org or e-mail Lillian G. Remer at lilli@prev.org). This package has been in use since 1995 and was one of the first available packages with spatial modeling capabilities. Current capabilities in Version 5.2, released in late 2005 (Ponicki and Gruenewald, 2005) include regular regression with spatial diagnostics, GLS models, pooled cross sectional and time-series models with and without temporal autocorrelations adjustments, Least Squares Dummy Variable and Random Effects models, as well as extensive outlier and influential case analyses. In addition, S[3] has a number of useful database management tools designed for spatial modeling, such as assembling block diagonal connection matrices for multisite cross sectional models or for pooled cross sectional and time-series models, transformations on the connection matrix, weighted data, and the construction of several kinds of spatial lag variables.

This discussion of software is by no means meant to be comprehensive; several of the sites mentioned here have more information about these and a number of other packages for spatial modeling. The packages discussed here are available and relatively easy to use, and will give you several ways to begin to explore the possibilities that spatial modeling can provide for your data and applications.

We will illustrate several kinds of spatial models using S[3] with some of the data we have previously used to illustrate coding and mapping through this book.

Our approach will be the same as before, showing you screen shots, commands, and step-by-step instructions for duplicating the analyses we show here.

Example: A Cross Sectional Spatial Model: Gang Crime and Alcohol Availability

A number of studies have suggested a link between violence and alcohol availability in a spatial analysis framework (Gruenewald at al., 2006; Gruenewald and Remer, 2006; Alaniz et al., 1998). This has led to the notion that alcohol policy may be an effective tool in crime and violence prevention (see Parker, forthcoming). One area of research on violence that has been of great concern to policy makers and researchers has been gang violence, and it has been an area in which very little in the way of effective prevention efforts have been documented (see Howell, 1998). An unaddressed question is whether or not the alcohol availability and violence link would also be found if the specific type of violence and crime involved street gang activities—if so, this could provide a potentially useful policy tool to combat gangs and gang activity through the regulation of alcohol availability. This could take the form of limiting new outlets in areas with a high level of gang activity, placing a moratorium on new outlets in certain areas or communities, policing current outlets to insure they are not selling to underage customers, or even revoking licenses and closing outlets that repeatedly violate state and local laws in their business practices—this would result in reduced outlet density. However, first our spatial model must provide some good evidence that there is a relationship net of other factors that are also associated with higher rates of gang violence and activity.

Figure 3.11 shows the basic spatial patterning between gang violence and gang activities (all arrests involving gangs such as tagging, gang injunction violations, gang-related drug offenses) and alcohol outlets in Riverside. The patterns on the map seem to indicate clustering of these two variables in a number of places in the city of Riverside. However, there are places where one variable occurs and not the other, so what is the relationship? We also know from the research literature on

FIGURE 3.11   **Gang activities (light) and alcohol outlets (off sale, dark), 2000**

Geocoded Gang Crime and Alcohol Outlets

gangs that a number of other factors influence the rate of gang violence and activity in a neighborhood, including parental supervision, the presence of law-abiding and successful role models, and the degree of general disorder in the neighborhood (see Klien and Maxson, 2006). As certain ethnic groups are associated with gangs, especially in poor neighborhoods, the percent of African Americans and Latinos should be held constant, as well as the proportion of the population in the young male category—prime recruits for gang membership. If outlet density has an important link to gang crime after these factors have been held constant, this would be good evidence of a link that could be used to address the gang problem.

S^3 requires some data preparation before it can begin to address this relationship. The basic form that the data needs to be in is referred to as a space delimited file. The structure of such a file is that each observation or spatial unit's data begins on a new line; that the first variable on each line is a unique identification number, and that between the values of each variable and the next is at least one blank space. Most statistical programs can export a file with these characteristics; the file shown in Figure 3.12 was produced with SPSS.

FIGURE 3.12   **A space delimited text file produced by SPSS**

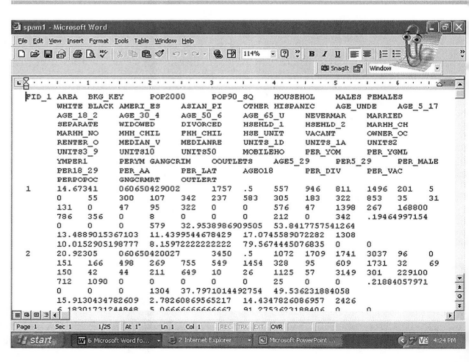

Notice that the first line contains the names of the variables, the first of which is FID_1; this labeling of the variables in the first line is optional, but is very useful as if you do not provide names, the program will provide helpful names like Y and X1, X2, X3, and so on.

The purpose of the ID numbers is to allow the program to insure that the data in the multiple files that are required for input in S^3 are properly linked. The data can be placed into as many as three separate files: one for the Y, dependent, or endogenous variable or variables (you can only analyze one dependent variable at a time, but if you have a number to predict or explain with similar sets of independent variables, you can input them into S^3 in one file and the program will ask you to select one for each analysis); one for the X, independent, or exogenous variables; and one for the connection or weight matrix that describes the structure of the space you are analyzing. In fact, you can have your independent and dependent variables in the same file, and just have the program input two copies for its use.

Once the data are ready, you can open the Mathematica Kernal program window, and call the S³ program to begin the run. Once you have told S³ where to find all the data files, everything the program understands is confirmed in the output file, both on screen (in Figure 3.13) and in the output file, which you can

FIGURE 3.13   **S³ data file summary and listing of selected dependent and independent variables**

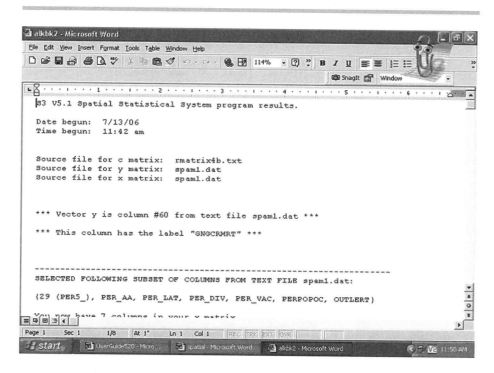

name according to your own wishes. You get the option to select columns from the Y and X variable lists to construct the exact subset of variables you wish to use in the current run. You can also add a constant to your model (Figure 3.14). You receive a printout of the univariate results, which is useful in order to make sure that the proper variables have been selected and the data are those you intend to model.

FIGURE 3.14   **Adding a constant to the analysis and univariate results**

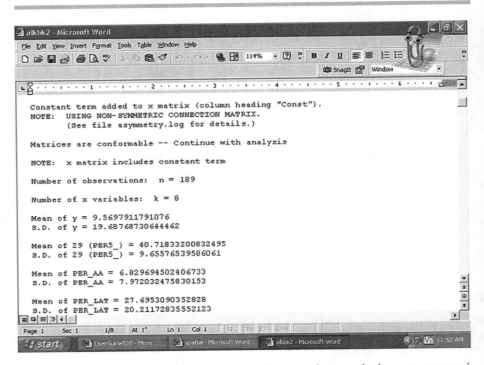

After an option to transform the connection matrix to make it more appropriate for the analysis, you can produce the Moran's I for the dependent variable weighted by the connection matrix, to assess at a basic level the degree to which spatial autocorrelation is a problem in these data, as shown in Figure 3.15. The output gives the value of Moran's I (referred to as the Moran Coefficient or MC),

FIGURE 3.15   **Moran's I results for gang crime**

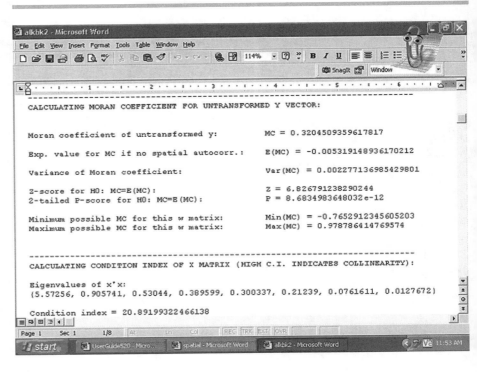

which in this case is 0.32. The output also provides a significance test, probability level, and a confidence interval around the estimate; in this case the value of Moran's I is highly significant, a not unexpected result given the maps and details we have examined previously. The output also provides the results of a multicollinearity check, based on the eigenvalues of the matrix of independent variables. The condition index, equal to the square root of the ratio of the largest eigenvalue to the smallest is a diagnostic test for too much inter correlation among the independent variables. This would imply a lack of independence among your independent variables, suggesting perhaps that one or more would be redundant for the model. You should have a good theoretical or empirical reason for each variable included, and this is important statistically to get the right set of variables included (the missing variable problem in spatial modeling was discussed previously). Usually the condition index has to be above 30 and closer to 100 to indicate a problem of this sort.

The next step is to run the standard regression model, assuming you have regular non-spatial data, and examine the residuals for the presence of spatial autocorrelation (Figure 3.16). The output gives some of the usual statistics for a regression model, including the coefficients and standard errors; the t test for significant is given in Figure 3.17.

FIGURE 3.16   **Standard regression results with spatial data**

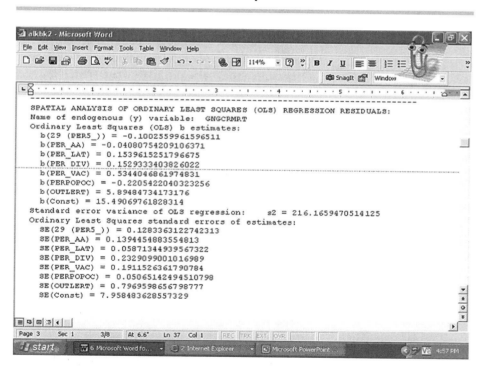

FIGURE 3.17   **More standard regression results and spatial diagnostics**

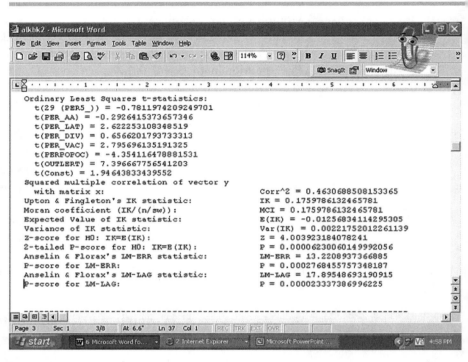

You can also see the spatial diagnostics in Figure 3.17. The t test values indicate that several of the net effects estimated here are significant, but recall the discussion about false positives when spatial autocorrelation is present. The output shows that the Moran's I on the residuals, although reduced from 0.32 on the raw gang crime rate, is now 0.17, and still statistically significant. So whatever spatial aspects captured by the effects of the other variables, including outlet density, these were not sufficient to fully account for the spatial patterns in these data. We need to examine a GLS model to properly estimate these effects with the contaminating impact of spatial association.

The Anselin and Florax (1995) statistics indicate that both the LM-ERR and the LM-LAG are significant, but the probability value for the LM-LAG is smaller than that for the LM-ERR, indicating that the autoregressive model is to be preferred. It would probably be worth while to run both models and compare the results; if the results are similar, this is strong evidence that you have found something reliable.

The next step is to run the GLS autoregressive model. The program will help you specify the model and select start values for the iterative process. The results of the GLS give you a sense of how much the estimates have been improved by accounting for the spatial autcorrelation in terms of statistical efficiency. This is taken to mean that a reduction in unexplained variance is efficient from a statistical point of view—the estimator with the lowest error is the most accurate and thus efficient. The efficiency gained from the GLS model can be shown by comparing the regular regression error variance with that of the spatial GLS; in this case the results show a modest 10 percent increase in efficiency for the GLS autoregressive model.

The t tests in Figure 3.18 from the GLS model replicate those from the regular regression model, and this gives us some confidence that our results are robust and stable under different sets of assumptions. We can now be more certain that

FIGURE 3.18   T tests from the GLS autoregressive model

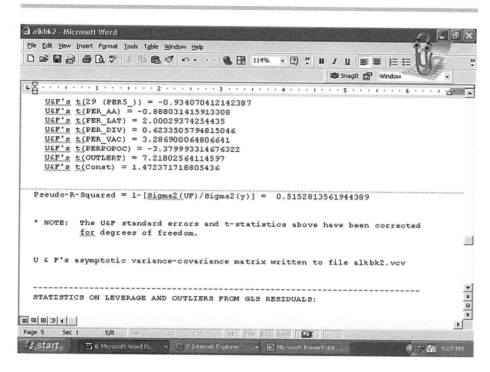

our findings, namely that alcohol outlet density has a positive and net effect on gang crime controlling for the effects of parental supervision, role models, disorder, ethnicity, and the availability of young males to join gangs.

Example: Multisite Studies in Spatial Modeling

One type of design that may be applicable to a number of situations is the case of a multisite spatial analysis. In a study reported in Alaniz et al. (1998), the relationship between alcohol availability and youth violence was investigated in three northern California communities: Redwood City, Union City, and Gilroy. The communities had some significant differences, and were selected originally to represent three different kinds of places: a small city in a largely rural area (Gilroy), a medium-sized city near smaller cities (Redwood City), and a largely residential city in which people commuted to larger cities nearby (Union City). The question in each, however, was the role of outlet density on youth violence.

This multisite design presents a unique challenge to a spatial model; one could run three separate analyses, but the number of units in each city limits the generalizability (14, 57, and 32, respectively), but pooling the cities into one analysis would allow for a more stable set of estimates (total number of units equals 103). However, the cities are not contiguous, so how can the spatial structure be represented?

S^3 provides an option to combine separate connection matrices into a block diagonal format that contains the connection pattern for each city connected in the matrix by an appropriate set of rows and columns of zeros where the units do not have contact. The data for the dependent and independent variables need to be simply appended onto one another in the same order that the three connection matrices have been linked. Near the beginning of the S^3 run, you have the option to create a block diagonal connection or weight matrix, as shown in Figure 3.19.

FIGURE 3.19   **S³ option to create block diagonal connection matrix**

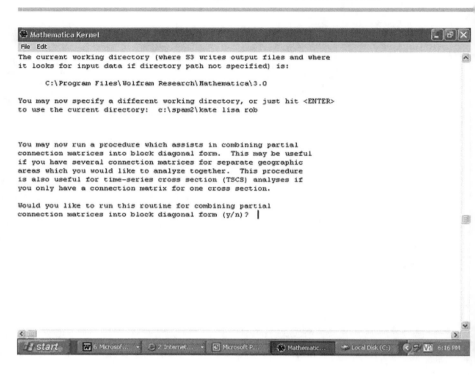

After adding each matrix in, the program gives you a chance to save the newly created block diagonal matrix under a new name so that it can be used in future analyses, as shown in Figure 3.20.

FIGURE 3.20   **Saving the block diagonal connection matrix**

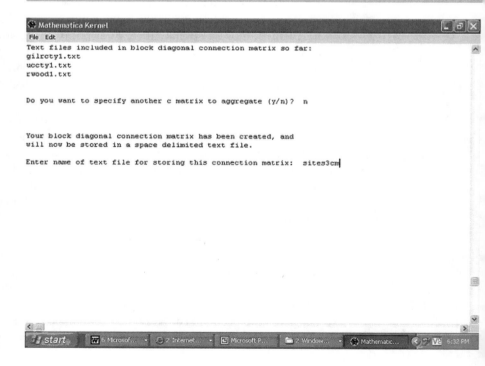

Now the analysis can proceed as before, with the appended variables' matrices in the same order as the three connection matrices were added to the block diagonal matrix. As you can see in Alaniz et al. (1998), the results indicated that outlet density was significant net of the other variables included in the model. In addition, the spatial model results showed some significant differences from the standard regression model, including the fact that one false positive uncovered was spatial autocorrelation which was accounted for properly, as being the impact of population on youth violence. In addition, the results showed that the presence of immigrants in the block group across all three sites was not a significant predictor of youth violence, an important finding given some of the current debate about the impact of immigrants in American communities.

Example: Pooled Cross Sectional and Time-Series Spatial Models

The capability of S^3 to conduct spatial models with pooled cross sectional and time-series data enhances the applicability of this package and allows you to apply spatial modeling to a significantly broader class of problems. We use as our example the impact of the gang prevention program in Riverside, Project Bridge, that we considered at the beginning of this section. By combining data across time we can track the impact of the intervention program and assess its outcome overall and in the specific places it was targeted. The example here presents six years' worth of data, so that we are pooling data from 133 block groups in the city of Riverside (1990 Census; several of the maps shown earlier in the book have 209 block groups from the 2000 Census) across six years, from 1994 to 1999; the interventions began in 1995, so we have a baseline year and four additional years after the beginning of the interventions.

The interventions were a combination of a number of activities and interactions, as detailed in Parker et al. (2004a); the project was a local implementation of Spergel's Comprehensive Model for Gang Prevention, Intervention, and Suppression (Spergel, 1999). The impact of the intervention was conceived of as a steady ramp, as in Figure 3.21.

FIGURE 3.21 **Intervention effects model for gang intervention program, Riverside**

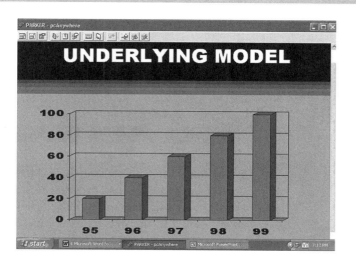

Alternative models were experimented with, but this one was consistent with the qualitative evidence about the nature of the program interventions and their activity, and produced stable and consistent estimates. The intervention was targeted in two broad areas across the city, as shown in Figure 3.2—the areas are referred to here as Arlanza and East Side; a third area, Casa Blanca, was specifically designated as a control area, and no intervention activities were engaged in with gang members or other youth in this third area.

The spatial model will first test the interventions together, that is, net of the other variables in the model: Did the two intervention areas have lower rates of gang activity than the rest of the city? We then test each intervention by itself against the control area and the rest of the city, which is essentially a test of whether or not each intervention area was significantly different from the other intervention area. The other factors considered in the model were unemployment, the percent of the adult population with less than 10 years of formal education (a poverty measure; see Loftin and Hill, 1974), percent of the residents who were foreign born, percent of the adults who were divorced (a measure of parental supervision), and the percent of Males between the ages of 16 and 24—the age of many active gang leaders and members.

After specifying the input matrices and constructing the block diagonal connection matrix if necessary, S^3 asks if you would like to use the pooled time-series cross sectional mode (TSCS), as shown in Figure 3.22.

FIGURE 3.22   **Requirements to run S^3 in time-series cross sectional mode**

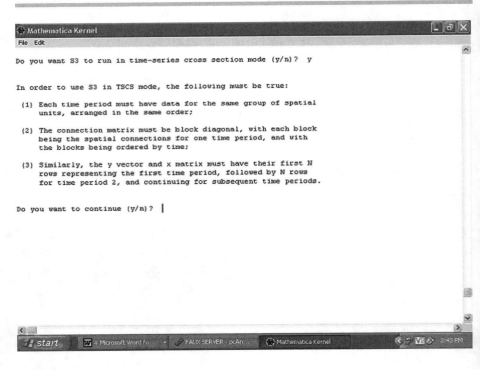

If you have not properly constructed the data files, you can exit the program and correct the problem. The program next asks you to confirm the number of time serial points you have and it then calculates the number of cross sections; you can then proceed to the step of calculating the Moran's I on the dependent variable, as shown in Figure 3.23.

FIGURE 3.23   **S³ in time-series cross sectional mode**

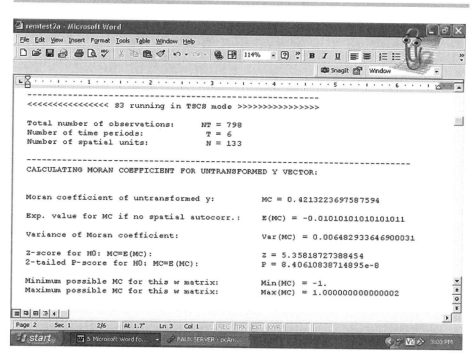

The next step is to compute the regular regression model and analyze the residuals for spatial autocorrelation; you have the option here of running the LSDV model, in which a unit specific dummy variable is specified for each cross section. You have the option of not seeing all those coefficients in the output, but remember that if you select this option, your coefficients are net of all those dummy variables. The alternative is to select the Random Effects Model, if the assumptions are warranted. Including the LSDV dummy variables can add to the computational time, and the Random Effects Model uses these estimates in the GLS model so that the computational time is increased significantly for this option.

If your data show temporal autocorrelation, you can select a Cochrane Orcutt lag structure for the error term to account for this; doing so precludes the Random Effects Model as these two models use similar transformations. Figure 3.24 shows the ordinary regression results.

FIGURE 3.24   **Time-series cross sectional regression results**

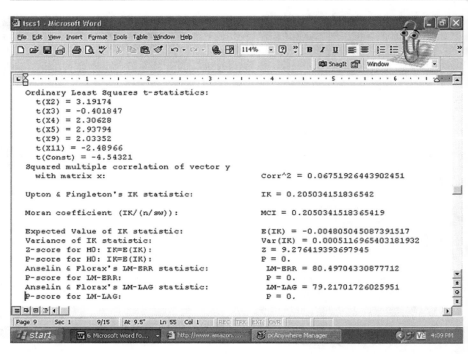

Notice that the Moran's I on the residuals is still significant, is reduced by about 50 percent from the corresponding value for the dependent variable alone. Although not very different, the Anselin and Florax tests suggest a nuisance model, consistent with the Random Effects Model. The results of this model are shown in Figure 3.25.

FIGURE 3.25   **GLS REM results for time-series cross section data**

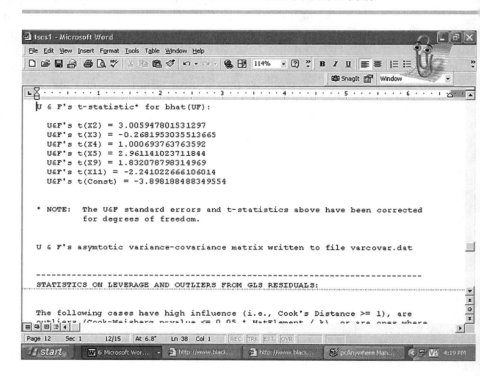

Variable X11 is the measure of the intervention's overall effect, and the results here show that the intervention has a negative and significant net effect on gang crime in Riverside between 1994 and 1999. Two other variables were found to increase gang crime: unemployment (X2) and the lack of parental supervision (X5) as measured by the percent of adults divorced in the block group.

The Hausman Test (Hausman, 1978) was insignificant, supporting the choice of the Random Effects Model over the LSDV, and the tests for temporal autocorrelation of the REM residuals were nonsignificant.

Spatial modeling can be a very powerful tool for understanding the way space impacts behavior and policy, and can be applied to a number of types of data and situations.

Example: Spatial Models: Limitations, Issues, and Emerging Developments

Like all statistical modeling approaches, spatial modeling has limitations. The usual set of assumptions that apply to standard linear modeling also apply here, and can be especially problematic. For example the assumption that the residual variances are randomly distributed is particularly problematic if there are large inter spatial unit variation in the observations. In pooled models, this is dealt with via the Random Effects versus LSDV choice, but in the cross sectional case the assumption is that whatever heterogeneity there is has been explained by the inclusion of the right independent variables—another version of the omitted variable problem discussed above. If the heterogeneity is due to spatial effects, in can be modeled; if not, it may undermine the stability of the results.

The problems discussed previously concerning the clustering of events within and across spatial unit boundaries do not get magically solved by multivariate spatial models. The problem of the distribution of observations on the variables we are relating in the model is still a difficult one, and could lead to false inferences. Using smaller units addresses this problem, as it minimizes the possibility of errors, but depending on the actual distribution of people and their behavior, problems could still arise.

Some of the additions to standard modeling which have helped to address some of its limitations, such as interaction terms, nonlinear measures and nonlinear models, have yet to be fully adopted in the spatial modeling framework as their interaction with the way spatial effects are modeled and these features is not well understood. Eventually analogous procedures to these and other models in common use in general may well be developed, but their absence in the spatial case limits the current applicability of spatial modeling. In addition, the impact of measurement error, so well addressed by the development of Structural Equation Models (Bollen, 1989), has yet to be addressed in any application of spatial models. This is a major shortcoming which will need to be addressed to increase the utility of spatial models in social and behavioral sciences.

Substantive Issues in Spatial Modeling

As a type of statistical modeling, spatial analysis is subject to all the same limitations and caveats as any quantitative analytical strategy. We have discussed the omitted variable problem, but the problem of making inferences is the same here as in research in general. A net effect of one variable on another, controlling for all the factors you can think of, surviving corrections for spatial autocorrelation, temporal autocorrelation, and other kinds of issues addressed by this approach are still subject to the limits of our conceptual and theoretical knowledge, the limits of our ability to capture what we really mean when collecting data, and our ability to properly interpret the findings. Finding an effect of professional role models on gang violence, or alcohol outlet density on youth violence is really the start of the puzzle rather than the answer. The question then becomes why and how? To use spatial models to address policy-related issues such as crime prevention and youth development we have to think very carefully about what the results mean, how they are limited by our thinking and expectations, and how they will be interpreted by policy makers. Adding a spatial dimension can be a big advantage in increasing our understanding, but we also must be careful how this new dimension will be used. If we find a link between minority population and crime in a certain area, law enforcement may wish to use this information to increase their activities in the neighborhood; this may result in some innocent people being affected as well as the offenders. In a free society like ours it is against our traditions and ideals to tell people they cannot go someplace they want to, unlike repressive regimes that limit access to certain areas based on ethnicity or gender. We need to make sure we really understand how space is having its impact, and what implications our findings have for the lives of the people who will be affected by those results.

New Developments in Spatial Modeling

One of the recent developments in statistical methods in the social sciences that has proved to be very successful and powerful for a whole class of problems spanning many disciplines has been the advances in hierarchical linear modeling and the dissemination of the popular software program HLM (Bryk and Raudenbush, 1992). A number of important conceptual and theoretical approaches in the social and behavioral sciences depend on the notion of context and its importance in behavioral and social outcomes, and yet there had been a great deal of methodological inadequacy in the standard approaches to incorporating context into standard models. Spatial modeling is one way to conceive of the impact of context, but there were many situations, such as in schools with classrooms, and corporations with branch offices, in which nonphysical context was important, and understanding the influence on one level of an organization of levels that were imbedded within the larger form was important. HLM is designed for just such situations, but it quickly became apparent that HLM could be applied to physical space, that is neighborhoods within cities. However, the original specification of the HLM model did not contain a spatial autocorrelation adjustment, a potentially problematic situation when HLM was applied to physical spaces with contiguous units. In a ground-breaking paper Sampson et al. (1999) solved this problem by adding a spatial component to an HLM specification through a two-stage procedure (1999: 646). Further integration of these two approaches is a promising new development for both spatial and hierarchical modeling techniques.

There are a number of other emerging developments in spatial modeling that deal with the fact that although we may have observations on a spatially ordered event or process, these observations are almost always incomplete, and the omitted information may be very important for understanding how space interacts with the other components of the processes and behaviors we wish to understand. Some of these approaches involve using simulations to model likely patterns in the omitted data and how the omitted data are likely to connect with the observed data. For example, Møller and Waagepetersen (2003) use Markov Chain Monte Carlo (MCMC) methods in point processing applications to enhance inferential ability in the presence of sparse data. These methods might be applicable to studying violence and other relatively rare events, not all of which are reported in data collection systems and may help to identify emerging hot spots long before the official data show such a concentration of detected events.

Another potentially interesting development is the application of Bayesian statistical approaches to reducing uncertainty in modeling spatial processes. Essentially the reasoning is that what we observe of events in space is part of the spatial process, but not all of it. It may be that from other studies we can make some inferences about the underlying processes that we cannot observe that ought to contribute to the distribution of events in space if we could measure all events; if we make such inferences and add the contribution of these processes to the ones we can directly observe this may yield a more realistic picture of the actual spatial processes. If we were studying property crime in a city, we might realize that police reports reflect only part of the underlying process that produces a distribution in space of these events. Perhaps a study of insurance-related claims shows that people typically do not report thefts below a certain threshold of loss, and we could use MCMC simulations to construct additional events at lower levels of loss to see how they would contribute to the pattern.

The Bayesian approach can also be useful as a way to incorporate information from alternative models into a spatial modeling process (Hoeting et al., 2002; Borgoni and Billari, 2003). The recognition of the multiple underlying sources of spatial processes that contribute to an observed set of events in space, and the understanding that we can only observe parts of these processes, suggests that we can systematically enhance our data and modeling with simulations and Bayesian decision making. However, Bayesian approaches are only as good as the credibility of the sources of information about the distributions of the missing aspects of the process (Burstyn and Kromhout, 2004). If we introduce data based on processes without strong prior empirical foundation, or, in the case of model selection, we average over well and poorly or improperly specified models, we may be doing more harm than good in this process.

In short, the current state of spatial modeling is appropriate and useful for a number of applications in social and behavioral sciences and in the area of policy research. Although there are limitations to the current standard approaches, new developments and research are extending the capability and applicability of spatial models to a wider and wider variety of problems and strengthening the ability of researchers and policy makers to use spatial modeling to understand the complex world around us and to support good decision making in public policy.

Conclusion

This book has provided you with a full introduction to the exciting and versatile field of Geographic Information Systems, given you a valuable and useful set of new skills, and hopefully challenged you to think more and more about the role that space plays in our lives, our behaviors, and our decision making. We have provided you with lots of hands-on experience in coding, mapping, and analysis, and if you have followed along on your computer, mapping and analyzing the data we have provided on the DVD and the book's website, you are an experienced GIS practitioner. The website has many additional data sets and exercises to further explore these techniques and approaches; we also urge you to use the models we have given you to build your own GIS databases, map your data, and conduct your own spatial modeling. This is the way to experience the power of GIS and the techniques we have discussed here.

We also hope that you take away from this experience increased ability to think critically about the maps and spatial analyses that are presented to you with increasing frequency—whether in the newspaper, the Web, on the TV news, or in your organization, company, city, or school system. Now that you know how these maps are made and how the models are built, you will see the problems, limitations, and uncertainties reflected in these GIS applications, and you will know the questions to ask in order to make these efforts better and to use them to improve your situation and that of those around you. If any of these outcomes result from your exposure to *GIS and Spatial Analysis for the Social Sciences*, our expectations will be fulfilled beyond hope. Thanks for persisting with us on this trip across space and time, and happy mapping into the future.

Appendix   **GIS Data Sources**

Listed below are some data sets relevant to the social sciences that are compatible with GIS analyses. This list is in no way considered exhaustive. Most of the data can be accessed at no charge, or for only a nominal fee. We provide this information with a caution to our readers that any data set can be made compatible with GIS as long as it contains some geospatial attribute such as an address, zip code, county, or region. As with any type of analytic technique it may be necessary to first do some preparation with your data before plugging it into a GIS analysis, but virtually any database can be used for this purpose. We present this list for your convenience, but readers should not feel limited to use only data sets that appear here for their own GIS projects.

United States Census Bureau
http://www.census.gov/main/www/access.html

General Social Survey
http://gss.norc.org/

National Archive of Criminal Justice Data
http://www.icpsr.umich.edu/NACJD/

United States Bureau of Justice Statistics
http://www.ojp.usdoj.gov/bjs/

Federal Bureau of Investigation
http://www.ojp.usdoj.gov/bjs/

United Nations Statistics Division
http://unstats.un.org/unsd/default.htm

United States Department of Labor
http://www.bls.gov/data/

Center for Disease Control
http://wonder.cdc.gov/

World Health Organization
http://www.who.int/whosis/en/

North American Transportation Atlas Data
http://www.bts.gov/publications/north_american_transportation_atlas_data/

Environmental Protection Agency
http://www.epa.gov/epahome/Data.html

United States Fish and Wildlife Service
http://wetlandsfws.er.usgs.gov/NWI/download.html

Federal Geographic Data Committee
http://www.fgdc.gov/dataandservices

The Geography Network
http://www.geographynetwork.com/data/index.html

The Odum Institute
http://152.2.32.107/odum/jsp/content_node.jsp?nodeid=7

Inter-University Consortium for Political and Social Research
http://www.icpsr.org/

Council of European Social Science Data Archives
http://extweb3.nsd.uib.no/cessda/home.html

Panel Study of Income Dynamics
http://psidonline.isr.umich.edu/

Statistical Abstract of the United States
http://www.census.gov/compendia/statab/

State Data Center
http://www.census.gov/sdc/www/

United Kingdom Data Archive
http://www.data-archive.ac.uk/

United Kingdom Government Statistics
http://www.statistics.gov.uk/

Center for International Earth Science Information Network
http://www.ciesin.org/index.html

United States Public Elementary-Secondary School Data
http://www.census.gov/govs/www/school.html

National Center for Education Statistics
http://nces.ed.gov/

References

Alaniz, M. L., Cartmill, R. S., and Parker, R. N. (1998) "Immigrants and Violence: The Importance of Neighborhood Context." *Hispanic Journal of Behavioral Sciences* 20(2): 155–174.

Allison, Paul D. (1999) *Multiple Regression*. Thousand Oaks, CA: Pine Forge Press.

Anselin, L. (1995) "Local Indicators of Spatial Association-LISA." *Geographical Analysis* 27: 93–115.

Anselin, L. and Florax, R. J. G. M. (1995) "Small Sample Properties of Tests for Spatial Dependence in Regression Models: Some Further Results." In L. Anselin and R. J. G. M. Florax (eds.), *New Directions in Spatial Econometrics*. New York: Springer.

Anselin, L., Ibnu Syabri, and Youngihn Kho (2005) "GeoDa: An Introduction to Spatial Data Analysis" *Geographical Analysis* 38(1): 5–22.

Bollen, Kenneth A. (1989) *Structural Equation Models with Latent Variables*. New York: Academic Press.

Borgoni, Riccardo and Billari, Francesco C. (2003) "Bayesian Spatial Analysis of Demographic Survey Data." *Demographic Research* 8: 61–92.

Bratton, William. (1998) *Turnaround: How America's Top Cop Reversed the Crime Epidemic*. New York: Random House.

Bryk, Anthony and Raudenbush, Stephen (1992) *Hierarchical Linear Models*. Newbury Park, CA: Sage Publications.

Burawoy, M. (2003) "Revisits: An Outline of a Theory of Reflexive Ethnography." *American Sociological Review* 68: 645–679.

Burstyn, Igor and Kromhout, Hans (2004) "A Critique of Bayesian Methods for Exposure Assessment." *Annals of Occupational Hygiene* 46: 429–491.

Cliff, A. D. and Ord, J. K. (1971) *Spatial Autocorrelation*. London: Pion.

Cornish, Drek B. and Clarke, Ronald V. (1987) "Understanding Crime Displacement: An Application of Rational Choice Theory." *Criminology* 25: 933–948.

Dewees, Maria A. and Parker, Karen F. (2003) "Women, Region and Types of Homicide." *Homicide Studies* 7: 368–393.

Duncan, O. D. (1961) "Socioeconomic Scores for Detailed Occupations [in the 1960 Census]." University of Chicago, Population Research and Training Center.

Felson, Marcus (1987) "Routine Activities and Crime Prevention in the Developing Metropolis." *Criminology* 25: 911–932.

Geolytics, Inc. (2003) Neighborhood Change Database: Census Tract Data 1970–2000. Machine readable data file.

Goodchild, M. F. and Janelle, D. G. (2004) "Thinking Spatially in the Social Sciences." In M. F. Goodchild and D. G. Janelle (eds.), *Spatially Integrated Social Science*. New York: Oxford University Press.

Greenblatt, J. C. (2000) "Patterns of Alcohol Use Among Adolescents and Associations with Emotional and Behavioral Problems." Washington, DC: SAMHSA, available online at: www.samhsa.gov/oas.

Gruenewald, P. J. and Remer, L. (2006) "Changes in Outlet Densities Affect Violence Rates." *Alcoholism: Clinical and Experimental Research* 30(7): 1184–1193.

Gruenewald, P. J., Freisthler, B., Remer, L., LaScala, E. A., and Treno, A. (2006) "Ecological Models of Alcohol Outlets and Violent Assaults: Crime Potentials and Geospatial Analysis." *Addiction* 101(5): 666–677.

Hagan, J., MacMillan, R., and Wheaton, B. (1996) "New Kid in Town: Social Capital and the Life Course Effects of Family Migration on Children." *American Sociological Review* 61: 368–385.

Hanushek, Eric and Jackson, J. (1977) *Statistical Methods for the Social Sciences*. New York: Academic Press.

Harris, David (1997) " 'Driving while Black' and All Other Traffic Offenses: The Supreme Court and Pretextual Traffic Stops." *Journal of Criminal Law and Criminology* 87(2).

Harris, T. and Weiner, D. (1996) "GIS and Society: The Social Implications of How People, Space, and Environment are Represented in GIS." Santa Barbara, CA: NCGIA Technical Report 96–97.

Hausman, J. A. (1978) "Specification Tests in Econmetrics." *Econometrica* 46(1): 1251–1271

Hoeting, J., Raftery, A. E., and Madigan, D. (2002) "A Method for Simultaneous Variable and Transformation Selection in Linear Regression." *Journal of Computational and Graphical Statistics* 11: 485–507.

Howell, J. C. (1998). "Promising Programs for Youth Gang Violence Prevention and Intervention." In R. Loeber and D. P. Farrington (eds.), *Serious and Violent Juvenile Offender*: Thousand Oaks, CA: Sage Publications.

Jensen, Jason L. (2004) "A Multipopulation Comparison of the Diffusion of Innovation of Public Organizations and Policies across Time and Space." *Policy Studies Journal* 32: 109–127.

Klein, Malcolm W. and Maxson, Cheryl L. (2006) *Street Gang Patterns and Policies*. London and New York: Oxford University Press.

Land, K. C. and Deane, G. (1992) "On the Large-Sample Estimation of Regression Models with Spatial or Network-Effects Terms: A Two-Stage Least Squares Approach." In P.V. Marsden (ed.), *Sociological Methodology*. New York: Blackwell.

Loftin, Colin K. and Hill, Robert H. (1974) "Regional Subculture and Homicide: An Examination of the Gastil-Hackney Thesis." *American Sociological Review* 39: 714–724.

Loftin, C. K. and Ward, S. K. (1983) "A Spatial Autocorrelation Model of the Effects of Population Density on Fertility." *American Sociological Review* 48: 121–128.

Ma, Jingsheng, Haining, Robert P., and Wise, Stephen M. (1997) SAGE: An

Integrated GIS for Health Data Analysis. Sheffield, UK: Sheffield Centre for Geographic Information and Spatial Analysis: http://www.shef.ac.uk/~scgisa/newscgisa/research.htm#methodology.

Matsueda, R. (1982) "Testing Control Theory and Differential Association: A Causal Modeling Approach." *American Sociological Review* 47: 489–504.

Møller, J. and Waagepetersen, R. (2003) *Statistical Inference and Simulation for Spatial Point Processes*. Boca Raton, FL: Chapman & Hall/CRC Press.

Moran, P. A. P. (1950) "Notes on Continuous Stochastic Phenomena." *Biometrika* 37: 17–23.

Parker, Robert Nash (Forthcoming) *Alcohol and Violence: The Nature of the Relationship and the Promise of Prevention*. Walnut Creek, CA: Alta Mira Press.

Parker, Robert Nash, Asencio, Emily K., Ho-Pih, Kay Kei, and Wojtalewicz, Celeste (2004a) "Evaluating a Comprehensive Gang Intervention." Riverside, CA: Presley Center for Crime and Justice, Research Paper.

Parker, R. N., Asencio, E. K., Seheult, O., Pih, K., Ross, H., Meade, H., et al. (2004b) "Racial Preference in Traffic Stops: A Geospatial Analysis of Driving While Black or Brown." Riverside, CA: Presley Center for Crime and Justice, Paper.

Parker, R. N., Luther, K., and Murphy, L. (Forthcoming) "Availability, Gang Violence, and Alcohol Policy: Gaining Support for Alcohol Regulation via Harm Reduction Strategies." *Contemporary Drug Problems*, in press.

Pitchford, Phil and Lisa O'Neill Hill (2002) "Delving into Disparities." The Press-Enterprise, February 24, p. A1.

Ponicki, William R. and Gruenewald, Paul J. (2005) S^3: *Spatial Statistical System User's Guide, Version 5.2*. Berkeley, CA: Pacific Institute for Research and Evaluation.

Ramirez, Deborah, McDevitt, Jack, and Farrel, Amy (2000) "A Resource Guide on Racial Profiling Data Collection Systems: Promising Practices and Lessons Learned." Draft. Northeastern University.

Sampson, R. J., Morenoff, J. D., and Earls, F. (1999) "Beyond Social Capital: Spatial Dynamics of Collective Efficacy for Children." *American Sociological Review* 64: 633–660.

Schroeder, Larry D., Sjoquist, David L., and Stephan Paula E., (1986) *Understanding Regression Analysis: An Introductory Guide*. Quantitative Applications in the Social Sciences, No. 57. Thousand Oaks, CA: Sage Publications.

Schulz, Kenneth (2006) "National Rivalries in the 20th Century." Presented to the Center for Advanced Studies in Behavioral Sciences.

Sherman, Lawrence W. and Berk, Richard (1984) "The Specific Deterrent Effects of Arrests for Domestic Assault." *American Sociological Review* 49(2): 261–272.

Sherman, Lawrence W., Gartin, Patrick R., and Buerger, Michael E. (1989) "Hot Spots of Predatory Crime: Routine Activity and the Criminology of Place." *Criminology* 27: 27–56.

Sorenson, Aage B.(1979) "A Model and a Metric for the Intergenerational Status Attainment Process." *American Journal of Sociology* 85: 361–384.

Spergel, I. A. (1996) *The Youth Gang Problem: A Community Approach*. New York: Oxford University Press.

Spergel, I. A. (1999) *Youth Gangs: Problems and Response*. New York: Oxford University Press.

Spergel, I. A. and Alexander, A. (1993) *National Youth Gang Suppression and Intervention Program*. Rockville, MD: Office of Juvenile Justice and Delinquency Prevention.

Stark, Rodney (1987) "Deviant Places: A Theory of the Ecology of Crime." *Criminology* 25: 893–910.

Sutherland, Edwin H. (1947) *Criminology*. 4th ed. Philadelphia, PA: Lippincott.

Walker, Jack L. (1973) Diffusion of Public Innovation Among the American States [Computer file]. Compiled by Jack L. Walker, University of Michigan, Institute of Public Policy Studies. ICPSR ed. Ann Arbor, MI: Inter-Consortium for Political and Social Research [producer and distributor].

Warren, P., Tomaskovic-Devey, D., Smith, W., Zingraff, M., and Mason, M. (2006) "Driving While Black: Bias Processes and Racial Disparity in Police Stops." *Criminology* 44: 709–738.

Wheaton, B. and Clarke, P. (2003) "Space Meets Time: Integrating Temporal and Contextual Influences on Mental Health in Early Adulthood." *American Sociological Review* 68: 680–706.

Index

3D Analyst 144, 145, 147, 150
3D maps: diffusion of innovation 141–56; socioeconomic conditions 156–9

Add All Values 162
Add Data: address locators 17; database format files 17–18, 111; diffusion of innovation 154–5; educational outcomes 190; immigration and unemployment 184, 187–8; new databases 8; new layers 7; poverty rates over time in New Orleans 131–5; thematic maps 52, 66
Add Field 67–8, 130–1, 145, 180
Add Renderer 152–3
Add Values 93
address locators 13–17, 22, 111; interactive geocoding 31; selecting 19–21; style 15
addresses: attribute table 10; databases 6–7, 10, 13, 15, 22; geocoding 4, 12–24, 25–9, 30–47; modifying 31, 32–3; range of 32, 37–8; unmatched 27, 30–1, 32, 33–4, 40, 46
Africa 174
African-Americans: gang-related crime 220; poverty rates over time in New Orleans 124–7, 128–35; racial profiling 62–75; *see also* ethnicity
aggregated data 123
Alaniz, M. L. 225, 227
alcohol availability 164–6, 205, 216, 219–27
algorithms 113
aliases 23
animations 200
Anselin, L. 115, 120, 207, 211, 215, 218, 224, 230
ArcScene 148, 149–50, 153, 158, 159
armed conflict 87–95, 174, 175
atlases 29, 31, 32, 34, 35
attribute table 10, 43; 3D maps 145–6, 147, 154; census data 138; diffusion of innovation 154–6; educational outcomes 191, 196, 197–8; homicide patterns 161–2; Hurricane Katrina's impact on education 170, 171; immigration and unemployment 180, 181, 182; poverty rates over time in New Orleans 129–31; rivalries between nations 90; subsetting data 98–101; thematic maps 54, 61–2, 66–7, 78
autocorrelation correlation between the values of one or more variables measured in the subunits of a space that arises because the subunits are arrayed in a common geographic space (spatial autocorrelation) or because the subunits are measured repeatedly over time ((time) serial autocorrelation) 208, 211, 212–14, 216, 222–4, 227, 229, 232

bar graphs 136, 140–1, 165, 166, 198–9
basemap files files used by the GIS application to determine where to place particular attributes based upon some specified geographic criteria xvi; educational outcomes 190–1, 193; Hurricane Katrina's impact on education 170; immigration and unemployment 179; join operation 170, 194, 195; traffic ticket data 65–6
Bayesian approaches 233
bias 46, 212
birth rate 85
block groups 6, 12; candidate selection 32; divorce rates 82; median rents 157–8; school planning 105–7, 109; tessellations 118–19; thematic maps 51, 66; violent incidents 23–4, 28, 29, 98, 113–15, 118–19, 211, 216
boundaries: category 80; geocoding 32, 34, 35; reference data 51–2; spatial modeling 206, 209, 212, 231; youth violence 112–13, 114–15, 116

Calculate Values 67, 146

candidate addresses 31–8, 40–2, 46

census data: ethnic groups 64; Hurricane Katrina's impact on education 170; poverty rates over time in New Orleans 124–7, 128, 129, 131–2, 134; residential patterns and ethnicity 136, 137–8, 139, 140; *see also* data files; U.S. Census Bureau

Charts submenu 132–4; *see also* bar graphs; pie charts

classification: crime 97; multivariate maps 87–95; thematic maps 80

clustering approach 113–23, 207, 208, 211

combining maps 110–11

condition index 223

connection matrix a matrix with the same dimensions as the number of subunits displayed on a map which contains information about the structure of the space and the geospatial relationship of the subunits to each other 208, 212, 218, 221–2, 225–7, 228

context 4–5, 232

correlation coefficients 207, 208, 213

Create Layer From Selected Features 104–5, 122, 140, 169, 193

crime: alcohol availability and youth violence 164–6, 205, 216, 219–27; classification of 97; data on xiv; homicide patterns 160–4; 'hot spots' 5, 81–2, 117, 119, 206, 233; juvenile 75–83, 112–13; Project Bridge 203–5; racial profiling 62–75, 205; rate 85; spatial modeling 232; *see also* gang-related crime; youth violence

Crime Prevention Through Environmental Design 206

cross sectional spatial data 216, 218, 219–25, 231

data collection 179, 206, 209

data files files that contain the attributes that the user is interested in analyzing along geographic boundaries xvi; address locators 15; converting 194–5; diffusion of innovation 155; educational outcomes 189, 194; immigration and unemployment 179, 180, 184, 187–8; spatial modeling 220–1, 228; thematic maps 51, 52–4; traffic ticket data 65–6; *see also* census data; databases

Data Management Tools 122

data mining 24, 65

Data View 56, 163, 179, 187

databases: 3D maps 154; adding database format file to map 18; adding new 8; address 6–7, 10, 13, 15, 22; complex 202–3; Neighborhood Change Database 124; saving spreadsheet in database format 17–18, 111, 154; street 5, 7, 9–10, 31–2; technology development xv; *see also* data files

death rate 85

Delete Field 181–2

diffusion of innovation 141–56

disaster relief 85, 166–73

Dissolve function 121–3

divorce rates 82–3, 84–5, 86–7, 112

Dot density 162, 163

drawing tool 38–9, 91, 93, 95, 110

dynamic maps maps which display data for a single space or a consistent set of subunits of a space across multiple periods 124–7, 141

Editor menu 47, 131, 147, 180–1

education: Hurricane Katrina impact on 166–73; policy and outcomes 188–200; school planning and projections 105–11

errors: geocoding 22, 24, 29, 36; spatial modeling 212–13, 215, 224

ethnicity: gang-related crime 105, 220; racial profiling 62–75; residential living patterns 135–41; youth violence 119–20

Excel 2, 17, 25, 91, 111, 154

Export Data 171, 196, 197–8

Export Map 48–50, 61

Extensions 144–5

false positive a finding in a statistical model that a cause or prediction is significant when in fact the effect of the cause or predictor is not significant. The reason the false positive appears to be significant is because some aspect of the spatial nature of the data involved bas been ignored or improperly modeled 212–13, 224, 227

Federal Bureau of Investigation (FBI) xiv, 97, 160, 164

Field Calculator 68, 146, 147

Florax, R. J. G. M. 215, 224, 230

formulas: building a selection formula 102; verification of 44, 102–3, 122

gang-related crime: Project Bridge 203–5, 227; spatial modeling 210–11, 219–31; subsetting 96, 97, 98, 102, 104–5; *see also* youth violence

Generalization 122
Generalized Least Squares (GLS)
   framework 213, 214, 216, 218, 224, 229,
   230
geocoding the process of converting address
   based or in general coordinate based
   information on the location of events,
   occurrences, institutions, etc., into
   mappable points on a **layer** in a mapping
   session: addresses 12–24; automatic 13,
   21, 22–3, 24, 26–8; basics of 3–12;
   examples 24–51; interactive 13, 23, 24,
   29–47; Options submenu 21–4, 27;
   school planning 111; thematic maps 75,
   77–8
GeoDa 218
geospatial modeling *see* **spatial modeling**
Get Unique Values 101, 122, 191
GIS (Geographic Information Systems):
   components of xv–xvi; definition of xiv,
   1; history of xiv–xv
GLS *see* Generalized Least Squares
   framework
graduated color scheme 54, 64, 69, 70,
   78–9, 176, 183
graduated symbols 54, 69, 184–5, 188

Hausman Test 231
health policy 174–5
HIV infections 174–5
HLM 232
homicide patterns 160–4
housing: high-rise 206; residential patterns
   and ethnicity 135–41; socioeconomic
   conditions 156–9
Hurricane Katrina 124, 128–31, 166–73

Identify tool 3–4, 45, 92, 173, 199
immigration 175–88, 201, 227
IMS *see* Internet Map Services
innovation 141–56
Insert menu 57–8, 60, 71
Internet Map Services (IMS) provide the
   ability to produce dynamic GIS
   applications and publish them on the
   Internet xvii
intersections 23, 24, 26, 35, 36

Jensen, Jason L. 141–2
Join submenu 76–8, 156, 170–1, 195–6
juvenile crime 75–83, 112–13; *see also*
   youth violence

labeling 10–11, 29, 70–1
Latinos: gang-related crime 220; racial

profiling 62–4, 69, 71–2, 73; residential
   patterns 136–41; youth violence 119–20;
   see also ethnicity
layer a map or data base that is part of a
   mapping session. Multiple layers can be
   available in a single mapping session, and
   the map and any data associated with a
   layer can be displayed and/or overlaid on
   other layers in the same mapping session:
   adding new 7; changing name of 162,
   169, 182–3, 184, 188, 193; changing order
   of 186–7, 188; Create Layer From
   Selected Features 104–5, 122, 140, 169,
   193; displaying 12; Export Data 196–8;
   overlay on existing maps 9; Paste Layer
   127; Select by Attributes 43–4; thematic
   maps 58, 76–8
Layer Properties: Add Renderer 152–3; bar
   graphs 140, 141, 166, 198; changing
   name of layer 162, 169, 182–3, 184, 188,
   193; homicide patterns 162; median rent
   calculation 159; pie charts 132, 133,
   134, 171–2; rate mapping 86; rivalries
   between nations 93; thematic maps 54,
   69, 71–2, 78, 79, 80, 82, 135
layoffs 177–8, 179, 187–8
Layout View 56–7, 60, 73, 74, 163, 173,
   187, 200
Least Squares Dummy Variable (LSDV)
   model 217, 218, 229, 231
Legend Item Selector 60–1
Legend Properties 59–60
Legend Wizard 58–9
legend a key to a map showing the
   definition and content of that displayed
   on a **thematic map** 56, 57–61, 71, 187,
   200
line color 91, 93, 94, 175
Line Properties 93
Local Moran I: clustering approach
   115–16, 118, 120; spatial modeling
   207–8, 211, 214–16, 217, 222–4, 228, 230
LSDV *see* Least Squares Dummy Variable
   model

magnifying glass tool 11, 38, 92, 107
map projections used to represent a three-
   dimensional curved surface such as the
   globe, or earth as a flat computer file, or
   flat map xvi
map scale the representation of the
   proportional ratio between distances on
   the map display and actual distances
   xvi–xvii, 169, 193
Mapquest 29, 31, 110

Markov Chain Monte Carlo (MCMC)
    methods 233
Microsoft Excel 2, 17, 25, 91, 111, 154
Microsoft PowerPoint 47, 49–50, 61
Microsoft Word 47
misspellings 22, 23
Møller, J. 233
Moran's I: clustering approach 115–16,
    118, 120; spatial modeling 207–8, 211,
    214–16, 217, 222–4, 228, 230
multisite spatial analysis 218, 225–7
multivariate maps 84–5, 128–59, 203;
    classification 87–95; combining 110–11;
    planning and projections 105–11;
    poverty rates over time in New Orleans
    128–35; residential patterns and
    ethnicity 135–41; subsetting 95–105
multivariate regression 201–2
murders 160–4

national rivalries 87–95, 174, 175
Neighborhood Change Database 124
New Orleans 124–7, 128–35
New York City Police Department 160
normalization forming a rate by using a
    variable measuring the population at risk
    of an event as the denominator and a
    count of the events occurring in a space
    or the subunits of a space over a specific
    time period 86, 95, 96, 165; *see* rate
    mapping
nuisance model 213, 215, 216, 230

OLS *see* Ordinary Least Squares model
Open Attribute Table 145
Options submenu 21–4, 145
Ordinary Least Squares (OLS) model 217

Parker, Robert Nash 62, 64, 65, 227
Paste Layer 127
Pearson's r 207, 208
peer networks 5
pie charts 128–9, 132–4, 171–2, 173
pin maps 2–3, 75; juvenile crime 76, 113,
    114; New York City Police Department
    160; school planning 111
planning: disaster planning and relief
    166–73; school planning 105–11
police: alcohol availability and youth
    violence 165; New York City Police
    Department 160; racial profiling 62, 64,
    65; youth violent contact with 95, 96
policy 5, 84, 159, 160–200; alcohol
    availability and youth violence 164–6,
    219; disaster planning and relief 166–73;

educational policy and outcomes
    188–200; health and world affairs 174–5;
    homicide patterns 160–4; immigration
    and unemployment 175–88; spatial
    modeling 205, 232, 233; urban housing
    137
pooled cross sectional and time-series design
    a research design that combines data for
    units of analysis across a set of units,
    e.g., states, counties, census tracks, block
    groups, etc. (cross sectional data) with
    data measured repeatedly across regular,
    uniform time periods such as months,
    years, quarters, etc. (time series data)
    216–17, 218, 227–31
poverty rates 124–7, 128–35, 137, 156
PowerPoint 47, 49–50, 61
Pre-Logic VBA Script Code 146, 147
Preview 58
Project Bridge 203–5, 227
proportional symbols 54

racial profiling 62–75, 205
Random Effects Model (REM) 217, 218,
    229, 230, 231
raster format data in the raster format is
    data stored as a series of cells with a
    single value contained in each cell xvii,
    120
rate mapping 85–7
reference data any data-base that provides
    basic geospatial data such as address
    locator files, census data and shape file
    combinations, or any other data-base
    that provides basic information necessary
    to construct a map or display
    information on a map 15, 51–2, 65–6
regression analysis 201–2, 207, 208, 212,
    213–15, 217, 223–4, 229–30
relative risk 85, 86, 87
REM *see* Random Effects Model
residential patterns 135–41
Review/Rematch submenu 27, 29, 30, 42,
    45
rivalries between nations 87–95, 174, 175
Routine Activity approach 206

S3 (Spatial Statistical Systems) 218, 219–31
SAGE 218
Sampson, R. J. 232
saving data 47–8, 187, 200; cluster analysis
    120; Export Data command 171, 196,
    197–8; Save As Layer File 193; thematic
    maps 61, 71, 73, 75
Scene Properties 150

schooling: educational policy and outcomes 188–200; Hurricane Katrina impact on 166–73; planning and projections 105–11

segregation 136, 137

Select by Attributes 42–4, 100–3, 121–2, 168, 191, 192

Select by Location 138–9

Selection tool: Create Layer From Selected Features 104–5, 122, 140, 169, 193; interactive geocoding 42–4

shape file a computer file containing the definition of a map of a location giving the shape of the map and most often including the definition of polygons that form subunits in the space in **vector format** 8, 53, 182

socioeconomic conditions 156–9, 189, 190

sociology 202

software 217–18

space: meaning of 206–7; measuring the impact of 207–8

space delimited files 220

spatial heterogeneity the concept that spatial locations are not independent of other spatial locations divided by boundaries such as county and state lines xvii, 231

spatial modeling any statistical modeling approach that involves relationships within and between variables arrayed in units of geographic space and/or which explicitly involves the nature and structure of the space in the statistical model 201–34; cross sectional 216, 219–25, 231; errors 212–13; limitations of 231; meaning of space 206–7; multisite studies 225–7; new developments 232–3; pooled cross sectional and time-series design 216–17, 227–31; relationships among variables 207–8; software choice 217–18; statistical issues 208–12; statistical modeling of spatial data 213–16; substantive issues 231–2; types of data 216–17

Spatial Statistics Tools 120

Spergel, Irving 203–4, 227

spreadsheets: aliases 23; saving in database format 17–18, 111, 154; school planning 110–11; traffic ticket data 65; *see also* Microsoft Excel

Start Editing 131, 146, 180–1

street databases 5, 7, 9–10, 31–2

street labeling 10–11, 29

subsetting 95–105, 111

Sutherland, - 4–5

symbol properties 39, 111, 198–9

Symbol Selector 184–5, 188

Symbology tab: Add Renderer 152; bar graphs 140, 165, 198; graduated symbols 184, 188; homicide patterns 162; pie charts 132–3, 171–2; Quantities 183, 184; rate mapping 86; rivalries between nations 93; thematic maps 54, 55, 69–70, 71–2, 78, 80, 82, 90, 135

t tests 224–5

teaching colleges 141–2, 143–56

tessellation a subunit of a geographic space constructed on the basis of the distribution of a variable or variables measuring the characteristics of the population or behavior of people in the subunit 113, 115–23, 210, 211

text tool 175

thematic map a map that shows the distribution of one or more variables across the space mapped or among the subunits of the space mapped 51–83; category boundaries 80, 112; constructing another map 73–4; creating 52–62; diffusion of innovation 142; gang-related violence 97, 104; Join submenu 76–8; juvenile crime 75–83, 114; Layout View 56–7; legends 56, 57–61; New York City Police Department 160; poverty rates over time in New Orleans 127, 129, 135; racial profiling 62–75; residential patterns and ethnicity 136; rivalries between nations 90; school planning 107, 110, 111; selecting a shape file 52–3; selecting variables to display 55, 72; Symbology tab options 54, 55, 69–70, 71–2, 78, 80, 82, 90; unemployment 183–4

time: diffusion of innovation 141–56; poverty rates over time in New Orleans 124–7, 128–35

TIN (triangular irregular network) 150–2, 157–8, 159

titles 56, 60–1, 71, 73, 187, 200

Toolbox 13

Tools 18, 19, 29, 45

traffic tickets 62–75

unemployment 166, 175–88, 201

Uniform Crime Report (UCR) 160, 162, 164

units of analysis 112–13; spatial modeling

206, 209, 211, 212; tessellations 113, 120, 122–3
urban residential patterns 135–41
U.S. Census Bureau xiv; address databases 6–7, 10; algorithms 113; block groups 5–6; boundaries 206, 209; sub-regions 1, 2; thematic maps 54; units of analysis 112; *see also* census data

vector format data in the vector format is data stored as geometries; vector data stores features as lines, points, or polygons that represent objects on a map xvii
Verify 44, 102–3, 122
violent incidents 23–4, 28, 29, 41, 45, 98, 112–20; *see also* youth violence

Waagepetersen, R. 233
Walker, Jack L. 141, 143, 154, 156
world maps 89–90
world rivalries 87–95, 174, 175

youth violence: alcohol availability 164–6, 205, 216, 219–27; clustering approach 113–23, 211; geocoding 5, 23–4; Project Bridge 203–5; spatial modeling 207, 210–11, 215, 219–31; subsetting 95–105; thematic maps 75–83; *see also* violent incidents

Z test 116, 117, 118, 120
zooming 92, 139; candidate addresses 31, 33, 34, 38, 46; selected features 44